War on Terrorism

War on Terrorism

Capt. Mithilesh K. Singh

PRASHANT PUBLISHING HOUSE
DELHI-110094

Published by :
Prashant Publishing House
C-34, 28 Foota Road, Gali-3,
West Karwal Nagar, Delhi-110094
Phone : 011-22963970, Mob. : 9810396373
e-mail.: prashantpublishinghouse@gmail.com

War on Terrorism

First Published 2016

ISBN 978-93-80565-75-0

PRINTED IN INDIA
Published by Mr. R.K. Jha M/s Prashant Publishing House and Published at H.S. Offset House Press, Delhi.

Contents

Preface

The War on Terror (WoT), also known as the Global War on Terrorism (GWOT), refers to the international military campaign that started after the September 11 attacks on the United States.

U.S. President George W. Bush first used the term "War on Terror" on 20 September 2001. The Bush administration and the western media have since used the term to argue a global military, political, legal, and conceptual struggle against both organizations designated terrorist and regimes accused of supporting them. It was originally used with a particular focus on countries associated with Islamic terrorismorganizations including al-Qaeda and like-minded organizations.

In 2013, President Barack Obama announced that the United States was no longer pursuing a War on Terror, as the military focus should be on specific enemies rather than a tactic. He stated, "We must define our effort not as a boundless 'Global War on Terror', but rather as a series of persistent, targeted efforts to dismantle specific networks of violent extremists that threaten America."

After the terrorist attacks of September 11, 2001, the Bush administration declared a worldwide "war on terror," involving open and covert military operations, new security legislation, efforts to block the financing of terrorism, and more. Washington called on other states to join in the fight against terrorism asserting that "either you are with us, or you are with the terrorists." Many governments joined this campaign, often adopting harsh new laws, lifting long-standing legal protections and stepping up domestic policing and intelligence work.

Critics charge that the "war on terrorism" is an ideology of fear and repression that creates enemies and promotes violence rather than mitigating acts of terror and strengthening security.

The worldwide campaign has too often become an excuse for governments to repress opposition groups and disregard international law and civil liberties. Governments should address terrorism through international cooperation, using international law and respecting civil liberties and human rights. Governments should also address the root causes of terrorism, notably political alienation due to prejudice, state-sponsored violence and poverty.

SIS is a symptom of the absence of legitimate government in Iraq and Syria. After all, Al Qaeda in Iraq was defeated in 2007 when Gen. David Petraeus allied with Sunni tribesmen. But the failure to follow through on this victory politically and the divisive sectarian character of the Iraqi government is what made possible the emergence of ISIS through alliances with those same Sunni tribes. In Syria, the Assad regime, with its barrel bombs, not to mention imprisonment and torture, kills many more people than ISIS, which moves into areas where governance is lacking and resistance is virtually nonexistent.

This book is a modest attempt to discuss all these issues.

—Editor

1

Introduction

It was with disbelief and shock that people around the world saw footage of the terrorist attacks in the US on on September 11, 2001 when the planes-turned-missiles slammed into the World Trade Center towers and damaged the Pentagon.

This ultimately resulted in the US declaring and waging a war on "terror". Osama Bin Laden was eventually tracked down and killed some 10 years later. But the way the war on terror has been conducted has led to many voicing concerns about the impact on civil liberties, the cost of the additional security focused changes, the implications of the invasions and wars in Iraq and Afghanistan, and more.

The War on Terror (WoT), also known as the Global War on Terrorism (GWOT), refers to the international military campaign that started after the September 11 attacks on the United States.

U.S. President George W. Bush first used the term *"War on Terror"* on 20 September 2001. The Bush administration and the western media have since used the term to argue a global military, political, legal, and conceptual struggle against both organizations designated terrorist and regimes accused of supporting them. It was originally used with a particular focus on countries associated with Islamic terrorismorganizations including al-Qaeda and like-minded organizations.

In 2013, President Barack Obama announced that the United States was no longer pursuing a War on Terror, as the military focus should be on specific enemies rather than a tactic. He stated, "We must define our effort not as a boundless 'Global War on

Terror', but rather as a series of persistent, targeted efforts to dismantle specific networks of violent extremists that threaten America."

Etymology

The phrase "War on Terror" has been used to specifically refer to the ongoing military campaign led by the U.S., UK and their allies against organizations and regimes identified by them as terrorist, and excludes other independent counter-terrorist operations and campaigns such as those by Russia and India. The conflict has also been referred to by names other than the War on Terror. It has also been known as:

- World War III
- World War IV (assuming the Cold War was World War III)
- Bush's War on Terror
- The Long War
- The Global War on Terror
- The War Against al-Qaeda.

History of the Name

In 1984, the Reagan Administration used the term "war against terrorism" as part of an effort to pass legislation that was designed to freeze assets of terrorist groups and marshal the forces of government against them. Author Shane Harris asserts this was a reaction to the 1983 Beirut barracks bombing, which killed 241 U.S. and 58 Frenchpeacekeepers.

The concept of America at war with terrorism may have begun on 11 September 2001 when Tom Brokaw, having just witnessed the collapse of one of the towers of the World Trade Center, declared "Terrorists have declared war on [America]."

On 16 September 2001, at Camp David, President George W. Bush used the phrase *war on terrorism* in an unscripted and controversial comment when he said, "This crusade – this war on terrorism – is going to take a while,... " Bush later apologized for this remark due to the negative connotations the term *crusade* has to people, e.g. of Muslim faith. The word *crusade* was not used again. On 20 September 2001, during a televised address to a joint session of congress, Bush stated that, "(o)ur 'war on terror' begins with al-Qaeda, but it does not end there. It will not end until every terrorist group of global reach has been found, stopped, and defeated."

In April 2007, the British government announced publicly that it was abandoning the use of the phrase "War on Terror" as they found it to be less than helpful. This was explained more recently by Lady Eliza Manningham-Buller. In her 2011 Reith lecture, the former head of MI5 said that the 9/11 attacks were "a crime, not an act of war. So I never felt it helpful to refer to a war on terror."

U.S. President Barack Obama has rarely used the term, but in his inaugural address on 20 January 2009, he stated "Our nation is at war, against a far-reaching network of violence and hatred." In March 2009 the Defense Department officially changed the name of operations from "Global War on Terror" to "Overseas Contingency Operation" (OCO). In March 2009, the Obama administration requested that Pentagon staff members avoid use of the term, instead using "Overseas Contingency Operation".Basic objectives of the Bush administration "war on terror", such as targeting al Qaeda and building international counterterrorism alliances, remain in place. In December 2012, Jeh Johnson, the General Counsel of the Department of Defense, stated that the military fight will be replaced by a law enforcement operation when speaking at Oxford University, predicting that al Qaeda will be so weakened to be ineffective, and has been "effectively destroyed", and thus the conflict will not be an armed conflict underinternational law. In May 2013, Obama stated that the goal is "to dismantle specific networks of violent extremists that threaten America"; which coincided with the U.S.Office of Management and Budget having changed the wording from "Overseas Contingency Operations" to "Countering Violent Extremism" in 2010.

The Rhetorical War on Terror

Because the actions involved in the "war on terrorism" are diffuse, and the criteria for inclusion are unclear, political theorist Richard Jackson has argued that "the 'war on terrorism' therefore, is simultaneously a set of actual practices—wars, covert operations, agencies, and institutions—and an accompanying series of assumptions, beliefs, justifications, and narratives—it is an entire language or discourse." Jackson cites among many examples a statement by John Ashcroft that "the attacks of September 11 drew a bright line of demarcation between the civil and the savage". Administration officials also described "terrorists" as hateful, treacherous, barbarous, mad, twisted, perverted, without faith, parasitical, inhuman, and, most commonly, evil. Americans, in contrast, were described as brave, loving, generous, strong, resourceful, heroic, and respectful of human rights.

Both the term and the policies it denotes have been a source of ongoing controversy, as critics argue it has been used to justify unilateral preventive war, human rights abuses and other violations of international law.

BACKGROUND

Precursor to the 11 September Attacks

The origins of al-Qaeda can be traced to the Soviet war in Afghanistan (December 1979 – February 1989). The United States, United Kingdom, Saudi Arabia, Pakistan, and the People's Republic of China supported the Islamist Afghan mujahadeen guerillas against the military forces of the Soviet Union and the Democratic Republic of Afghanistan. A small number of "Afghan Arab" volunteers joined the fight against the Soviets, includingOsama bin Laden, but there is no evidence they received any external assistance. In May 1996 the group World Islamic Front for Jihad Against Jews and Crusaders (WIFJAJC), sponsored by bin Laden (and later re-formed as al-Qaeda), started forming a large base of operations in Afghanistan, where the Islamist extremist regime of theTaliban had seized power earlier in the year. In February 1998, Osama bin Laden signed a fatwâ, as head of al-Qaeda, declaring war on the West and Israel, later in May of that same year al-Qaeda released a video declaring war on the U.S. and the West.

On 7 August 1998, al-Qaeda struck the U.S. embassies in Kenya and Tanzania, killing 224 people, including 12 Americans. In retaliation, U.S. President Bill Clintonlaunched Operation Infinite

Reach, a bombing campaign in Sudan and Afghanistan against targets the U.S. asserted were associated with WIFJAJC, although others have questioned whether a pharmaceutical plant in Sudan was used as a chemical warfare plant. The plant produced much of the region's antimalarial drugs and around 50% of Sudan's pharmaceutical needs. The strikes failed to kill any leaders of WIFJAJC or the Taliban.

Next came the 2000 millennium attack plots, which included an attempted bombing ofLos Angeles International Airport. On 12 October 2000, the USS Cole bombing occurred near the port of Yemen, and 17 U.S. Navy sailors were killed.

11 September 2001 Attacks

On the morning of 11 September 2001, 19 Islamic men affiliated with al-Qaeda hijacked four airliners all bound for California. Once the hijackers assumed control of the airliners, they told the passengers that they had the bomb on board and would spare the lives of passengers and crew once their demands were met – no passenger and crew actually suspected that they would use the airliners as suicide weapons since it had never happened before in history. The hijackers – members of al-Qaeda's Hamburg cell– intentionally crashed two airliners into the Twin Towers of the World Trade Center inNew York City, New York, killing the 147 civilians and the ten hijackers on board the airliners. Both buildings collapsed within two hours from fire damage related to the crashes, destroying nearby buildings and damaging others, and killing 2,192 civilians, 71 law enforcement officers, and 343 firefighters who were in the towers and on the ground.

The hijackers crashed a third airliner into the Pentagon in Arlington County, Virginia, just outside Washington D.C., killing 70 civilians and 55 military personnel who were in the building, as well as 59 civilians and the five hijackers on board. 39 civilians, a law enforcement officer, and four hijackers died when the fourth plane crashed into a field near Shanksville, Pennsylvania, after some of its passengers and flight crew attempted to retake control of the plane, which the hijackers had redirected toward Washington D.C., to target the White House, or the U.S. Capitol. No flights had survivors.

A total of 2,977 victims and 19 hijackers perished in the attacks, making it the worst terrorist attack to ever take place on U.S. soil (and the worst act of international terrorism to take place on U.S. soil) and also the deadliest foreign attack on U.S. soil since the Japanese carried out a surprise air raid on Pearl Harbor on 7 December 1941.

U.S. OBJECTIVES

The Authorization for Use of Military Force Against Terrorists or "AUMF" was made law on 14 September 2001, to authorize the use of United States Armed Forces against those responsible for the attacks on 11 September 2001. It authorized the President to use all necessary and appropriate force against those nations, organizations, or persons he determines planned, authorized, committed, or aided the terrorist attacks that occurred on 11 September 2001, or harbored such organizations or persons, in order to prevent any future acts of international terrorism against the United States by such nations, organizations or persons. Congress declares this is intended to constitute specific statutory authorization within the meaning of section 5(b) of the War Powers Resolution of 1973.

The George W. Bush administration defined the following objectives in the War on Terror:

1. Defeat terrorists such as Osama bin Laden, Abu Musab al-Zarqawi and demolish their organizations
2. Identify, locate and demolish terrorists along with their organizations
3. Deny sponsorship, support and sanctuary to terrorists
    1. End the state sponsorship of terrorism
    2. Establish and maintain an international standard of accountability with regard to combating terrorism
    3. Strengthen and sustain the international effort to combat terrorism
    4. Work with willing and able states
    5. Enable weak states
    6. Persuade reluctant states

7. Compel unwilling states
8. Interdict and disorder material support for terrorists
9. Abolish terrorist sanctuaries and havens

4. Diminish the underlying conditions that terrorists seek to exploit
    1. Partner with the international community to strengthen weak states and prevent (re)emergence of terrorism
    2. Win the war of ideals
5. Defend U.S. citizens and interests at home and abroad
    1. Integrate the National Strategy for Homeland Security
    2. Attain domain awareness
    3. Enhance measures to ensure the integrity, reliability, and availability of critical, physical, and information-based infrastructures at home and abroad
    4. Implement measures to protect U.S. citizens abroad
    5. Ensure an integrated incident management capability

U.S. AND NATO-LED MILITARY OPERATIONS

Operation Active Endeavour

Operation Active Endeavour is a naval operation of NATO started in October 2001 in response to the 11 September attacks. It operates in the Mediterranean and is designed to prevent the movement of militants or weapons of mass destruction and to enhance the security of shipping in general.

Operation Enduring Freedom

Operation Enduring Freedom is the official name used by the Bush administration for the War in Afghanistan, together with three smaller military actions, under the umbrella of the Global War on Terror. These global operations are intended to seek out and destroy any al-Qaeda fighters or affiliates.

Operation Enduring Freedom – Afghanistan

On 20 September 2001, in the wake of the 11 September attacks, George W. Bush delivered an ultimatum to the Taliban government of Afghanistan, the Islamic Emirate of Afghanistan, to turn over

Osama bin Laden and al-Qaeda leaders operating in the country or face attack. The Taliban demanded evidence of bin Laden's link to the 11 September attacks and, if such evidence warranted a trial, they offered to handle such a trial in an Islamic Court. The U.S. refused to provide any evidence.

Subsequently, in October 2001, U.S. forces (with UK and coalition allies) invaded Afghanistan to oust the Taliban regime. On 7 October 2001, the official invasion began with British and U.S. forces conducting airstrike campaigns over enemy targets. Kabul, the capital city of Afghanistan, fell by mid-November. The remaining al-Qaeda and Taliban remnants fell back to the rugged mountains of eastern Afghanistan, mainly Tora Bora. In December, Coalition forces (the U.S. and its allies) fought within that region. It is believed that Osama bin Laden escaped into Pakistan during the battle.

In March 2002, the U.S. and other NATO and non-NATO forces launched Operation Anaconda with the goal of destroying any remaining al-Qaeda and Taliban forces in the Shah-i-Kot Valley and Arma Mountains of Afghanistan. The Taliban suffered heavy casualties and evacuated the region.

The Taliban regrouped in western Pakistan and began to unleash an insurgent-style offensive against Coalition forces in late 2002. Throughout southern and eastern Afghanistan, firefights broke out between the surging Taliban and Coalition forces. Coalition forces responded with a series of military offensives and an increase in the amount of troops in Afghanistan. In February 2010, Coalition forces launched Operation Moshtarak in southern Afghanistan along with other military offensives in the hopes that they would destroy the Taliban insurgency once and for all. Peace talks are also underway between Taliban affiliated fighters and Coalition forces. In September 2014, Afghanistan and the United States signed a security agreement, which permits United States and NATO forces to remain in Afghanistan until at least 2024. The United States and other NATO and non-NATO forces are planning to withdraw; with the Taliban claiming it has defeated the United States and NATO, and the Obama Administration viewing it as a victory. In December 2014, ISAF encasing its colors, and Resolute Support began as the NATO operation in Afghanistan. Continued

United States operations within Afghanistan will continue under the name "Operation Freedom's Sentinel".

Operation Enduring Freedom – Philippines

In January 2002, the United States Special Operations Command, Pacific deployed to thePhilippines to advise and assist the Armed Forces of the Philippines in combating Filipino Islamist groups. The operations were mainly focused on removing the Abu Sayyaf group and Jemaah Islamiyah (JI) from their stronghold on the island of Basilan. The second portion of the operation was conducted as a humanitarian program called "Operation Smiles". The goal of the program was to provide medical care and services to the region of Basilan as part of a "Hearts and Minds" program. Joint Special Operations Task Force – Philippines disbanded in June 2014,ending a 14-year mission. After JSOTF-P disbanded, as late as November 2014, American forces continued to operate in the Philippines under the name "PACOM Augmentation Team".

Operation Enduring Freedom – Horn of Africa

This extension of Operation Enduring Freedom was titled OEF-HOA. Unlike other operations contained in Operation Enduring Freedom, OEF-HOA does not have a specific organization as a target. OEF-HOA instead focuses its efforts to disrupt and detect militant activities in the region and to work with willing governments to prevent the reemergence of militant cells and activities.

In October 2002, the Combined Joint Task Force - Horn of Africa (CJTF-HOA) was established inDjibouti at Camp Lemonnier. It contains approximately 2,000 personnel including U.S. military and special operations forces (SOF) and coalition force members, Combined Task Force 150 (CTF-150).

Task Force 150 consists of ships from a shifting group of nations, including Australia, Canada, France, Germany, Italy, Netherlands, Pakistan, New Zealand and the United Kingdom. The primary goal of the coalition forces is to monitor, inspect, board and stop suspected shipments from entering the Horn of Africa region and affecting the United States' Operation Iraqi Freedom.

Included in the operation is the training of selected armed forces units of the countries of Djibouti, Kenya and Ethiopia in counter-terrorism and counter-insurgency tactics. Humanitarian efforts conducted by CJTF-HOA include rebuilding of schools and medical clinics and providing medical services to those countries whose forces are being trained.

The program expands as part of the Trans-Saharan Counterterrorism Initiative as CJTF personnel also assist in training the armed forces of Chad, Niger, Mauritania and Mali. However, the War on Terror does not include Sudan, where over 400,000 have died in an ongoing civil war.

On 1 July 2006, a Web-posted message purportedly written by Osama bin Laden urgedSomalis to build an Islamic state in the country and warned western governments that the al-Qaeda network would fight against them if they intervened there.

Somalia has been considered a "failed state" because its official central government was weak, dominated by warlords and unable to exert effective control over the country. Beginning in mid-2006, the Islamic Courts Union (ICU), an Islamist faction campaigning on a restoration of "law and order" through Sharia law, had rapidly taken control of much of southern Somalia.

On 14 December 2006, the U.S. Assistant Secretary of State Jendayi Frazer claimed al-Qaeda cell operatives were controlling the Islamic Courts Union, a claim denied by the ICU.

By late 2006, the UN-backed Transitional Federal Government (TFG) of Somalia had seen its power effectively limited to Baidoa, while the Islamic Courts Union controlled the majority of southern Somalia, including the capital of Mogadishu. On 20 December 2006, the Islamic Courts Union launched an offensive on the government stronghold of Baidoa, and saw early gains before Ethiopia intervened in favor of the government.

By 26 December, the Islamic Courts Union retreated towards Mogadishu, before again retreating as TFG/Ethiopian troops neared, leaving them to take Mogadishu with no resistance. The ICU then fled to Kismayo, where they fought Ethiopian/TFG forces in the Battle of Jilib. The Prime Minister of Somalia claimed that three "terror suspects" from the 1998 United States embassy bombings are being sheltered in Kismayo. On 30 December 2006, al-Qaeda deputy leader Ayman al-Zawahiri called upon Muslims worldwide to fight against Ethiopia and the TFG in Somalia.

On 8 January 2007, the U.S. launched the Battle of Ras Kamboni by bombing Ras Kamboni using AC-130 gunships.

On 14 September 2009, U.S. Special Forces killed two men and wounded and captured two others near the Somali village of Baarawe. Witnesses claim that helicopters used for the operation launched from French-flagged warships, but that could not be confirmed. A Somali-based al-Qaida affiliated group, the Al-Shabaab, has confirmed the death of "sheik commander" Saleh Ali Saleh Nabhan along with an unspecified number of militants. Nabhan, a Kenyan, was wanted in connection with the 2002 Mombasa attacks.

Operation Enduring Freedom - Trans Sahara

The conflict in northern Mali began in January 2012 with radical Islamists (affiliated to al-Qaeda) advancing into northern Mali. The Malian government had a hard time maintaining full control over their country. The fledgling government requested support from the international community on combating the Islamic militants. In January 2013, France intervened on behalf of the Malian government's request and deployed troops into the region. They launched Operation Serval on 11 January 2013, with the hopes of dislodging the al-Qaeda affiliated groups from northern Mali.

Iraq

Iraq had been listed as a State sponsor of terrorism by the U.S. since 1990, when Saddam Hussein invaded Kuwait. Iraq had also been on the list from 1979 to 1982; it was removed so that the U.S. could provide material support to Iraq in its war with Iran. Hussein's regime had proven to be a problem for the UN and Iraq's neighbors due to its use of chemical weapons against Iranians andKurds in the 1980s.

Iraqi no-fly Zones

Following the ceasefire agreement that suspended hostilities (but not officially ended) in the 1991Gulf War, the United States and its allies instituted and began patrolling Iraqi no-fly zones, to protect Iraq's Kurdish and Shi'a Arab population—both of which suffered attacks from the Hussein regime before and after the Gulf War—in Iraq's northern and southern regions, respectively. U.S. forces continued in combat zone deployments through November 1995 and launched Operation Desert Foxagainst Iraq in 1998 after it failed to meet U.S. demands of "unconditional cooperation" in weapons inspections.

In the aftermath of Operation Desert Fox, during December 1998, Iraq announced that it would no longer respect the no-fly zones and resumed its attempts to shoot down U.S. aircraft.

Operation Iraqi Freedom

The Iraq War began in March 2003 with an air campaign, which was immediately followed by a U.S.-led ground invasion. The Bush administration stated the invasion was the "serious consequences" spoken of in the UNSC Resolution 1441, partially on the basis of Iraq possessing weapons of mass destruction. The Bush administration also stated the Iraq war was part of the War on Terror, something later questioned or contested.

The first ground attack came at the Battle of Umm Qasr on 21 March 2003 when a combined force of British, American and Polish forces seized control of the port city of Umm Qasr. Baghdad, Iraq's capital city, fell to American forces in April 2003 and Saddam Hussein's government quickly dissolved. On 1 May 2003, Bush announced that major combat operations in Iraq had ended. However, an insurgency arose against the U.S.-led coalition and the newly developing Iraqi military and post-Saddam government. The insurgency, which included al-Qaeda affiliated groups, led to far more coalition casualties than the invasion. Other elements of the insurgency were led by fugitive members of President Hussein's Ba'ath regime, which included Iraqi nationalists andpan-Arabists. Many insurgency leaders are Islamists and claim to be fighting a religious war to reestablish the Islamic Caliphate of centuries past. Iraq's former president, Saddam Hussein was captured by U.S. forces in December 2003. He was executed in 2006.

In 2004, the insurgent forces grew stronger. The U.S. conducted attacks on insurgent strongholds in cities like Najaf and Fallujah.

In January 2007, President Bush presented a new strategy for Operation Iraqi Freedom based uponcounter-insurgency theories and tactics developed by General David Petraeus. The Iraq War troop surge of 2007 was part of this "new way forward" and, along with U.S. backing of Sunni groups it had previously sought to defeat, has been credited with a widely recognized dramatic decrease in violence by up to 80%.

Operation New Dawn

The war entered a new phase on 1 September 2010, with the official end of U.S. combat operations. The last U.S. troops exited Iraq on 18 December 2011.

OPERATION INHERENT RESOLVE (SYRIA AND IRAQ)

In a major split in the ranks of Al Qaeda's organization, the Iraqi franchise, known as Al Qaeda in Iraq covertly invaded Syria and the Levant and began participating in the ongoing Syrian Civil War, gaining enough support and strength to re-invade Iraq's western provinces under the name of theIslamic State of Iraq and the Levant (ISIS/ISIL), taking over much of the country in a blitzkrieg-like action and combining the Iraq insurgency and Syrian Civil War into a single conflict. Due to their extreme brutality and a complete change in their overall ideology, Al Qaeda's core organization in Central Asia eventually denounced ISIS and directed their affiliates to cut off all ties with this organization. Many analysts believe that because of this schism, Al Qaeda and ISIL are now in a competition to retain the title of the world's most powerful terrorist organization.

The Obama administration began to reengage in Iraq with a series of airstrikes aimed at ISIS beginning on 10 August 2014. On 9 September 2014 President Obama said that he had the authority he needed to take action to destroy the militant group known as the Islamic State of Iraq and the Levant, citing the 2001 Authorization for Use of Military Force Against Terrorists, and thus did not require additional approval from Congress. The following day on 10 September 2014 President Barack Obama made a televised speech about ISIL, which he stated "Our objective is clear: We will degrade, and ultimately destroy, ISIL through a comprehensive and sustained counter-terrorism strategy". Obama has authorized the deployment of additional U.S. Forces into Iraq, as well as authorizing direct military operations against ISIL within Syria. On the night of 21/22 September the United States, Saudi Arabia, Bahrain, the UAE, Jordan and Qatar started air attacks against ISIS in Syria.

In October 2014, it was reported that the U.S. Department of Defense considers military operations against ISIL as being under Operation Enduring Freedom in regards to campaign medal awarding. On 15 October, the military intervention became known as "Operation Inherent Resolve".

OTHER MILITARY OPERATIONS

Fighting in Pakistan

Following the 11 September 2001 attacks, former President of Pakistan Pervez Musharraf sided with the U.S. against the Taliban government in Afghanistan after an ultimatum by then U.S. President George W. Bush. Musharraf agreed to give the U.S. the use of three airbases for Operation Enduring Freedom. United States Secretary of State Colin Powell and other U.S. administration officials met with Musharraf. On 19 September 2001, Musharraf addressed the people of Pakistan and stated that, while he opposed military tactics against the Taliban, Pakistan risked being endangered by an alliance of India and the U.S. if it did not cooperate. In 2006, Musharraf testified that this stance was pressured by threats from the U.S., and revealed in his memoirs that he had "war-gamed" the United States as an adversary and decided that it would end in a loss for Pakistan.

On 12 January 2002, Musharraf gave a speech against Islamic extremism. He unequivocally condemned all acts of terrorism and pledged to combat Islamic extremism and lawlessness within Pakistan itself. He stated that his government was committed to rooting out extremism and made it clear that the banned militant organizations would not be allowed to resurface under any new name. He said, "the recent decision to ban extremist groups promoting militancy was taken in the national interest after thorough consultations. It was not taken under any foreign influence".

In 2002, the Musharraf-led government took a firm stand against the jihadi organizations and groups promoting extremism, and arrested Maulana Masood Azhar, head of the Jaish-e-Mohammed, andHafiz Muhammad Saeed, chief of the Lashkar-e-Taiba, and took dozens of activists into custody. An official ban was imposed on the groups on 12 January. Later that year, the Saudi born Zayn al-Abidn Muhammed Hasayn Abu Zubaydah was arrested by Pakistani officials during a series of joint U.S.-Pakistan raids. Zubaydah is said to have been a high-ranking al-Qaeda official with the title of operations chief and in charge of running al-Qaeda training camps. Other prominent al-Qaeda members were arrested in the following two years, namely Ramzi bin al-Shibh, who is known to have been a financial backer of al-Qaeda operations, and Khalid Sheikh Mohammed, who at the time of his capture was the third highest-ranking official in al-Qaeda and had been directly in charge of the planning for the 11 September attacks.

In 2004, the Pakistan Army launched a campaign in the Federally Administered Tribal Areas of Pakistan's Waziristan region, sending in 80,000 troops. The goal of the conflict was to remove the al-Qaeda and Taliban forces in the region.

After the fall of the Taliban regime many members of the Taliban resistance fled to the Northern border region of Afghanistan and Pakistan where the Pakistani army had previously little control. With the logistics and air support of the United States, the Pakistani Army captured or killed numerous al-Qaeda operatives such as Khalid Sheikh Mohammed, wanted for his involvement in the USS Cole bombing, the Bojinka plot, and the killing of *Wall Street Journal* reporter Daniel Pearl.

The United States has carried out a campaign of Drone attacks on targets all over the Federally Administered Tribal Areas. However, thePakistani Taliban still operates there. To this day it's estimated that 15 U.S. soldiers were killed while fighting al-Qaeda and Taliban remnants in Pakistan since the War on Terror began.

Osama bin Laden, who was of many founders of al-Qaeda, his wife, and son, were all killed on 2 May 2011, during a raid conducted by theUnited States special operations forces in Abbottabad, Pakistan.

The use of drones by the Central Intelligence Agency in Pakistan to carry out operations associated with the Global War on Terror sparks debate over sovereignty and the laws of war. The U.S. Government uses the CIA rather than the U.S. Air Force for strikes in Pakistan in order to avoid breaching sovereignty through military invasion. The United States was criticized by a report on drone warfare and aerial sovereignty for abusing the term 'Global War on Terror' to carry out military operations through government agencies without formally declaring war.

Fighting in Yemen

The United States has also conducted a series of military strikes on al-Qaeda militants in Yemen since the War on Terror began.Yemen has a weak central government and a powerful tribal system that leaves large lawless areas open for militant training and operations. Al-Qaida has a strong presence in the country.

The U.S., in an effort to support Yemeni counter-terrorism efforts, has increased their military aid package to Yemen from less than $11 million in 2006 to more than $70 million in 2009, as well as providing up to $121 million for development over the next three years.

Fighting in Kashmir

In a 'Letter to American People' written by Osama bin Laden in 2002, he stated that one of the reasons he was fighting America is because of its support of India on the Kashmir issue. While on a trip to Delhi in 2002, U.S. Secretary of Defense Donald Rumsfeld suggested that Al-Qaeda was active in Kashmir, though he did not have any hard evidence. An investigation in 2002 unearthed evidence that Al-Qaeda and its affiliates were prospering in Pakistan-administered Kashmir with tacit approval of Pakistan's National Intelligence agency Inter-Services Intelligence. A team of

Special Air Service and Delta Force was sent into Indian-administered Kashmir in 2002 to hunt for Osama bin Laden after reports that he was being sheltered by the Kashmiri militant group Harkat-ul-Mujahideen.

U.S. officials believed that Al-Qaeda was helping organize a campaign of terror in Kashmir in order to provoke conflict between India and Pakistan. Fazlur Rehman Khalil, the leader of the Harkat-ul-Mujahideen, signed al-Qaeda's 1998 declaration of holy war, which called on Muslims to attack all Americans and their allies. Indian sources claimed that In 2006, Al-Qaeda claimed they had established a wing in Kashmir; this worried the Indian government. India also claimed that Al-Qaeda has strong ties with the Kashmir militant groups Lashkar-e-Taiba and Jaish-e-Mohammed in Pakistan.

While on a visit to Pakistan in January 2010, U.S. Defense secretary Robert Gates stated that Al-Qaeda was seeking to destabilize the region and planning to provoke a nuclear war between India and Pakistan.

In September 2009, a U.S. Drone strike reportedly killed Ilyas Kashmiri, who was the chief of Harkat-ul-Jihad al-Islami, a Kashmiri militant group associated with Al-Qaeda. Kashmiri was described by Bruce Riedel as a 'prominent' Al-Qaeda member, while others described him as the head of military operations for Al-Qaeda. Waziristan had now become the new battlefield for Kashmiri militants, who were now fighting NATO in support of Al-Qaeda. On 8 July 2012, Al-Badar Mujahideen, a breakaway faction of Kashmir centric terror group Hizbul Mujahideen, on conclusion of their two-day Shuhada Conference called for mobilisation of resources for continuation of jihad in Kashmir.

American Military Intervention in Cameroon

In October 2015, the US began deploying 300 military personnel to Cameroon, with the invitation of the Cameroonian government, to support African forces in a non-combat role in their fight against ISIS insurgency in that country. The troops' primary missions will revolve around providing intelligence support to local forces as well as conducting reconnaissance flights.

INTERNATIONAL MILITARY SUPPORT

The invasion of Afghanistan is seen to have been the first action of this war, and initially involved forces from the United States, the United Kingdom, and the Afghan Northern Alliance. Since the initial invasion period, these forces were augmented by troops and aircraft from Australia, Canada, Denmark, France, Italy, Netherlands, New Zealand and Norway amongst others. In 2006, there were about 33,000 troops in Afghanistan.

On 12 September 2001, less than 24 hours after the 11 September attacks in New York City and Washington, D.C., NATO invoked Article 5 of the North Atlantic Treaty and declared the attacks to be an attack against all 19 NATO member countries. Australian Prime Minister John Howard also declared that Australia would invoke the ANZUS Treaty along similar lines.

In the following months, NATO took a wide range of measures to respond to the threat of terrorism.

On 22 November 2002, the member states of the Euro-Atlantic Partnership Council (EAPC) decided on a Partnership Action Plan against Terrorism, which explicitly states, "EAPC States are committed to the protection and promotion of fundamental freedoms and human rights, as well as the rule of law, in combating terrorism."

NATO started naval operations in the Mediterranean Sea designed to prevent the movement of terrorists or weapons of mass destruction as well as to enhance the security of shipping in general called Operation Active Endeavour.

Support for the U.S. cooled when America made clear its determination to invade Iraq in late 2002. Even so, many of the "coalition of the willing" countries that unconditionally supported the U.S.-led military action have sent troops to Afghanistan, particular neighboring Pakistan, which has disowned its earlier support for the Taliban and contributed tens of thousands of soldiers to the conflict. Pakistan was also engaged in the War in North-West Pakistan (Waziristan War). Supported by U.S. intelligence, Pakistan was attempting to remove the Taliban insurgency and al-Qaeda element from the northern tribal areas.

International Security Assistance Force

December 2001 saw the creation of the NATO-led International Security Assistance Force (ISAF) to assist the Afghan Transitional Administration and the first post-Taliban elected government. With a renewed Taliban insurgency, it was announced in 2006 that ISAF would replace the U.S. troops in the province as part of Operation Enduring Freedom.

The British 16th Air Assault Brigade (later reinforced by Royal Marines) formed the core of the force in southern Afghanistan, along with troops and helicopters from Australia, Canada and the Netherlands. The initial force consisted of roughly 3,300 British, 2,000 Canadian, 1,400 from the Netherlands and 240 from Australia, along with special forces from Denmark and Estonia and small contingents from other nations. The monthly supply of cargo containers through Pakistani route to ISAF in Afghanistan is over 4,000 costing around 12 billion in Pakistani Rupees.

TERRORIST ATTACKS AND FAILED PLOTS SINCE 9/11

Al-Qaeda

Since 9/11, Al-Qaeda and other affiliated radical Islamist groups have executed attacks in several parts of the world where conflicts are not taking place. Whereas countries like Pakistan have suffered hundreds of attacks killing tens of thousands and displacing many more.

- The 2002 Bali bombings in Indonesia were committed by various members of Jemaah Islamiyah, an organization linked to Al-Qaeda.
- The 2003 Casablanca bombings were carried out by Salafia Jihadia, an Al-Qaeda affiliate.
- After the 2003 Istanbul bombings, Turkey charged 74 people with involvement, including Syrian Al-Qaeda member Loai al-Saqa.
- The 2004 Madrid train bombings in Spain were "inspired by" Al-Qaeda, though no direct involvement has been established.

- The 7 July 2005 London bombings in the United Kingdom were perpetrated by 4 homegrown terrorists, one of whom appeared in an edited video with a known Al-Qaeda operative, though the British government denies Al-Qaeda involvement.
- Al Qaeda claimed responsibility for the 11 April 2007 Algiers bombings in Algeria.
- The 2007 Glasgow International Airport attack in the United Kingdom was carried out by a pair of bombers whose laptops and suicide notes included videos and speeches referencing Al-Qaeda, though no direct involvement was established.
- The 2009 Fort Hood shooting in the United States was committed by Nidal Malik Hasan, who had been in communication with Anwar al-Awlaki, though the Department of Defense classifies the shooting as an incidence of workplace violence.
- Morocco blames Al-Qaeda for the 2011 Marrakech bombing, though Al-Qaeda denies involvement.
- The 2012 Toulouse and Montauban shootings in France were committed by Mohammed Merah, who reportedly had familial ties to Al-Qaeda, along with a history of petty crime and psychological issues. Merah claimed ties to Al-Qaeda, though French authorities deny any connection.
- To date, no one has been convicted for the 2012 U.S. Consulate attack in Benghazi in Libya and no one has claimed responsibility. Branches of Al-Qaeda, Al-Qaeda affiliates, and individuals "sympathetic to Al-Qaeda" are blamed.
- The gunmen in the 2015 *Charlie Hebdo* shooting in Paris identified themselves as belonging to Al-Qaeda's branch in Yemen.

There may also have been several additional planned attacks that were not successful.

- 2004 financial buildings plot (United States and the United Kingdom)

- 21 July 2005 London bombings (United Kingdom)
- 2006 Toronto terrorism plot (Canada)
- 2006 transatlantic aircraft plot involving liquid explosives carried onto commercial airplanes
- 2006 Hudson River bomb plot (United States)
- 2007 Fort Dix attack plot (United States)
- 2007 London car bombs (United Kingdom)
- 2007 John F. Kennedy International Airport attack plot (United States)
- 2009 Bronx terrorism plot (United States)
- 2009 New York City Subway and United Kingdom plot (United States and the United Kingdom)
- 2009 Northwest Airlines Flight 253 bombing plot (United States)
- 2010 Stockholm bombings (Sweden)
- 2010 Times Square car bombing attempt (United States)
- 2010 cargo plane bomb plot (United States)
- 2010 Portland car bomb plot (United States)
- 2011 Manhattan terrorism plot (United States)
- 2013 VIA Rail Canada terrorism plot (Canada)

Islamic State of Iraq and the Levant (ISIL)

- 2013 Reyhanlý bombings in Turkey that led to 52 deaths and the injury of 140 people.
- 2014 Canadian parliament shootings, an ISIL-inspired attack on Canada's parliament, resulting in the death of a Canadian soldier, as well as that of the perpetrator.
- 2015 Porte de Vincennes siege perpetrated by Amedy Coulibaly in Paris, which led to four deaths and the injury of nine others.
- 2015 Corinthia Hotel attack on 27 January in Libya that led to 10 deaths.
- 2015 Sana'a mosque bombings on 20 March that led to the death of 142 and injury of 351 people.
- 2015 Curtis Culwell Center attack on 3 May 2015, that led to the injury of one security officer.

- 2015 November 2015 Paris attacks on the 13th that left at least 132 dead and injured at least 352 civilians, caused France to be put under a state of emergency, close its borders and deploy three French contingency plans. Islamic State claimed responsibility for the attacks, with French President François Hollande later stated the attacks were carried out "by the Islamic state with internal help".

So far, there has been only one failed plot by ISIL:

- 2014 mass-beheading plot in Australia

U.S. MILITARY AID TO OTHER COUNTRIES

Pakistan

In the three years before the attacks of 11 September, Pakistan received approximately US$9 million in American military aid. In the three years after, the number increased to US$4.2 billion, making it the country with the maximum funding post 9/11.

Brahamdagh Bugti stated in a 2008 interview that he would accept aid from India, Afghanistan, and Iran in defending Baluchistan.Pakistan has repeatedly accused India of supporting Baloch rebels, and Wright-Neville writes that outside Pakistan, some Western observers also believe that India secretly funds the Balochistan Liberation Army (BLA).

POST 9/11 EVENTS INSIDE THE UNITED STATES

In addition to military efforts abroad, in the aftermath of 9/11 the Bush Administration increased domestic efforts to prevent future attacks. Various government bureaucracies that handled security and military functions were reorganized. A new cabinet-level agency called the United States Department of Homeland Security was created in November 2002 to lead and coordinate the largest reorganization of the U.S. federal government since the consolidation of the armed forces into the Department of Defense.

The Justice Department launched the National Security Entry-Exit Registration System for certain male non-citizens in the U.S., requiring them to register in person at offices of the Immigration and Naturalization Service.

The USA PATRIOT Act of October 2001 dramatically reduces restrictions on law enforcement agencies' ability to search telephone, e-mail communications, medical, financial, and other records; eases restrictions on foreign intelligence gathering within the United States; expands the Secretary of the Treasury's authority to regulate financial transactions, particularly those involving foreign individuals and entities; and broadens the discretion of law enforcement and immigration authorities in detaining and deporting immigrants suspected of terrorism-related acts. The act also expanded the definition of terrorism to include domestic terrorism, thus enlarging the number of activities to which the USA PATRIOT Act's expanded law enforcement powers could be applied. A new Terrorist Finance Tracking Program monitored the movements of terrorists' financial resources (discontinued after being revealed by *The New York Times*). Global telecommunication usage, including those with no links to terrorism, is being collected and monitored through the NSA electronic surveillance program. The Patriot Act is still in effect.

Political interest groups have stated that these laws remove important restrictions on governmental authority, and are a dangerous encroachment on civil liberties, possible unconstitutional violations of the Fourth Amendment. On 30 July 2003, the American Civil Liberties Union (ACLU) filed the first legal challenge against Section 215 of the Patriot Act, claiming that it allows the FBI to violate a citizen's First Amendment rights, Fourth Amendment rights, and right to due process, by granting the government the right to search a person's business, bookstore, and library records in a terrorist investigation, without disclosing to the individual that records were being searched. Also, governing bodies in a number of communities have passed symbolic resolutions against the act.

In a speech on 9 June 2005, Bush said that the USA PATRIOT Act had been used to bring charges against more than 400 suspects, more than half of whom had been convicted. Meanwhile, the ACLU quoted Justice Department figures showing that 7,000 people have complained of abuse of the Act.

The Defense Advanced Research Projects Agency (DARPA) began an initiative in early 2002 with the creation of the Total

Information Awareness program, designed to promote information technologies that could be used in counter-terrorism. This program, facing criticism, has since been defunded by Congress.

By 2003, 12 major conventions and protocols were designed to combat terrorism.

These were adopted and ratified by a number of states. These conventions require states to co-operate on principal issues regarding unlawful seizure of aircraft, the physical protection of nuclear materials, and the freezing of assets of militant networks.

In 2005, the UN Security Council adopted Resolution 1624 concerning incitement to commit acts of terrorism and the obligations of countries to comply with international human rights laws.

Although both resolutions require mandatory annual reports on counter-terrorism activities by adopting nations, the United States and Israel have both declined to submit reports.

In the same year, the United States Department of Defense and the Chairman of the Joint Chiefs of Staff issued a planning document, by the name "National Military Strategic Plan for the War on Terrorism", which stated that it constituted the "comprehensive military plan to prosecute the Global War on Terror for the Armed Forces of the United States...including the findings and recommendations of the 9/11 Commission and a rigorous examination with the Department of Defense".

On 9 January 2007, the House of Representatives passed a bill, by a vote of 299–128, enacting many of the recommendations of the 9/11 Commission.

The bill passed in the U.S. Senate, by a vote of 60–38, on 13 March 2007 and it was signed into law on 3 August 2007 by President Bush. It became Public Law 110-53. In July 2012, U.S. Senate passed a resolution urging that the Haqqani Network be designated a foreign terrorist organisation.

The Office of Strategic Influence was secretly created after 9/11 for the purpose of coordinating propaganda efforts, but was closed soon after being discovered. The Bush administration implemented the Continuity of Operations Plan (or Continuity of

Government) to ensure that U.S. government would be able to continue in catastrophic circumstances.

Since 9/11, extremists made various attempts to attack the United States, with varying levels of organization and skill. For example, vigilant passengers aboard a transatlantic flight prevented Richard Reid, in 2001, and Umar Farouk Abdulmutallab, in 2009, from detonating an explosive device.

Other terrorist plots have been stopped by federal agencies using new legal powers and investigative tools, sometimes in cooperation with foreign governments.

Such thwarted attacks include:

- The 2001 shoe bomb plot
- A plan to crash airplanes into the U.S. Bank Tower (aka Library Tower) in Los Angeles
- The 2003 plot by Iyman Faris to blow up the Brooklyn Bridge in New York City
- The 2004 Financial buildings plot, which targeted the International Monetary Fund and World Bank buildings in Washington, D.C., theNew York Stock Exchange and other financial institutions
- The 2004 Columbus Shopping Mall Bombing Plot
- The 2006 Sears Tower plot
- The 2007 Fort Dix attack plot
- The 2007 John F. Kennedy International Airport attack plot
- The New York Subway Bombing Plot and 2010 Times Square car bombing attempt

The Obama administration has promised the closing of the Guantanamo Bay detention camp, increased the number of troops inAfghanistan, and promised the withdrawal of its troops from Iraq.

CASUALTIES

According to Joshua Goldstein, an international relations professor from the American University, The Global War on Terror has seen fewer war deaths than any other decade in the past century.

Costs

A March 2011 Congressional report estimated spending related to the war through fiscal year 2011 at $1.2 trillion, and that spending through 2021 assuming a reduction to 45,000 troops would be $1.8 trillion. A June 2011 academic report covering additional areas of spending related to the war estimated it through 2011 at $2.7 trillion, and long term spending at $5.4 trillion including interest.

Criticism

Criticism of the War on Terror addresses the issues, morality, efficiency, economics, and other questions surrounding the War on Terror and made against the phrase itself, calling it a misnomer.

The notion of a "war" against "terrorism" has proven highly contentious, with critics charging that it has been exploited by participating governments to pursue long-standing policy/military objectives, reduce civil liberties, and infringe upon human rights.

It is argued that the term war is not appropriate in this context (as in War on Drugs), since there is no identifiable enemy, and that it is unlikely international terrorism can be brought to an end by military means.

Other critics, such as Francis Fukuyama, note that "terrorism" is not an enemy, but a tactic; calling it a "war on terror", obscures differences between conflicts such as anti-occupation insurgents and international mujahideen.

With a military presence in Iraq and Afghanistan and its associated collateral damage Shirley Williams maintains this increases resentment and terrorist threats against the West. There is also perceived U.S. hypocrisy, media induced hysteria, and that differences in foreign and security policy have damaged America's image in most of the world.

OTHER WARS ON TERROR

In the 2010s, China has also been engaged in its own War on Terror, predominantly a domestic campaign in response to violent actions byUighur separatist movements in the Xinjiang conflict. This campaign was largely criticized in international media due to the perception that it unfairly targets and persecutes Chinese Muslims, potentially resulting in negative backlash from China's predominantly MuslimUighur population.

Russia has also been engaged in its own, also largely internally focused, counter-terrorism campaign often termed a war on terror. LikeChina's war on terror, Russia's has also been focused on separatist and Islamist movements that use political violence to achieve their ends.

2

Criticism of the War on Terror

Criticism of the War on Terror addresses the morals, ethics, efficiency, economics, as well as other issues surrounding the War on Terror. It also touches upon criticism against the phrase itself, which was branded as a misnomer. The notion of a "war" against "terrorism" has proven highly contentious, with critics charging that participating governments exploited it to pursue long-standing policy/military objectives, reduce civil liberties, and infringe upon human rights. It is argued that the term war is not appropriate in this context (as inWar on Drugs), since there is no identifiable enemy and that it is unlikely international terrorism can be brought to an end by military means.

Other critics, such as Francis Fukuyama, note that "terrorism" is not an enemy, but a tactic: calling it a "war on terror" obscures differences between conflicts such as anti-occupation insurgents and international mujahideen. With a military presence in Iraq andAfghanistan and its associated collateral damage Shirley Williams maintains this increases resentment and terrorist threats against the West. Other criticism include United States hypocrisy, media induced hysteria, and that changes in American foreign and security policy have shifted world opinion against the US.

Terminology

Various critics dubbed the term "War on Terror" as nonsensical. For example, billionaire activist investor George Soros criticized the term "War on Terror" as a "false metaphor." Linguist George Lakoff of the Rockridge Institute argued that there cannot literally be a war on terror, since terror is an abstract noun. "Terror cannot be destroyed by weapons or signing a peace treaty. A war on terror has no end."

Jason Burke, a journalist who writes about radical Islamic activity, describes the terms "terrorism" and "war against terrorism" in this manner:

There are multiple ways of defining terrorism and all are subjective. Most define terrorism as 'the use or threat of serious violence' to advance some kind of 'cause'. Some state clearly the kinds of group ('sub-national', 'non-state') or cause (political, ideological, religious) to which they refer. Others merely rely on the instinct of most people when confronted with an act that involves innocent civilians being killed or maimed by men armed with explosives, firearms or other weapons. None is satisfactory and grave problems with the use of the term persist. Terrorism is after all, a tactic. The term 'war on terrorism' is thus effectively nonsensical. As there is no space here to explore this involved and difficult debate, my preference is, on the whole, for the less loaded term 'militancy'. This is not an attempt to condone such actions, merely to analyze them in a clearer way.

Perpetual War

Former U.S. President George W. Bush articulated the goals of the War on Terror in a September 20, 2001 speech, in which he said that it "will not end until every terrorist group of global reach has been found, stopped and defeated." In that same speech, he called the war "a task that does not end", an argument he reiterated in 2006 State of The Union address.

Preventive War

One justification given for the invasion of Iraq was to prevent terroristic, or other attacks, by Iraq on the United States or other nations. This can be viewed as a conventional warfare realization of the War on Terror.

A major criticism leveled at this justification is that it does not fulfill one of the requirements of a just war and that in waging war preemtively, the United States undermined international law and the authority of the United Nations, particularly the United Nations Security Council.

On this ground, by invading a country that did not pose an imminent threat without UN support, the U.S. violated international law, including theUN Charter and the Nuremberg principles, therefore committing a war of aggression, which is considered a war crime.

Additional criticism raised the point that the United States might have set a precedent, under the premise of which any nation could justify the invasion of other states.

Richard N. Haass, president of the Council on Foreign Relations, argues that on the eve of U.S. intervention in 2003, Iraq represented, at best, a gathering threat and not an imminent one. In hindsight he notes that Iraq did not even represent a gathering threat.

"The decision to attack Iraq in March 2003 was discretionary: it was a war of choice. There was no vital American interests in imminent danger and there were alternatives to using military force, such as strengthening existing sanctions."

However, Haass argues that U.S. intervention in Afghanistan in 2001 began as a war of necessity—vital interests were at stake—but morphed "into something else and it crossed a line in March 2009, when President Barack Obama` decided to sharply increase American troop levels and declared that it was U.S. policy to 'take the fight to the Taliban in the south and east' of the country." Afghanistan, according to Haass, eventually became a war of choice.

WAR ON TERROR SEEN AS PRETEXT

Some have argued that part of the War on Terror has little to do with its stated purpose, since Iraq had nothing to do with the September 11 attacks and the invasion was carried out on the basis of faulty or doctored intelligence. Excerpts from an April 2006 report compiled from sixteen U.S. government intelligence agencies has strengthened the claim that engaging in Iraq has increased terrorism in the region.

Domestic Civil Liberties

In the United Kingdom, critics have claimed that the Blair government had used the War on Terror as a pretext to radically curtail civil liberties, some enshrined in law since Magna Carta. For example, the detention-without-trial in Belmarsh prison: controls on free speech through laws against protests near Parliament and laws banning the "glorification" of terrorism: and reductions in checks on police power, as in the case of Jean Charles de Menezes andMohammed Abdul Kahar.

Former Liberal Democrat Leader Sir Menzies Campbell has also condemned Blair's inaction over the controversial U.S. practice of extraordinary rendition, arguing that the human rights conventions to which the UK is a signatory (e.g. European Convention on Human Rights) impose on the government a "legal obligation" to investigate and prevent potential torture and human rights violations.

Unilateralism

U.S. President George W. Bush's remark of November 2001 claiming that "You're either with us or you are with the terrorists," has been a source of criticism. Thomas A. Keaney of Johns Hopkins University's Foreign Policy Institute said "it made diplomacy with a number of different countries far more difficult because obviously there are different problems throughout the world."

As a War against Islam

Since the War on Terror revolved primarily around the United States and other NATO states intervening in the internal affairs of Muslim countries (i.e. in Iraq, Afghanistan, etc.) and organisations, it has been labelled a war against Islam by ex-United States Attorney GeneralRamsey Clark, among others. After his release from Guantanamo in 2005, ex-detainee Moazzam Begg appeared in the Islamist propaganda video *21st Century CrUSAders* and claimed the U.S. was engaging in a new crusade:

I think that history is definitely repeating itself and for the Muslim world and I think even a great part of the non-Muslim world now, are beginning to recognize that there are ambitions that the United States has on the lands and wealth of nations of Islam.

Methods

Critics believe that interrogation methods employed by U.S. forces in places such asGuantanamo Bay and Abu Ghraib were immoral and unethical, making them no better than theinsurgents they are trying to find. The War on Terrorism has been effectively called an act of terrorism in itself by some who point to incidents such as the Bagram torture and prisoner abusescandal, the Abu Ghraib torture and prisoner abuse scandal, the alleged use of chemical weaponsagainst terrorists in Fallujah, and the use of military force to disperse anti-American demonstrations in Iraq.

Aiding Terrorism

Each month, there are more suicide terrorists trying to kill Americans and their allies in Afghanistan, Iraq, as well as other Muslim countries than in all the years before 2001*combined*. From 1980 to 2003, there were 343 suicide attacks around the world and at most 10 percent were anti-American inspired. Since 2004, there have been more than 2,000, over 91 percent against U.S. and allied forces in Afghanistan, Iraq, as well as other countries.

Robert Pape

University of Chicago professor and political scientist, Robert Pape has written extensive work onsuicide terrorism and states that it is triggered by military occupations, not extremist ideologies. In works such as *Dying to Win: The Strategic Logic of Suicide Terrorism* and *Cutting the Fuse*, he uses data from an extensive terrorism database and argues that by increasing military occupations, the US government is increasing terrorism. Pape is also the director and founder of the Chicago Project on Security and Terrorism (CPOST), a database of every known suicide terrorist attack from 1980 to 2008.

In 2006, a National Intelligence Estimate stated that the war in Iraq has increased the threat of terrorism. The estimate was compiled by 16 intelligence agencies and was the first assessment of global terrorism since the start of the Iraq war.

Cornelia Beyer explains how terrorism increased as a response to past and present military intervention and occupation, as well as to 'structural violence'. Structural violence, in this instance, refers to economic conditions of backwardness which are attributed to the economic policies of the Western nations, the United States in particular.

British Liberal Democrat politician Shirley Williams wrote that the United States and United Kingdom governments "must stop to think whether it is sowing the kind of resentment which is the seedbed of future terrorism." The United Kingdom ambassador to Italy, Ivor Roberts, echoed this criticism when he stated that President Bush was "the best recruiting sergeant ever for al Qaeda." The United States also granted "protected persons" status under the Geneva Convention to the Mojahedin-e-Khalq, an Iranian group classified by theU.S. Department of State as a terrorist organization, sparking criticism. Other critics further noted that the American government granted political asylum to several alleged terrorists and terrorist organizations that seek to overthrow Fidel Castro's regime, while the American government claims to be anti-terrorism.

Hypocrisy of the Bush Administration

The alleged mastermind behind the September 11, 2001 attacks was part of the Mujahedin who were sponsored, armed, trained and aided by the CIA to fight the Soviet Union after it intervened in Afghanistan in 1979.

Venezuela accused the U.S. government of having a double standard towards terrorism for giving safe haven to Luis Posada Carriles.Some Americans also commented on the selective use of the term War on Terrorism, including 3 star general William Odom, formerly President Reagan's NSA Director, who wrote:

"As many critics have pointed, out, terrorism is not an enemy. It is a tactic. Because the United States itself has a long record of supporting terrorists and using terrorist tactics, the slogans of today's war on terrorism merely makes the United States look hypocritical to the rest of the world. A prudent American president would end the present policy of "sustained hysteria" over potential terrorist attacks..treat terrorism as a serious but not a strategic problem, encourage Americans to regain their confidence and refuse to let al Qaeda keep us in a state of fright."

Misleading Information

Critics argued that some politicians supporting the War on Terror are motivated by reasons other than those they publicly state. Others accuse those politicians of cynically misleading the public to achieve their own ends. For instance, in the months leading up to the invasion of Iraq, President Bush and members of his administration indicated that they possessed information which demonstrated a link between Saddam Hussein and al-Qaeda. Published reports of the links began in late December 1998.

In January 1999, *Newsweek*magazine published a story about Saddam Hussein and al-Qaeda joining forces to attack U.S. interests in the Gulf Region.

ABC News broadcast a story of this link soon after. Polls suggested that a majority of Americans believed that Saddam Hussein was linked to theattacks of September 11, 2001. However, despite shifting public opinion, the Bush Administration believed that there was the possibility of a potential collaboration between al Qaeda and Saddam Hussein's Ba'ath regime following the U.S. led invasion of Afghanistan. Amnesty International Irene Khan criticized the use of pro-humanitarian arguments by Coalition countries prior to its 2003 invasion of Iraq, writing in an open letter: "This selective attention to human rights is nothing but a cold and calculated manipulation of the work of human rights activists. Let us not forget that these same governments turned a blind eye to Amnesty International's reports of widespread human rights violations in Iraq before the Gulf War."

Torture by Proxy

The term "torture by proxy" is used by some critics to describe situations in which the CIA and other US agencies transferred supposed terrorists, whom they captured during their efforts in the 'War on terrorism', to countries known to employ torture as an interrogation technique. Some also claimed that US agencies knew torture was employed, even though the a transfer of anyone to anywhere for the purpose of torture is a violation of US law.

Nonetheless, Condoleezza Rice (then the United States Secretary of State) stated that:

"the United States has not transported anyone and will not transport anyone, to a country when we believe he will be tortured. Where appropriate, the United States seeks assurances that transferred persons will not be tortured."

This US programme also prompted several official investigations in Europe into alleged secret detentions and unlawful inter-state transfers involving Council of Europe member states, including those related with the so-called War on Terrorism. A June 2006 report from the Council of Europe estimated that 100 people were kidnapped by the CIA on EU territory with the cooperation of Council of Europe members and rendered to other countries, often after having transited through secret detention centres ("black sites"), some located in Europe, utilised by the CIA. According to the separate European Parliament report of February 2007, the CIA has conducted 1,245 flights, many of them to destinations where these alleged 'terrorists' could face torture, in violation of article 3 of the United Nations Convention Against Torture.

RELIGIONISM AND ISLAMOPHOBIA

One aspect of the criticism regarding the rhetoric justifying the War on Terror was religionism, or more specifically Islamophobia. Theologian Amir Hussain, who studies contemporary Muslims societies in North America, defines this concept as a stereotyping of all followers of Islam as real or potential terrorists due to alleged hateful and violent teaching of their religion. He goes on to argue that "Islam is reduced to the concept of jihad and Jihad is reduced to terror against the West." This line of argument echoes Edward Said's famous piece *Orientalism* in which he argued that the United States sees the Muslims and Arabs in an essentialized caricatures – as oil supplies or potential terrorists.

Decreasing International Support

In 2002, strong majorities supported the U.S.-led War on Terror in Britain, France, Germany, Japan, India and Russia, according to a sample survey conducted by the Pew Research Center. By 2006, supporters of the effort were in the minority in Britain (49%), Germany (47%), France (43%) and Japan (26%). Although a majority of Russians still supported the War on Terror, that majority had decreased by 21%. Whereas 63% of Spaniards supported the War on Terror in 2003, only 19% of the population indicated support in 2006. 19% of the Chinese population still supports the War on Terror and less than a fifth of the populations of Turkey, Egypt, as well as Jordan support the efforts. The report also indicated that Indian public support for the War on Terror has been stable. Andrew Kohut, while speaking to theU.S. House Committee on Foreign Affairs, noted that and according to the Pew Research Center polls conducted in 2004, "the ongoing conflict in Iraq continues to fuel anti-American sentiments. America's global popularity plummeted at the start of military action in Iraq and the U.S. presence there remains widely unpopular."

Marek Obrtel, former Lieutenant Colonel in Field Hospital with Czech Republic army, returned his medals which he received during his posting in Afghanistan War for NATO operations. He criticized the War on Terror as describing the mission as "deeply ashamed that I served a criminal organization such as NATO, led by the USA and its perverse interests around the world."

Role of U.S. Media

Researchers in communication studies and political science found that American understanding of the "War onTerror" is directly shaped by how mainstream news media reports events associated with the conflict. In *Bush's War: Media Bias and Justifications for War in a Terrorist Age* political communication researcher Jim A. Kuypers illustrated "how the press failed America in its coverage on the War on Terror." In each comparison, Kuypers "detected massive bias on the part of the press." This researcher called the mainstream news media an "anti-democratic institution" in his conclusion. "What has essentially happened since 9/11 has been that Bush has repeated the same themes and framed those themes the same whenever discussing the War on Terror," said Kuypers. "Immediately following 9/11, the mainstream news media (represented by CBS, ABC, NBC, *USA Today, The New York Times,* as well as *The Washington Post*) did echo Bush, but within eight weeks it began to intentionally ignore certain information the president was sharing and instead reframed the president's themes or intentionally introduced new material to shift the focus."

This goes beyond reporting alternate points of view, which is an important function of the press. "In short," Kuypers explained, "if someone were relying only on the mainstream media for information, they would have no idea what the president actually said. It was as if the press were reporting on a different speech." The study is essentially a "comparative framing analysis." Overall, Kuypers examined themes about 9-11 and the War on Terror that President Bush used and compared them to themes that the press used when reporting on what he said.

"Framing is a process whereby communicators, consciously or unconsciously, act to construct a point of view that encourages the facts of a given situation to be interpreted by others in a particular manner," wrote Kuypers. These findings suggest that the public is misinformed about government justification and plans concerning the War on Terror.

Others have also suggested that press coverage contributed to a public confused and misinformed on both the nature and level of the threat to the U.S. posed by terrorism. In his book, *Trapped in the War on Terror* political scientist Ian S. Lustick, claimed, "The media have given constant attention to possible terrorist-initiated catastrophes and to the failures and weaknesses of the government's response." Lustick alleged that the War on Terror is disconnected from the real but remote threat terrorism poses and that the generalized War on Terror began as part of the justification for invading Iraq, but then took on a life of its own, fueled by media coverage. Scott Atran writes that "publicity is the oxygen of terrorism" and the rapid growth of international communicative networks renders publicity even more potent, with the result that "perhaps never in the history of human conflict have so few people with so few actual means and capabilities frightened so many."

Media researcher Stephen D. Cooper's analysis of media criticism *Watching the Watchdog: Bloggers As the Fifth Estate* contains several examples of controversies concerning mainstream reporting of the War on Terror. Cooper found that bloggers' criticisms of factual inaccuracies in news stories or bloggers' discovery of the mainstream press' failure to adequately verify facts before publication caused many news organizations to retract or change news stories.

Cooper found that bloggers specializing in criticism of media coverage advanced four key points:

- Mainstream reporting of the War on Terror has frequently contained factual inaccuracies. In some cases, the errors go uncorrected: moreover, when corrections are issued they usually are given far less prominence than the initial coverage containing the errors.
- The mainstream press has sometimes failed to check the provenance of information or visual images supplied by Iraqi "stringers" (local Iraqis hired to relay local news).
- Story framing is often problematic: in particular, "man-in-the-street" interviews have often been used as a representation of public sentiment in Iraq, in place of methodologically sound survey data.
- Mainstream reporting has tended to concentrate on the more violent areas of Iraq, with little or no reporting of the calm areas.

David Barstow won the 2009 Pulitzer Prize for Investigative Reporting by connecting the Department of Defense to over 75 retired generals supporting the Iraq War on television and radio networks. The Department of Defense recruited retired generals to promote the war to the American public. Barstow also discovered undisclosed links between some retired generals and defense contractors. He reported that "the Bush administration used its control over access of information in an effort to transform the analysts into a kind of media Trojan horse".

British Objections

The Director of Public Prosecutions and head of the Crown Prosecution Service in the UK, Ken McDonald, Britain's most senior criminal prosecutor, stated that those responsible for acts of terrorism such as the 7 July 2005 London bombings are not "soldiers" in a war, but "inadequates" who should be dealt with by the criminal justice system. He added that a "culture of legislative restraint" was needed in passing anti-terrorism laws and that a "primary purpose" of the violent attacks was to tempt countries such as Britain to "abandon our values." He stated that in the eyes of the UK criminal justice system, the response to terrorism had to be "proportionate and grounded in due process and the rule of law":

London is not a battlefield. Those innocents who were murdered...were not victims of war. And the men who killed them were not, as in their vanity they claimed on their ludicrous videos, 'soldiers'. They were deluded, narcissistic inadequates. They were criminals. They were fantasists. We need to be very clear about this. On the streets of London there is no such thing as a war on terror. The fight against terrorism on the streets of Britain is not a war. It is the prevention of crime, the enforcement of our laws and the winning of justice for those damaged by their infringement.

Stella Rimington, former head of the British intelligence service MI5 criticised the War on Terror as a "huge overreaction" and had decried the militarization and politicization of U.S. efforts to be the wrong approach to terrorism. David Miliband, former UK foreign secretary, has similarly called the strategy a "mistake". Nigel Lawson, former Chancellor of the Exchequer, called for Britain to end its involvement in the War in Afghanistan, describing the mission as "wholly unsuccessful and indeed counter-productive."

CRITICAL INFRASTRUCTURE PROTECTION IN THE FIGHT AGAINST TERRORISM

The potential for catastrophic terrorist attacks that affect critical infrastructures is increasing. The consequences of an attack on the industrial control systems of critical infrastructure could vary widely. It is commonly assumed that a successful cyber attack would cause few, if any, casualties, but might result in loss of vital infrastructure service. For example, a successful cyber-attack on the public telephone switching network might deprive customers of telephone service while technicians reset and repaired the switching network. An attack on a chemical or liquid natural gas facility's control systems might lead to more widespread loss of lives as well as significant physical damage.

Another type of catastrophic infrastructure failure might be when one part of the infrastructure leads to the failure of other parts, causing widespread cascade effect. Such failure might occur due to the synergistic effect of infrastructure industries on each other. A simple example might be an attack on electrical utilities where electricity distribution was disrupted; sewage treatment plants and waterworks could also fail, as the turbines and other electrical apparatuses in these facilities might shut down.

Cascade events can be very damaging too, causing widespread utility outages. The blackouts in North-America and Europe during the last two years have put in evidence the vulnerability of energy infrastructures and consequently the need to find effective measures to prevent/or to mitigate the consequences derived from a major supply disruption. This use of cyberterrorism could also result in an amplification of the physical attack's effects. An example of this might be a conventional bombing attack on a building combined with a temporary denial of electrical or telephone service. The resulting degradation of emergency response, until back-up electrical or communication systems can be brought into place and used, could increase the number of casualties and public panic.

COUNTERMEASURES TO CYBER-TERRORISM OF CRITICAL

Goals of the Special Action Plan

The goal of this action plan is to protect the critical infrastructure from attacks of cyber-terrorism, which have the potential for large impacts on people's lives and on the economic activities of business using telecommunications networks and information systems. The government, primarily the Cabinet Secretariat, in close cooperation with the private sector, is working hard to implement this plan. In addition, as an objective of this plan, there are efforts to enhance the voluntary, independent participation by the businesses and regional public organizations associated with the critical infrastructure areas in the private sector (hereafter, called private sector critical infrastructure operators). Furthermore, the government will provide the necessary cooperation when the private sector critical infrastructure operators implement the plan.

The Threat of Cyber Terrorism

Many businesses and government activities have come to depend on information systems. It is also expected that there will be an acceleration in the use of information technologies and networking. For the critical infrastructure, like power supply, transportation, and electronic control, information systems also have a crucial role in maintaining public safety and stable supplies of indispensable services for the economic activities of business and the daily lives of the people.

An electronic attack using telecommunications networks and information systems (called a "cyber attack") on these important information systems that are fundamental to the critical infrastructure, has the potential to disrupt people's lives and business activities, as well as to cause large amounts of damage, placing people's lives at risk. This kind of attack, unlike a physical attack, can be made from a single computer by a person with the ability to intrude the information system. There is also the fear that systematic, large-scale attacks could be made for the purpose of causing disruption and confusion to business activities and people's lives.

Overseas, there have been cases of damage to financial information systems, and individuals known as hackers intruding critical information systems, denial-of-service attacks (DoS attack), as well as instances of large amounts of damage caused by the spread of computer viruses; so it is clear that this threat is already becoming a reality. The United States is developing a congressional plan to handle the threat of financial damage, confusion, injury or death caused by attacks on critical networks by terrorist groups or criminal organizations having advanced technical skills. Connections via the Internet and other networks continue to develop, and interdependence increases. There is also increasing standardization and commonality in the specifications of information systems. These trends increase the threat of cyber attacks, even on information systems that currently face little danger from outside intrusion. In addition, there is always the possibility of such attacks being made by inside personnel. It must be recognized that even an information system that is not connected to any other networks is not immune to the danger of an outside attack.

Critical Infrastructure Fields

At the present time, the critical infrastructure fields that are considered likely to have the largest impact on financial activities and people's daily lives in the event of a cyber-terrorist attack are telecommunications, finance, aviation, railroads, electrical power, gas, and government/administrative services (including regional public organizations).

The ministries and agencies with jurisdiction over each of these critical infrastructure areas are making efforts to appropriately implement this plan for each of the areas. In order to protect the critical infrastructure of Japan from the threat of cyber-terrorism it is also important for fields other than these critical infrastructure fields to refer to this special action plan and strengthen the countermeasures as needed.

Preventing Damage (Raising Security Level)

In order to prevent damage, risk analysis will be performed for the information systems of the target critical infrastructures, and measures will be implemented as needed according to the importance of the information system. It is also necessary to continually raise security level in each of the fields with critical infrastructure.

(1) Raising security level in private sector critical infrastructure fields

- Private sector critical infrastructure operators are working to raise security level by referring to "Guidelines for IT Security Policy" (issued July 18, 2000 by the IT Security Promotion Committee), the guidelines on information security from the various ministries and agencies, and the

OECD security guidelines, and establishing risk analysis and information security policies.

- When private sector critical infrastructure fields as well as regional public organizations (hereafter called "private sector, etc.") use information system with a common standard specification, or are connected to other information systems, there shall be proper handling of the shared risk for that field. To achieve this, investigations shall be made to establish countermeasure guidelines for these private sector, etc. groups.
- In order for the government to contribute to improving security level for the private sector, etc., efforts are being made to provide information, advice, and instruction, and to support the efforts of the private sector etc. groups.

(2) *Raising security level to establish electronic government*

- The various ministries and agencies implementing the necessary measures to improve security level, starting by establishing an electronic government foundation by 2003, and following the policies established according to the "Guidelines for IT Security Policy".
- The special advisory team of the Cabinet Secretariat is providing technical surveys and advice on security countermeasures for information systems for the various ministries and agencies.

Establish and Enhance Communication and Coordination Systems between Government and the Private Sector

For the various critical infrastructure fields, it is necessary to establish and enhance systems for the government and private sector to coordinate prevention, response, and sharing of security data (data required to improve security) as well as warning information (information needed for emergency response and warnings, such as data on the occurrence of cyber attacks).

Particularly, as the threat of cyber terrorism grows, it is necessary to quickly establish a communication and coordination system between government and the private sector to handle cyber terrorism, and based on the situation in each field, it is necessary to develop the next level of systems, within one year of establishing this plan.

(1) Communication and coordination systems for private sector etc. critical infrastructure groups

Build a communication and coordination system between operators associated with cyber-terrorism countermeasures, while making use of existing communication mechanisms, to fulfill the following roles.

- Collect, distribute and share the common security information in the various fields, as well as the warning information.
- A communication system for when a cyber attack occurs, or when there is a danger of such an attack
- Implement unified, centralized communications for the government and related agencies

(2) Communication and coordination systems with other critical infrastructure operators

In cases of interconnection to other information systems and operators of important infrastructure in other fields through networks, develop, as needed, the communication and cooperation systems for cyber-terrorism countermeasures.

(3) Establishing a communication and cooperation system for government

The government, centering on the Cabinet Secretariat, will fill the following roles in developing the communication and cooperation systems

- Collecting, distributing and sharing security information and warning information
- Collecting information when a cyber-attack occurs, or when there is a danger of such an attack
- Within government departments, communication with related agencies and the private sector etc. critical infrastructure groups

(4) Handling of data

For the information collection and sharing, the appropriate data will be provided by the private sector etc. critical infrastructure groups. To achieve this, there must be efforts made to build a relationship of trust between all interested parties, such as obtaining a consensus on handling this data rigorously and correctly.

(5) Cooperation with private sector etc. critical infrastructure groups

The government will make efforts to cooperate with the private sector etc. critical infrastructure groups, including providing security and warning information.

Detection of Cyber Attacks and Emergency Response Through Government and Private Sector Cooperation

In addition to determining the measures to be taken for each of the critical infrastructure fields in the event of a cyber attack, or when there is a danger of such an attack, it is necessary to strengthen the response capabilities of the government and private sector overall.

(1) Detection of cyber attacks

- The government and private sector etc. critical infrastructure operators shall determine in advance the appropriate handling measures for the situation, including type and extent of the damage, and locations, in the event that damage occurs to a key information system, assuming that it is difficult to judge whether it is a cyber attack, based on adequate consideration of the potential scenarios.
- The government and private sector etc. critical infrastructure operators will collect security data and warning data from government agencies, organizations related to information security, and information system vendors, etc.

(2) Establishing an emergency response plan

- To establish countermeasures and an emergency response plan in the event of a cyber attack, or when there is a danger of such an attack on the private sector etc. critical infrastructure operators, investigate while making use of the communications systems established as described in section 5. (Expected issues for the emergency response plan)

Communication, containment of damage, verification of safety, recovery (temporary measures), prevention of recurrence, etc.

Furthermore, it is important that this plan outlines the procedures over time after a cyber attack is detected, so that it is possible to respond quickly.

- The actions during an emergency will sometimes require a high-level judgement, so procedures like the emergency response plan will be determined so that the appropriate persons, having the proper authority and responsibility, can make decisions quickly.

(3) Information and communication procedures during an emergency

- In the event of a cyber-attack, or when there is an information indicating a danger of such an attack, the emergency information communication procedure is as follows.

(a) Communication of information related to the cyber attack

1. The ministry, agency or private sector, etc. critical infrastructure operator that is subject to a cyber attack, or obtains information indicating the danger of such an attack, in addition to quickly taking the appropriate steps, will also provide the relevant information to the specified personnel in other key private sector infrastructure fields, local government offices, and related agencies.
2. The ministries and agencies that receive this information will provide guidance and advice to the private sector, etc. critical infrastructure operators subjected to the attack, as well as informing the Cabinet Secretariat of the relevant information.
3. The Cabinet Secretariat will coordinate the related ministries and agencies, and collect information.

(b) Communication of warning information

4. The Cabinet Secretariat notifies the various ministries and agencies of warning information when it is necessary based on the contents of the information indicating an attack or the danger of an attack.
5. When the various ministries and agencies receive warnings from the Cabinet Secretariat, they will quickly notify the local private sector etc. critical infrastructure operators.
   - The government and private sector, etc. critical infrastructure operators will run drills of cyber terrorism countermeasures as necessary.
   - In the event that people's lives or business economic activities are affected due to damage from an attack, the government and private sector, etc. critical infrastructure operators will make every effort to quickly provide the relevant information to those involved.

(4) Strengthening the government's emergency response system

- In the event of a cyber attack, or when there is a danger of such an attack, the Cabinet Secretariat will collect information and coordinate the cooperation and efforts of the various ministries, as well as organizing the ministries and agencies for the action guidelines when it is necessary for the government to take action.
- The Cabinet Secretariat will establish the required communications systems with the cooperation of the various ministries and agencies. In addition, the information gathering system and the response systems for cyber terrorism will be enhanced by the various ministries and agencies.

Establish Foundations of Information Security

Training of personnel, research and development, widespread application, and appropriate laws and regulations on information security fundamentals is required in order to further develop countermeasures to cyber terrorism.

To provide protection from cyber attacks on critical infrastructure, the operators and users of general information systems, not just those of the key systems, must be aware of the threat of cyber attacks, deepen their understanding of the need for security measures, and take the necessary security countermeasures so that there is a widespread general awareness and effort to handle this issue.

(1) Promote development of human resources

- The government and private sector, etc. critical infrastructure operators will work to continuously train educate personnel, and to develop specialists in security technology.

(2) Promote research and development

- The government and private sector, etc. critical infrastructure operators will promote cooperation and communication between the government and the private sector on research of the technology, countermeasures, threat analysis, and development of the required technology to build a strong foundation against the threat of cyber terrorism.

(3) Promote widespread application

- The government will announce the occurrences of illegal access, publicize information on defense against illegal access, and raise general awareness on cyber terrorism threats both inside and outside Japan.
- The government will promote research and study of information security for the personnel of the private sector, etc. critical infrastructure operators.

(4) Add and revise legislation

- The government will consider changes to the law, such as the basic criminal law, from the perspective of maintaining safety for the telecommunications networks and international harmony.

International Cooperation

Cyber attacks can be made without regard for national

boundaries, so international cooperation and coordination is required in order to handle such attacks.

- The government and private sector, etc. key infrastructure operators will work to accumulate information from information security organizations outside Japan.
- The government will promote cooperation with the international organizations related to cyber-terrorism of the OECD and G8.
- The government will work to strengthen international cooperation, information exchanges and shared training with the counterparts in other nations.

Action Plan Revisions

This action plan is the first version, focused on establishing a means of communication and coordination between the government and the private sector. The government will periodically review and revise this plan as required, according to future progress and developments.

WE ARE LOSING THE WAR ON TERROR

The ground truth about the spread of terrorism will be a hard one for many Americans to swallow after 13 costly years of war. Terrorism is spreading worldwide. Our enemies have sustained our blows, adapted, and grown. Two questions loom large as a consequence: Where did we go wrong and what do we do now?

Recent headlines and new studies support the conclusion that global terror trends are heading in an ever more dangerous direction. In early June, the Rand Corporation released a study that detailed the growing threat. It reports that in 2007, there were 28 Salafi-jihadist groups like al Qaeda. As of last year, there were 49. In 2007, these groups conducted 100 attacks. Last year, they conducted 950. The study estimates that there were between 18,000 and 42,000 such terrorists active seven years ago. The low-end estimate for last year, at 44,000, is higher than the top estimate for 2007, and the new high-end estimate is 105,000. The administration rightly argues that "core al Qaeda" has sustained "huge" damage. But "core al Qaeda" no longer poses the principle threat to the

U.S. homeland. That comes, according to the Rand report, from al Qaeda in the Arabian Peninsula. As Rand summarizes the report: "Since 2010, there has been a 58 percent increase in the number of jihadist groups, a doubling of jihadist fighters and a tripling of attacks by Al Qaeda affiliates.

The most significant threat to the United States, the report concludes, comes from terrorist groups operating in Yemen, Syria, Afghanistan and Pakistan."

As legitimate as the questions that have emerged in the Bowe Bergdahl case may be, they are secondary to the deteriorating situation associated with the war the recently released prisoner went to Afghanistan to fight.

There is no denying that the contempt for Congress shown in failing to inform it of the deal — even as perhaps 100 in the administration knew of it — starkly reveals the cynicism behind last year's faux deferral to Congress on Syria.

But it would be far more cynical to continue with the Obama team's variation on the "mission accomplished" misrepresentations of his predecessor. The war in Iraq was not over or won when we said it was. Nor is the war on terror won or the threat it poses resolved simply by no longer using the term or suggesting our goal was merely to inflict damage on the tiny fraction of terrorists who were associated with the 9/11 attacks. The reality is that we are still fighting the last war on terror even as a new set of risks loom and are made worse by our minimizing their implications for political purposes.

In its recent assessment, "Country Reports on Terrorism 2013," the State Department acknowledged the trend. It observes that last year attacks worldwide increased almost by half, from 6,700 to 9,700. Nearly 18,000 people died and nearly 33,000 were injured. While the report hails allied forces for making progress combating al Qaeda's core in the AfPak region, it also notes that the group's affiliates are becoming more dangerous.

The report takes particular note of the threat posed by foreign extremists in Syria, which has become a kind of petri dish in which a growing global terror threat is being cultivated. Estimates on the number of such fighters range from7,000 to over 20,000. The news that one recent suicide bomber in Syria was an American and that one of the attackers behind the recent shooting at the Jewish Museum of Belgium spent time in Syria suggests how this threat may evolve over time. It's not unlikely that, if left unchecked, the long-term consequences of a cadre of fighters trained in Syria who will soon return to their home countries will be one of the darkest legacies of that war — a legacy that may well echo the long-term costs associated with training jihadists in the battle against the Russians in Afghanistan in the 1980s, among whom, of course, was Osama bin Laden.

Sleepwalking Into a Trap

On just one day this week, Pakistani Taliban claimed credit for an attack on Karachi's international airport that killed 30 people, while in Baluchistan 23 Shiite pilgrims were killed in gun and bomb attacks. (A follow-up attack on the Karachi airport's security academy occurred less than 48 hours later.) That same day, 52 people were killed in bombings in Baghdad. Elsewhere that day a female suicide bomber attacked a barracks in Nigeria. Scores more died in the fighting in Syria — many at the hands of the government, to be sure, but many also as victims of extremists.

Such attacks pass with little more than perfunctory comment from our leaders or the media. Yet we are numbed to such attacks at our peril. We compound the risk associated with such numbing by rationalizing them away. The Rand report notes that the number of "near abroad" attacks is up while the number of "far abroad" attacks has gone down. This is a way of saying that the threat to the U.S. homeland appears to be less from these fragmented, decentralized groups. The report also suggests that such groups are more easily defeated or turned against one another. The State Department presented its report with comments from its spokesperson that "the numbers [of attacks] against Americans have been very low for a long time and have continued to go down."

That fewer Americans are being killed and fewer terrorists are seeking to hit targets on U.S. soil is no doubt a very good thing. Much credit for producing such an outcome is due to the U.S. intelligence community and our military for reducing those risks to our homeland security establishment and the private sector organizations with which they must collaborate to be successful. But it would be as dangerous today to interpret current trends as being positive because one particular past enemy is in decline or because at the moment the risk to Americans at home is lower as it was for top officials to underappreciate the threat posed by bin Laden immediately before the 9/11 attacks.

That's the dangerous trap into which we risk falling. By overly focusing on narrowly addressing the threats identified with the attacks 13 years ago, we risk creating precisely the same conditions that led to those attacks… and ignoring other, perhaps more serious, emerging threats.

For example, serious threats exist to U.S. interests that are not threats to the homeland. The disintegration of Syria is such a threat. The creation of a failed state bordering Israel, Lebanon, Jordan, Turkey, and Iraq poses deep and lasting risks to the region. One manifestation of how such a threat can spread is visible right now in Iraq, where ISIS (the Islamic State of Iraq and the Levant), a group that cut its teeth in the Syria conflict, has just seized control of much of Iraq's second largest city, Mosul.

This compounds ISIS gains in Fallujah and across Anbar province. Should the Iraqi government fail to regain control of this region, the consequences of an extremist rump state on Jordan's eastern border and of conflict with Kurds in the north are grave. Such a scenario is quite possible, in fact; 11 years after the United States went to war with Iraq we could be on the verge of seeing it fracture into an extr

emist Sunni state in the west and an Iranian puppet state in the east — perhaps the worst possible outcome we could have envisioned. It raises the question: What is the opposite of "mission accomplished?" And another: Who lost Iraq? (That the destabilization that caused this was triggered by an Afghan-based extremist's group attack on the United States is illustrative of how unpredictable, convoluted, and widespread the aftershocks of terror attacks can be.)

This last point in turn should lead to the recognition that the cultivation of extremist threats within failed states like Syria or weak states like Iraq, Yemen, or Libya or those in sub-Saharan Africa seems certain to produce a new generation of jihadists who will soon pose a threat worldwide. That such groups have gained important footholds in Libya, Mali, Nigeria, and in the Horn of Africa should be very worrying to us. While they seem like distant places and the damage is not now being visited on Americans, what will be the cost in terms regional stability, access to vital resources, flows of immigrants and refugees to new countries that can ill-afford to house them, etc.?

The Risks Posed by National Narcissism

In the wake of the 9/11 attacks we had a number of reactions to the trauma it caused. Some were natural — like seeking to exact a punishment on those behind the attacks. Some were sound national security policy — like seeking to keep the attackers from ever attacking us again, and increasing the tools we have to anticipate or mitigate future risks. Some were dangerously ill-considered — like invading Iraq. Some were damaging to our national standing — like surveillance overreach or the use of torture. Today, we are learning the lessons of this period of reaction, this era in which so many of our initiatives seemed to be driven by fear of a future attack. That is why it would be both ironic and perilous for us to fail to learn one of the first lessons of what happened on 9/11, which is that in today's globalized, technologically empowered world, there is no such thing as a distant problem. All can make their way to our doorstep with lightning speed.

This does not mean we must intervene everywhere against everyone. The first War on Terror was clearly mismanaged in many sometimes profoundly damaging ways. Indeed, some of our best antidotes to the risk posed by terror are not war at all but good intelligence, good police work, and a renewed focus on economic, social, and institutional development. Certainly, invading and destabilizing extraneous countries only makes matters worse.

One of the most pervasive problems behind the first War on Terror was national narcissism — the sense that now that this problem that had afflicted so many for so long had taken a big enough toll on us, it was all about us, entirely up to us to handle in whatever way we saw fit, the laws of nations and the international community be damned. But there is another insidious consequence of such nationalism. It is the mistaken belief — the one that afflicted us prior to 9/11 and was one of its proximate causes — that if such problems did not impact our shores and our people, they never would; they weren't our concern. We can't let such a view delude us into complacency now.

As Seth Jones, the author of the Rand report, has said, "Based on these threats, the United States cannot afford to withdraw or remain disengaged from key parts of North Africa, the Middle East and South Asia. After more than a decade of war in Afghanistan and Iraq, it may be tempting for the U.S. to turn its attention elsewhere and scale back on counterterrorism efforts. But [our] research indicates that the struggle is far from over."

We dare not drop our guard. And we must find ways to work even more vigorously with the international community, with our allies, with stable regional governments upon which we can depend and with whom we can collaborate, to do whatever we can to reverse this disturbing recent trend. President Barack Obama's West Point speech — which suggested that we could now safely start to hand off such issues to partners on the ground — has, in the case of Pakistan and Iraq, been debunked within the last few days. We cannot put this effort on autopilot and forget about it. Instead we must develop new strategies and new active and committed alliances — like finding ways to work more closely with the Chinese, who face a similar threat at home, reinvigorating how the Atlantic Alliance works together on such issues, and working more closely with the more moderate Sunni states in the Middle East. Our new efforts will require more aid (and unlike with some of our Syria promises, aid that is swiftly delivered when it can make a difference). They will mean more technical assistance and training. More shared intelligence. More military support and, yes, action when it is the only and best available option. And above all it will mean instilling the sense of urgency that should be associated with any endeavor, like this one to protect our citizens and interests, in which we are so clearly losing ground.

3

September 11 Attacks and Terrorism

It is now over a decade since the terrorist attacks in the US, simply dubbed "9-11" shocked the world, and ushered in a global "war on terror". And looking back, what has the US to show for its decade of effort? Has it been winning the war on terror? It depends how it is measured. The killing of Osama Bin Laden was of course a major success. But the cost of vengeance (instead of justice) has also been high:

- A further turn towards hatred and a rise in those who think most Muslims are terrorists, that Islam is a threat to the world, etc.
- Wars that have seen far more than the 3,500 deaths that the US saw, and a self-fulfilling prophecy; creating more anger and resentment against the US, more potential terrorists, and the complete opposite of what the neo-cons wanted; global downturn and US decline instead consolidating their power and position in the world.
- Over 6,000 US soldiers killed in wars in Afghanistan and Iraq. Possibly 100 times that number of civilians in those countries (in Iraq, at an early point, there was an estimated range of 400,000 to 900,000 civilian deaths, which of course Bush had to reject, claiming it used flawed techniques, even though it used estimation techniques his own government agencies taught others to use).

The rest of Jim Lobe's article provides a useful summary of why Bush's focus on Iraq (under the clearly false and fearmongering excuses of weapons of mass destruction and links to terrorism), instead of tackling terrorism, was "perhaps the single-most disastrous foreign policy decision by a U.S. president in the past decade, if not the past century." This is because it allowed the Taliban to regroup in Afghanistan leading to more expensive military operations and strengthening Al Qaeda's resolve further. Meanwhile, various US actions in Iraq and elsewhere damaged its reputation around the world.

9/11

The early morning attacks on New York City and Washington, DC, blasted American security and drove the country into the type of grief and fear not felt since Pearl Harbor. For several days, Americans sought collective comfort in candlelight vigils; movie theaters were empty and churches were full. Yet grief soon gave way to anger and a search for answers and retribution. Who had committed this act of terrorism? How quickly could we respond? How soon would justice be served?

Most Americans assumed that the answer to the first question would be found among the usual suspects.

Secretary of Defense Donald Rumsfeld immediately concluded that the attack must have come from Iraq. Its half-mad dictator, Saddam Hussein, had chafed for a decade under the sanctions imposed by the United States after the Persian Gulf War of 1991. Rumsfeld ordered his aides to begin collecting evidence implicating Saddam in the attack, and to alert him as soon as they had built a case strong enough to justify a retaliatory attack on Iraq.

Others suggested that Iran must be involved. Recent years had witnessed a slight thaw in American-Iranian relations—some trade and travel restrictions had been removed, and in 2000 talks were held between members of the US Congress and Iran's parliament. But more than two decades of ill will and powerful memories of the 1979 attack on the American embassy in Tehran (and the hostage crisis that followed) led many to believe that Iran had resumed its attack against America.

For others, a more amorphous collection of Islamic terrorists leapt immediately to mind. The Palestinian Liberation Organization, Hamas, and Hezbollah all had long terrorist histories—most aimed at Israel but some aimed at the United States. Most Americans knew little about these organizations and the differences and similarities among them. But against the backdrop of 9/11, few felt the need to sort out the nuances of these radical organizations.

Even after the 9/11 terrorists were identified as members of Al Qaeda—Osama Bin Laden's organization of Sunni Islamic militants based in Afghanistan—many continued to search for links to a larger community of Middle Eastern enemies. President George W. Bush identified Iran as part of an "axis of evil" in his 2002 State of the Union Address, even though thousands of Iranians had marched in the streets of Tehran in demonstrations of sympathy with America following the 9/11 attacks and Iranian government officials cooperated fully when America launched its invasion of Afghanistan in late 2001. American government officials also engaged in an extensive, and now widely discredited, investigation of links between Iraq and Al Qaeda as it later prepared to invade Iraq and remove Hussein from power.

There may have been legitimate reasons for some initial confusion. The Middle East is a complex web of religious groups, nationalisms and ethnic rivalries, conflicting goals, and historical tensions. Forced by the attacks on New York and Washington, DC, to sort it all out in this moment of crisis may have been asking too much. But charting an enduring solution to the problem of United States-Middle East tensions requires that we unravel the threads and examine the long and complex history that has left peace so illusive in the region and the United States so frequently hated.

We must understand, for example, the United States' complex relationship with Israel—both America's long history of support for the Jewish state *and* America's repeated efforts to win recognition among Israel's Arab and Persian neighbors as an honest broker, a fair mediator of the region's conflicts.

We must also attempt to understand why Iranians refer to the United States as the "great Satan"—why America was held responsible for the crimes of an old Iranian monarch, the Shah, ousted in 1979 by the Shiite factions still in power today, and why the nation is so intent on resisting American pressures to curtail its nuclear program.

We must understand why oil, the region's most valuable resource, has become a political tool, rather than just a freely traded commodity—why Middle Eastern countries have used their oil to lash out at the western nations that rely on it and, in the process, bring vast wealth to the region.

These are not simple stories, and they may not lead to the discovery of a miracle solution to either terrorism or instability in the Middle East. But they may help us understand why the surprise attacks of 9/11—as undeniably horrific and unjustifiable as they were—perhaps should not have come as a complete surprise, and why the complications of subsequent American actions in Afghanistan and Iraq should have been anticipated.

The September 11 attacks (also referred to as September 11, September 11th, or9/11) were a series of four coordinated terrorist attacks by the Islamic terrorist group al-Qaeda on the United States on the morning of Tuesday, September 11, 2001. The attacks consisted of suicide attacks used to target symbolic U.S. landmarks.

Four passenger airliners—which all departed from airports on the U.S. East Coast bound forCalifornia—were hijacked by 19 al-Qaeda terrorists to be flown into buildings. Two of the planes, American Airlines Flight 11 and United Airlines Flight 175, were crashed into theNorth and South towers, respectively, of the World Trade Center complex in New York City. Within an hour and 42 minutes, both 110-story towers collapsed, with debris and the resulting fires causing partial or complete collapse of all other buildings in the World Trade Center complex, including the 47-story 7 World Trade Center tower, as well as significant damage to ten other large surrounding structures. A third plane, American Airlines Flight 77, was crashed into the Pentagon (the headquarters of the United States Department of Defense) in Arlington County, Virginia, leading to a partial collapse in the Pentagon's western side. The fourth plane, United Airlines Flight 93, initially was steered toward Washington, D.C., but crashed into a field near Shanksville, Pennsylvania, after its passengers tried to overcome the hijackers. In total, the attacks claimed the lives of 2,996 people (including the 19 hijackers) and caused at least $10 billion in property and infrastructure damage and $3 trillion in total costs. It was the deadliest incident for firefighters and law enforcement officers in the history of the United States, with 343 and 72 killed respectively.

Suspicion for the attack quickly fell on al-Qaeda. The United States responded to the attacks by launching the War on Terror and invading Afghanistan to depose the Taliban, which had harbored al-Qaeda. Many countries strengthened their anti-terrorism legislationand expanded the powers of law enforcement and intelligence agencies to prevent terrorist attacks. Although al-Qaeda's leader, Osama bin Laden, initially denied any involvement, in 2004 he claimed responsibility for the attacks. Al-Qaeda and bin Laden cited U.S. support of Israel, the presence of U.S. troops in Saudi Arabia, and sanctions against Iraq as motives. Having evaded capture for almost a decade, bin Laden was located and killed by members of the U.S. military in May 2011.

The destruction of the World Trade Center and nearby infrastructure caused serious damage to the economy of Lower Manhattan and had a significant effect on global markets, closingWall Street until September 17 and the civilian airspace in the U.S. and Canada until September 13. Many closings, evacuations, and cancellations followed, out of respect or fear of further attacks. Cleanup of the World Trade Center site was completed in May 2002, and the Pentagon was repaired within a year. On November 18, 2006, construction of One World Trade Center began at the World Trade Center site. The building was officially opened on November 3, 2014. Numerous memorials have been constructed, including the National September 11 Memorial & Museum in New York City, the Pentagon Memorial in Arlington County, Virginia, and the Flight 93 National Memorial in a field near Shanksville, Pennsylvania.

BACKGROUND

Al-Qaeda

The origins of al-Qaeda can be traced to 1979 when the Soviet Union invaded Afghanistan. Osama bin Laden traveled to

Afghanistan and helped organize Arabmujahideen to resist the Soviets. Under the guidance of Ayman al-Zawahiri, bin Laden became more radical. In 1996, bin Laden issued his first *fatwâ,* calling for American soldiers to leave Saudi Arabia.

In a second *fatwâ* in 1998, bin Laden outlined his objections to American foreign policy with respect to Israel, as well as the continued presence of American troops in Saudi Arabia after the Gulf War. Bin Laden used Islamic texts to exhort Muslims to attack Americans until the stated grievances are reversed. Muslim legal scholars "have throughout Islamic history unanimously agreed that the jihad is an individual duty if the enemy destroys the Muslim countries", according to bin Laden.

Osama Bin Laden

Bin Laden, who orchestrated the attacks, initially denied but later admitted involvement. Al Jazeerabroadcast a statement by bin Laden on September 16, 2001, stating, "I stress that I have not carried out this act, which appears to have been carried out by individuals with their own motivation." In November 2001, U.S. forces recovered a videotape from a destroyed house in Jalalabad, Afghanistan. In the video, bin Laden is seen talking to Khaled al-Harbi and admits foreknowledge of the attacks. On December 27, 2001, a second bin Laden video was released. In the video, he said, "It has become clear that the West in general and America in particular have an unspeakable hatred for Islam.... It is the hatred of crusaders. Terrorism against America deserves to be praised because it was a response to injustice, aimed at forcing America to stop its support for Israel, which kills our people.... We say that the end of the United States is imminent, whether Bin Laden or his followers are alive or dead, for the awakening of the Muslim umma (nation) has occurred", but he stopped short of admitting responsibility for the attacks. The transcript refers several times to the United States specifically targeting Muslims.

Shortly before the U.S. presidential election in 2004, in a taped statement, bin Laden publicly acknowledged al-Qaeda's involvement in the attacks on the U.S. and admitted his direct link to the attacks. He said that the attacks were carried out because, "we are free ... and want to regain freedom for our nation. As you undermine our security we undermine yours." Bin Laden said he had personally directed his followers to attack the World Trade Center. Another video obtained by Al Jazeera in September 2006 shows bin Laden with Ramzi bin al-Shibh, as well as two hijackers, Hamza al-Ghamdi and Wail al-Shehri, as they make preparations for the attacks. The U.S. never formally indicted bin Laden for the 9/11 attacks but he was on the FBI's Most Wanted List for the bombings of the U.S. Embassies in Dar es Salaam, Tanzania, and Nairobi, Kenya. After a 10-year manhunt, bin Laden was killed by American special forces in a compoundin Abbottabad, Pakistan on May 2, 2011.

Khalid Sheikh Mohammed

The journalist Yosri Fouda of the Arabic television channel Al Jazeera reported that, in April 2002, Khalid Sheikh Mohammed admitted his involvement, along with Ramzi bin al-Shibh. The9/ 11 Commission Report determined that the animosity towards the United States felt by Mohammed, the principal architect of the 9/ 11 attacks, stemmed from his "violent disagreement with U.S. foreign policy favoring Israel". Mohammed was also an adviser and financier of the 1993 World Trade Center bombing and the uncle of Ramzi Yousef, the lead bomber in that attack.

Mohammed was arrested on March 1, 2003, in Rawalpindi, Pakistan, by Pakistani security officials working with the CIA, then transported to Guantanamo Bay and interrogated using methods including waterboarding. During U.S. hearings at Guantanamo Bay in March 2007, Mohammed again confessed his responsibility for the attacks, stating he "was responsible for the 9/11 operation from A to Z" and that his statement was not made under duress.

Other al-Qaeda Members

In "Substitution for Testimony of Khalid Sheikh Mohammed" from the trial of Zacarias Moussaoui, five people are identified as having been completely aware of the operation's details. They are bin Laden, Khalid Sheikh Mohammed, Ramzi bin al-Shibh, Abu Turab al-Urduni, and Mohammed Atef. To date, only peripheral figures have been tried or convicted for the attacks.

On September 26, 2005, the Spanish high court sentenced Abu Dahdah to 27 years in prison for conspiracy on the 9/11 attacks and being a member of the terrorist organization al-Qaeda. At the same time, another 17 al-Qaeda members were sentenced to penalties of between six and eleven years. On February 16, 2006, the Spanish Supreme Court reduced the Abu Dahdah penalty to 12 years because it considered that his participation in the conspiracy was not proven.

Also, in 2006, Moussaoui, who some originally suspected might have been the assigned 20th hijacker, was convicted for the lesser role of conspiracy to commit acts of terrorism and air piracy. He is serving a life sentence without parole in the United States. Mounir el-Motassadeq, an associate of the Hamburg-based hijackers, is serving 15 years in Germany for his role in helping the hijackers prepare for the attacks.

The Hamburg cell in Germany included radical Islamists who eventually came to be key operatives in the 9/11 attacks. Mohamed Atta,Marwan al-Shehhi, Ziad Jarrah, Ramzi bin al-Shibh, and Said Bahaji were all members of al-Qaeda's Hamburg cell.

Motives

Osama bin Laden's declaration of a holy war against the United States, and a 1998 *fatwâ* signed by bin Laden and others, calling for the killing of Americans, are seen by investigators as evidence of his motivation. In bin Laden's November 2002 "Letter to America", he explicitly stated that al-Qaeda's motives for their attacks include:

- U.S. support of Israel
- support for the "attacks against Muslims" in Somalia
- support of Russian "atrocities against Muslims" in Chechnya
- pro-American governments in the Middle East (who "act as your agents") being against Muslim interests
- support of Indian "oppression against Muslims" in Kashmir
- the presence of U.S. troops in Saudi Arabia
- the sanctions against Iraq

After the attacks, bin Laden and al-Zawahiri released additional video tapes and audio tapes, some of which repeated those reasons for the attacks. Two particularly important publications were bin Laden's 2002 "Letter to America", and a 2004 video tape by bin Laden.

Bin Laden interpreted Muhammad as having banned the "permanent presence of infidels in Arabia". In 1996, bin Laden issued a *fatwâ*calling for American troops to leave Saudi Arabia. In 1998, al-Qaeda wrote, "for over seven years the United States has been occupying the lands of Islam in the holiest of places, the Arabian Peninsula, plundering its riches, dictating to its rulers, humiliating its people, terrorizing its neighbors, and turning its bases in the Peninsula into a spearhead through which to fight the neighboring Muslim peoples."

In a December 1999 interview, bin Laden said he felt that Americans were "too near to Mecca", and considered this a provocation to the entire Muslim world. One analysis of suicide terrorism suggested that without U.S. troops in Saudi Arabia, al-Qaeda likely would not have been able to get people to commit to suicide missions.

In the 1998 *fatwâ*, al-Qaeda identified the Iraq sanctions as a reason to kill Americans, condemning the "protracted blockade" among other actions that constitute a declaration of war against "Allah, his messenger, and Muslims." The *fatwâ* declared that "the ruling to kill the Americans and their allies – civilians and military – is an individual duty for every Muslim who can do it in any country in which it is possible to do it, in order to liberate the al-Aqsa Mosque and the holy mosque of Mecca from their grip, and in order for their [the Americans'] armies to move out of all the lands of Islam, defeated and unable to threaten any Muslim."

Bin Laden claimed, in 2004, that the idea of destroying the towers had first occurred to him in 1982, when he witnessed Israel's bombardment of high-rise apartment buildings during the 1982 Lebanon War. Some analysts, including Mearsheimer and Walt, also claim that one motivation for the attacks was U.S. support of Israel. In 2004 and 2010, bin Laden again connected the September 11 attacks with U.S. support of Israel, although most of the letter expressed bin Laden's disdain for President Bush and bin Laden's hope to "destroy and bankrupt" the U.S.

Other motives have been suggested in addition to those stated by bin Laden and al-Qaeda, including western support of Islamic and non-Islamic authoritarian regimes in Saudi Arabia, Iran, Egypt, Iraq, Pakistan and northern Africa, and the presence of western troops in some of these countries. Some authors suggest the "humiliation" resulting from the Islamic world falling behind the Western world – this discrepancy rendered especially visible by the globalization trend and a desire to provoke the U.S. into a broader war against the Islamic world in the hope of motivating more allies to support al-Qaeda. Similarly, others have argued that 9/11 was a strategic move with the objective of provoking America into a war that would incite a pan-Islamic revolution.

Planning of the Attacks

The idea for the attacks came from Khalid Sheikh Mohammed, who first presented it to Osama bin Laden in 1996. At that time, bin Laden and al-Qaeda were in a period of transition, having just relocated back to Afghanistan from Sudan. The 1998 African Embassy bombings and bin Laden's 1998 fatwâ marked a turning point, as bin Laden became intent on attacking the United States.

In late 1998 or early 1999, bin Laden gave approval for Mohammed to go forward with organizing the plot. A series of meetings occurred in early 1999, involving Mohammed, bin Laden, and his deputyMohammed Atef. Atef provided operational support for the plot, including target selections and helping arrange travel for the hijackers. Bin Laden overruled Mohammed, rejecting some potential targets such as the U.S. Bank Tower in Los Angeles because, "there was not enough time to prepare for such an operation".

Bin Laden provided leadership and financial support for the plot, and was involved in selecting participants. Bin Laden initially selected Nawaf al-Hazmi and Khalid al-Mihdhar, both experienced jihadists who had fought in Bosnia. Hazmi and Mihdhar arrived in the United States in mid-January 2000. In spring 2000, Hazmi and Mihdhar took flying lessons in San Diego, California, but both spoke little English, performed poorly with flying lessons, and eventually served as secondary – or "muscle" – hijackers.

In late 1999, a group of men from Hamburg, Germany arrived in Afghanistan, including Mohamed Atta,Marwan al-Shehhi, Ziad Jarrah, and Ramzi bin al-Shibh. Bin Laden selected these men because they were educated, could speak English, and had experience living in the West. New recruits were routinely screened for special skills and al-Qaeda leaders consequently discovered that Hani Hanjour already had a commercial pilot's license.

Hanjour arrived in San Diego on December 8, 2000, joining Hazmi. They soon left for Arizona, where Hanjour took refresher training. Marwan al-Shehhi arrived at the end of May 2000, while Atta arrived on June 3, 2000, and Jarrah arrived on June 27, 2000. Bin al-Shibh applied several times for a visa to the United States, but as a Yemeni, he was rejected out of concerns he would overstay his visa and remain as an illegal immigrant. Bin al-Shibh stayed in Hamburg, providing coordination between Atta and Mohammed. The three Hamburg cell members all took pilot training in South Florida.

In spring 2001, the secondary hijackers began arriving in the United States. In July 2001, Atta met with bin al-Shibh in Spain, where they coordinated details of the plot, including final target selection. Bin al-Shibh also passed along bin Laden's wish for the attacks to be carried out as soon as possible.

ATTACKS

Early on the morning of September 11, 2001, 19 hijackers took control of four commercial airliners (two Boeing 757 and two Boeing 767) en route to California (three headed to LAXin Los Angeles, and one to San Francisco) after takeoffs from Boston, Massachusetts;Newark, New Jersey; and Washington, D.C. Large planes with long flights were selected for hijacking because they would be heavily fueled.

The four flights were:

- American Airlines Flight 11: a Boeing 767 aircraft, departed Boston's Logan Airport at 7:59 a.m. en route to Los Angeles with a crew of 11 and 76 passengers, not including five hijackers. The hijackers flew the plane into the North Tower of the World Trade Center at 8:46 a.m.

- United Airlines Flight 175: a Boeing 767 aircraft, departed Logan Airport at 8:14 a.m. en route to Los Angeles with a crew of nine and 51 passengers, not including five hijackers. The hijackers flew the plane into the South Tower of the World Trade Center at 9:03 a.m.
- American Airlines Flight 77: a Boeing 757 aircraft, departed Washington Dulles International Airport in Virginia at 8:20 a.m. en route to Los Angeles with a crew of six and 53 passengers, not including five hijackers. The hijackers flew the plane into the Pentagon at 9:37 a.m.
- United Airlines Flight 93: a Boeing 757 aircraft, departed Newark International Airport at 8:42 a.m. en route to San Francisco, with a crew of seven and 33 passengers, not including four hijackers. As passengers attempted to subdue the hijackers, the aircraft crashed into the ground near Shanksville, Pennsylvania, at 10:03 a.m.

Media coverage was extensive during the attacks and aftermath, beginning moments after the first crash into the World Trade Center.

Events

At 8:46 a.m., five hijackers crashed American Airlines Flight 11 into the northern facade of the World Trade Center's North Tower (1 WTC), and at 9:03 a.m., another five hijackers crashed United Airlines Flight 175 into the southern facade of the South Tower (2 WTC). Five hijackers flew American Airlines Flight 77 into the Pentagon at 9:37 a.m.

A fourth flight, United Airlines Flight 93, under the control of four hijackers, crashed near Shanksville, Pennsylvania, southeast of Pittsburgh, at 10:03 a.m. after the passengers fought the hijackers. Flight 93's target is believed to have been either the Capitol or the White House. Flight 93's cockpit voice recorder revealed crew and passengers tried to seize control of the plane from the hijackers after learning through phone calls that Flights 11, 77, and 175 had been crashed into buildings that morning. Once it became evident to the hijackers that the passengers might regain control of the plane, the hijackers rolled the plane and intentionally crashed it.

Some passengers and crew members who called from the aircraft using the cabin airphone service and mobile phones provided details: several hijackers were aboard each plane; they used mace, tear gas, or pepper spray to overcome attendants; and some people aboard had been stabbed. Reports indicated hijackers stabbed and killed pilots, flight attendants, and one or more passengers. In their final report, the 9/11 Commission found the hijackers had recently purchased multi-function hand tools and assorted knives and blades. A flight attendant on Flight 11, a passenger on Flight 175, and passengers on Flight 93 said the hijackers had bombs, but one of the passengers said he thought the bombs were fake. The FBI found no traces of explosives at the crash sites, and the 9/11 Commission concluded that the bombs were probably fake.

Three buildings in the World Trade Center collapsed due to fire-induced structural failure. The South Tower collapsed at 9:59 a.m. after burning for 56 minutes in a fire caused by the impact of United Airlines Flight 175 and the explosion of its fuel. The North Tower collapsed at 10:28 a.m. after burning for 102 minutes. When the North Tower collapsed, debris fell on the nearby 7 World Trade Center building (7 WTC), damaging it and starting fires. These fires burned for hours, compromising the building's structural integrity, and 7 WTC collapsed at 5:21 p.m. The west side of the Pentagon sustained significant damage.

At 9:42 a.m., the Federal Aviation Administration (FAA) grounded all aircraft within the continental U.S., and aircraft already in flight were told to land immediately. All international civilian aircraft were either turned back or redirected to airports in Canada or Mexico, and all international flights were banned from landing on United States territory for three days. The attacks created widespread confusion among news organizations and air traffic controllers. Among the unconfirmed and often contradictory news reports aired throughout the day, one of the most prevalent said a car bomb had been detonated at the U.S. State Department's headquarters in Washington, D.C.Another jet—Delta Air Lines

Flight 1989—was suspected of having been hijacked, but the aircraft responded to controllers and landed safely in Cleveland, Ohio.

In a April 2002 interview, Khalid Sheikh Mohammed and Ramzi bin al-Shibh, who are believed to have organized the attacks, said Flight 93's intended target was the United States Capitol, not the White House. During the planning stage of the attacks, Mohamed Atta, the hijacker and pilot of Flight 11, thought the White House might be too tough a target and sought an assessment from Hani Hanjour (who hijacked and piloted Flight 77). Mohammed said al-Qaeda initially planned to target nuclear installations rather than the World Trade Center and the Pentagon, but decided against it, fearing things could "get out of control". Final decisions on targets, according to Mohammed, were left in the hands of the pilots.

Casualties

The attacks resulted in the deaths of 2,996 people and the injuries of 6,000+ others. The 2,996 death toll included 265 on the four planes (from which there were no survivors), 2,606 in the World Trade Center and in the surrounding area, and 125 at the Pentagon. Nearly all of those who perished were civilians with the exceptions of 72 law enforcement officers, 343 firefighters, 55 military personnel, and the 19 terrorists who died in the attacks. After New York, New Jersey lost the most state citizens, with the city of Hoboken having the most citizens that died in the attacks. More than 90 countries lost citizens in the September 11 attacks. The attacks of September 11, 2001, marked it the worst terrorist attack in world history and the deadliest foreign attack on American soil since the Japanese surprise attack on Pearl Harbor on December 7, 1941.

In Arlington County, 125 Pentagon workers lost their lives when Flight 77 crashed into the western side of the building. Of these, 70 were civilians and 55 were military personnel, many of them who worked for the United States Army or theUnited States Navy. The Army lost 47 civilian employees, six civilian contractors, and 22 soldiers, while the Navy lost six civilian employees, three civilian contractors, and 33 sailors. Seven Defense Intelligence Agency (DIA) civilian employees were also among the dead in the attack, as well as an Office of the Secretary of Defense (OSD) contractor. Lieutenant General Timothy Maude, an Army Deputy Chief of Staff, was the highest-ranking military official killed at the Pentagon.

In New York City, more than 90% of the workers and visitors who died in the towers had been at or above the points of impact. In the North Tower, 1,355 people at or above the point of impact were trapped and died of smoke inhalation, fell or jumped from the tower to escape the smoke and flames, or were killed in the building's eventual collapse. The destruction of all three staircases in the tower when Flight 11 hit made it impossible for anyone above the impact zone to escape. 107 people below the point of impact died as well.

In the South Tower, one stairwell, Stairwell A, was left intact after Flight 175 hit, allowing 14 people located on the floors of impact (including one man who saw the plane coming at him) and four more from the floors above to escape. New York City 911 operators who received calls from individuals inside the tower were not well informed of the situation as it rapidly unfolded and as a result, told callers not to descend the tower on their own. In total 630 people died in that tower, fewer than half the number killed in the North Tower. Casualties in the South Tower were significantly reduced by some occupants deciding to start evacuating as soon as the North Tower was struck.

At least 200 people fell or jumped to their deaths from the burning towers (as exemplified in the photograph *The Falling Man*), landing on the streets and rooftops of adjacent buildings hundreds of feet below. Some occupants of each tower above the point of impact made their way toward the roof in hope of helicopter rescue, but the roof access doors were locked. No plan existed for helicopter rescues, and the combination of roof equipment and thick smoke and intense heat prevented helicopters from approaching. A total of 411 emergency workers died as they tried to rescue people and fight fires. The New York City Fire Department (FDNY) lost 343 firefighters, including a chaplain, two paramedics, and a fire marshal. The New York City Police Department(NYPD) lost 23 officers. The Port Authority Police

Department (PAPD) lost 37 officers. Eight emergency medical technicians (EMTs) and paramedics from private emergency medical services units were killed.

Damage

Along with the 110-floor Twin Towers, numerous other buildings at the World Trade Center site were destroyed or badly damaged, including WTC buildings 3 through 7 and St. Nicholas Greek Orthodox Church. The North Tower, South Tower, the Marriott Hotel (3 WTC), and 7 WTC were completely destroyed. The U.S. Customs House (6 World Trade Center), 4 World Trade Center, 5 World Trade Center, and both pedestrian bridges connecting buildings were severely damaged. The Deutsche Bank Building on 130 Liberty Street was partially damaged and demolished some years later, starting in 2007. The two buildings of the World Financial Center also suffered damage.

The Deutsche Bank Building across Liberty Street from the World Trade Center complex was later condemned as uninhabitable because of toxic conditions inside the office tower, and wasdeconstructed. The Borough of Manhattan Community College's Fiterman Hall at 30 West Broadway was condemned due to extensive damage in the attacks, and is being rebuilt. Other neighboring buildings (including 90 West Street and the Verizon Building) suffered major damage but have been restored. World Financial Center buildings, One Liberty Plaza, the Millenium Hilton, and 90 Church Street had moderate damage and have since been restored. Communications equipment on top of the North Tower was also destroyed, but media stations were quickly able to reroute the signals and resume their broadcasts.

The Pentagon was severely damaged by the impact of American Airlines Flight 77 and ensuing fires, causing one section of the building to collapse. As the airplane approached the Pentagon, its wings knocked down light poles and its right engine hit a power generator before crashing into the western side of the building. The plane hit the Pentagon at the first-floor level. The front part of the fuselage disintegrated on impact, while the mid and tail sections kept moving for another fraction of a second. Debris from the tail section penetrated furthest into the building, breaking through 310 feet (94 m) of the three outermost of the building's five rings.

Rescue efforts

The New York City Fire Department deployed 200 units (half of the department) to the World Trade Center. Their efforts were supplemented by numerous off-duty firefighters and emergency medical technicians. The New York City Police Department sent Emergency Service Units and other police personnel, and deployed its aviation unit. Once on the scene, the FDNY, NYPD, and PAPD did not coordinate efforts and performed redundant searches for civilians. As conditions deteriorated, the NYPD aviation unit relayed information to police commanders, who issued orders for its personnel to evacuate the towers; most NYPD officers were able to safely evacuate before the buildings collapsed. With separate command posts set up and incompatible radio communications between the agencies, warnings were not passed along to FDNY commanders.

After the first tower collapsed, FDNY commanders issued evacuation warnings; however, due totechnical difficulties with malfunctioning radio repeater systems, many firefighters never heard the evacuation orders. 9-1-1 dispatchers also received information from callers that was not passed along to commanders on the scene. Within hours of the attack, a substantial search and rescue operation was launched. After months of around-the-clock operations, the World Trade Center site was cleared by the end of May 2002.

AFTERMATH OF ATTACK

Immediate Response

At 8:32 a.m., FAA officials were notified Flight 11 had been hijacked and they in turn notified theNorth American Aerospace Defense Command (NORAD). NORAD scrambled two F-15s from Otis Air National Guard Base in Massachusetts and they were airborne by 8:53 a.m. Because of slow and confused communication from FAA officials, NORAD had 9 minutes' notice that Flight 11 had been hijacked, and no notice about any of the other flights before they crashed. After both of the Twin Towers had already been hit, more fighters were scrambled from Langley Air Force Base in Virginia at 9:30 a.m. At 10:20 a.m. Vice President Dick Cheney issued orders to shoot down any commercial aircraft that could be positively identified as being hijacked. However, these instructions were not relayed in time for the fighters to take action. Some fighters took to the air without live ammunition, knowing that to prevent the hijackers from striking their intended targets, the pilots might have to intercept and crash their fighters into the hijacked planes, possibly ejecting at the last moment.

For the first time in U.S. history, SCATANA was invoked, thus stranding tens of thousands of passengers across the world. The FAA closed American airspace to all international flights, causing about five hundred flights to be turned back or redirected to other countries. Canada received 226 of the diverted flights and launched Operation Yellow Ribbon to deal with the large numbers of grounded planes and stranded passengers.

The 9/11 attacks had immediate effects upon the American people. Police and rescue workers from around the country took leaves of absence, traveling to New York City to help recover bodies from the twisted remnants of the Twin Towers. Blood donations across the U.S. surged in the weeks after 9/11.

The deaths of adults in the attacks resulted in over 3,000 children losing a parent. Subsequent studies documented children's reactions to these actual losses and to feared losses of life, the protective environment in the aftermath of the attacks, and effects on surviving caregivers.

Domestic Reactions

Following the attacks, President Bush's approval rating soared to 90%. On September 20, 2001, he addressed the nation and a joint session of the United States Congress regarding the events of September 11 and the subsequent nine days of rescue and recovery efforts, and described his intended response to the attacks. New York City mayor Rudy Giuliani's highly visible role won him high praise in New York and nationally.

Contingency plans for the continuity of governmentand the evacuation of leaders were implemented soon after the attacks.

However, Congress was not told that the United States had been under a continuity of government status until February 2002.

In the largest restructuring of the U.S. government in contemporary history, the United States enacted the Homeland Security Act of 2002, creating the Department of Homeland Security. Congress also passed the USA PATRIOT Act, saying it would help detect and prosecute terrorism and other crimes. Civil liberties groups have criticized the PATRIOT Act, saying it allows law enforcement to invade the privacy of citizens and that it eliminates judicial oversight of law enforcement and domestic intelligence. In an effort to effectively combat future acts of terrorism, the National Security Agency (NSA) was given broad powers. NSA commenced warrantless surveillance of telecommunications, which was sometimes criticized since it permitted the agency "to eavesdrop on telephone and e-mail communications between the United States and people overseas without a warrant". In response to requests by various intelligence agencies, the United States Foreign Intelligence Surveillance Court permitted an expansion of powers by the U.S. government in seeking, obtaining, and sharing information on U.S. citizens as well as non-U.S. people from around the world.

Hate Crimes

Shortly after the attacks, President Bush made a public appearance at Washington's largest Islamic Center and acknowledged the "incredibly valuable contribution" that millions of American Muslims made to their country and called for them "to be treated with respect." However, numerous incidents of harassment and hate crimes against Muslims and South Asians were reported in the days following the attacks. Sikhs were also targeted because Sikh males usually wear turbans, which are stereotypically associated with Muslims. There were reports of attacks on mosques and other religious buildings (including the firebombing of a Hindu temple), and assaults on people, including one murder: Balbir Singh Sodhi, a Sikh mistaken for a Muslim, was fatally shot on September 15, 2001, in Mesa, Arizona.

According to an academic study, people perceived to be Middle Eastern were as likely to be victims of hate crimes as followers of Islam during this time. The study also found a similar increase in hate crimes against people who may have been perceived as Muslims, Arabs, and others thought to be of Middle Eastern origin. A report by the South Asian American advocacy group known as South Asian Americans Leading Together, documented media coverage of 645 bias incidents against Americans of South Asian or Middle Eastern descent between September 11 and 17. Various crimes such as vandalism, arson, assault, shootings, harassment, and threats in numerous places were documented.

Muslim American Response

Muslim organizations in the United States were swift to condemn the attacks and called "upon Muslim Americans to come forward with their skills and resources to help alleviate the sufferings of the affected people and their families". These organizations included the Islamic Society of North America, American Muslim Alliance, American Muslim Council, Council on American-Islamic Relations, Islamic Circle of North America, and the Shari'a Scholars Association of North America. Along with monetary donations, many Islamic organizations launched blood drives and provided medical assistance, food, and shelter for victims.

International Reactions

The attacks were denounced by mass media and governments worldwide. Across the globe, nations offered pro-American support and solidarity. Leaders in most Middle Eastern countries, and Afghanistan, condemned the attacks. Iraq was a notable exception, with an immediate official statement that, "the American cowboys are reaping the fruit of their crimes against humanity". While the government of Saudi Arabia officially condemned the attacks, privately many Saudis favored bin Laden's cause. As in the United States, the aftermath of the attacks saw tensions increase in other countries between Muslims and non-Muslims.

United Nations Security Council Resolution 1368 condemned the attacks, and expressed readiness to take all necessary steps to respond and combat all forms of terrorism in accordance with their Charter. Numerous countries introduced anti-terrorism legislation and froze bank accounts they suspected of al-Qaeda ties. Law enforcement and intelligence agencies in a number of countries arrested alleged terrorists.

British Prime Minister Tony Blair said Britain stood "shoulder to shoulder" with the United States. A few days later, Blair flew to Washington to affirm British solidarity with the United States. In a speech to Congress, nine days after the attacks, which Blair attended as a guest, President Bush declared "America has no truer friend than Great Britain." Subsequently, Prime Minister Blair embarked on two months of diplomacy to rally international support for military action; he held 54 meetings with world leaders and travelled more than 40,000 miles (60,000 km).

Tens of thousands of people attempted to flee Afghanistan following the attacks, fearing a response by the United States. Pakistan, already home to many Afghan refugees from previous conflicts, closed its border with Afghanistan on September 17, 2001. Approximately one month after the attacks, the United States led a broad coalition of international forces to overthrow the Taliban regime from Afghanistan for their harboring of al-Qaeda. Though Pakistani authorities were initially reluctant to align themselves with the United States against the Taliban, they permitted the coalition access to their military bases, and arrested and handed over to the U.S. over 600 suspected al-Qaeda members.

The U.S. set up the Guantanamo Bay detention camp to hold inmates they defined as "illegal enemy combatants". The legitimacy of these detentions has been questioned by the European Union and human rights organizations.

Military Operations

At 2:40 p.m. in the afternoon of September 11, Secretary of Defense Donald Rumsfeld was issuing rapid orders to his aides to look for evidence of Iraqi involvement. According to notes taken by senior policy official Stephen Cambone, Rumsfeld asked for, "Best info fast. Judge whether good enough hit S.H." (Saddam Hussein) "at same time. Not only UBL" (Osama bin Laden). Cambone's notes quoted Rumsfeld as saying, "Need to move swiftly – Near term target needs – go massive – sweep it all up. Things related and not." In a meeting at Camp David on September

15 the Bush administration rejected the idea of attacking Iraq in response to 9/11.

The NATO council declared the attacks on the United States were an attack on all NATO nations which satisfied Article 5 of the NATO charter. This marked the first invocation of Article 5, which had been written during the Cold War with an attack by the Soviet Union in mind. Australian Prime Minister John Howard who was in Washington D.C. during the attacks invoked Article IV of theANZUS treaty. The Bush administration announced a War on Terror, with the stated goals of bringing bin Laden and al-Qaeda to justice and preventing the emergence of other terrorist networks. These goals would be accomplished by imposing economic and military sanctions against states harboring terrorists, and increasing global surveillance and intelligence sharing.

On September 14, 2001, the U.S. Congress passed the Authorization for Use of Military Force Against Terrorists. Still in effect, it grants the President the authority to use all "necessary and appropriate force" against those whom he determined "planned, authorized, committed or aided" the September 11th attacks, or who harbored said persons or groups.

On October 7, 2001, the War in Afghanistan began when U.S. and British forces initiated aerial bombing campaigns targeting Taliban and al-Qaeda camps, then later invaded Afghanistan with ground troops of the Special Forces. This eventually led to the overthrow of the Taliban rule of Afghanistan on December 9, 2001 by U.S. led coalition forces. Conflict in Afghanistan between the Taliban insurgencyand the Afghan forces backed by NATO Resolute Support Mission is ongoing. The Philippines and Indonesia, among other nations with their own internal conflicts with Islamic terrorism, also increased their military readiness.

EFFECTS AND HEALTH ISSUES

Hundreds of thousands of tons of toxic debris containing more than 2,500 contaminants, including known carcinogens, were spread across Lower Manhattan due to the collapse of the Twin Towers. Exposure to the toxins in the debris is alleged to have contributed to fatal or debilitating illnesses among people who were at ground zero. The Bush administration ordered the Environmental Protection Agency (EPA) to issue reassuring statements regarding air quality in the aftermath of the attacks, citing national security, but the EPA did not determine that air quality had returned to pre-September 11 levels until June 2002.

Health effects extended to residents, students, and office workers of Lower Manhattan and nearbyChinatown. Several deaths have been linked to the toxic dust, and the victims' names were included in the World Trade Center memorial. Approximately 18,000 people have been estimated to have developed illnesses as a result of the toxic dust.

There is also scientific speculation that exposure to various toxic products in the air may have negative effects on fetal development. A notable children's environmental health center is currently analyzing the children whose mothers were pregnant during the WTC collapse, and were living or working nearby. A study of rescue workers released in April 2010 found that all those studied had impaired lung functions, and that 30–40% were reporting little or no improvement in persistent symptoms that started within the first year of the attack.

Years after the attacks, legal disputes over the costs of illnesses related to the attacks were still in the court system. On October 17, 2006, a federal judge rejected New York City's refusal to pay for health costs for rescue workers, allowing for the possibility of numerous suits against the city. Government officials have been faulted for urging the public to return to lower Manhattan in the weeks shortly after the attacks. Christine Todd Whitman, administrator of the EPA in the aftermath of the attacks, was heavily criticized by a U.S. District Judge for incorrectly saying that the area was environmentally safe. Mayor Giuliani was criticized for urging financial industry personnel to return quickly to the greater Wall Street area.

The United States Congress passed the James L. Zadroga 9/11 Health and Compensation Act on December 22, 2010, and PresidentBarack Obama signed the act into law on January 2, 2011. It allocated $4.2 billion to create the World Trade Center Health Program, which provides testing and treatment for people suffering from long-term health problems related to the 9/11 attacks. The WTC Health Program replaced preexisting 9/11-related health programs such as the Medical Monitoring and Treatment Program and the WTC Environmental Health Center program.

According to a new study, pregnant women living near the World Trade Center during the 9/11 terror attacks experienced higher-than-normal negative birth outcomes. The study by Princeton University's Woodrow Wilson School of Public and International Affairs found that these mothers were more likely to give birth prematurely and deliver babies with low birth weights. Their babies were also more likely to be admitted to neonatal intensive care units after birth (especially baby boys), according to the study led by the Wilson School's Janet Currie and Hannes Schwandt.

Economic Impact on US

The attacks had a significant economic impact on United States and world markets. The stock exchanges did not open on September 11 and remained closed until September 17. Reopening, theDow Jones Industrial Average (DJIA) fell 684 points, or 7.1%, to 8921, a record-setting one-day point decline. By the end of the week, the DJIA had fallen 1,369.7 points (14.3%), at the time its largest one-week point drop in history. In 2001 dollars, U.S. stocks lost $1.4 trillion in valuation for the week.

In New York City, about 430,000 job-months and $2.8 billion dollars in wages were lost in the three months after the attacks. The economic effects were mainly on the economy's export sectors.The city's GDP was estimated to have declined by $27.3 billion for the last three months of 2001 and all of 2002. The U.S. government provided $11.2 billion in immediate assistance to the Government of New York City in September 2001, and $10.5 billion in early 2002 for economic development and infrastructure needs.

Also hurt were small businesses in Lower Manhattan near the World Trade Center, 18,000 of which were destroyed or displaced, resulting in lost jobs and their consequent wages. Assistance was provided by Small Business Administration loans, federal government Community Development Block Grants, and Economic Injury Disaster Loans. Some 31,900,000 square feet (2,960,000 m^2) of Lower Manhattan office space was damaged or destroyed. Many wondered whether these jobs would return, and if the damaged tax base would recover. Studies of the economic effects of 9/11 show the Manhattan office real-estate market and office employment were less affected than first feared, because of the financial services industry's need for face-to-face interaction.

North American air space was closed for several days after the attacks and air travel decreased upon its reopening, leading to a nearly 20% cutback in air travel capacity, and exacerbating financial problems in the struggling U.S. airline industry.

The September 11 attacks also led to the U.S. wars in Afghanistan and Iraq, as well as additional homeland security spending, totaling at least $5 trillion.

Society and Cultural

The impact of 9/11 extends beyond geopolitics into society and culture in general. Immediate responses to 9/11 included greater focus on home life and time spent with family, higher church attendance, and increased expressions of patriotism such as the flying of flags. The radio industry responded by removing certain songs from playlists, and the attacks have subsequently been used as background, narrative or thematic elements in film, television, music and literature. Already-running television shows as well as programs developed after 9/11 have reflected post-9/11 cultural concerns. 9/11 conspiracy theories have become social phenomena, despite lack of support from expert scientists, engineers, and historians. 9/11 has also had a major impact on the religious faith of many individuals; for some it strengthened, to find consolation to cope with the loss of loved ones and overcome their grief; others started to question their faith or lost it entirely, because they could not reconcile it with their view of religion.

The culture of America succeeding the attacks is noted for heightened security and an increased demand thereof, as well as paranoia andanxiety regarding future terrorist attacks that includes most of the nation. Psychologists have also confirmed that there has been an increased amount of national anxiety in commercial air travel.

Government Policies Toward Terrorism

As a result of the attacks, many governments across the world passed legislation to combat terrorism. In Germany, where several of the 9/11 terrorists had resided and taken advantage of that country's liberal asylum policies, two major anti-terrorism packages were enacted.

The first removed legal loopholes that permitted terrorists to live and raise money in Germany. The second addressed the effectiveness and communication of intelligence and law enforcement. Canada passed the Canadian Anti-Terrorism Act, that nation's first anti-terrorism law. The United Kingdom passed the Anti-terrorism, Crime and Security Act 2001 and the Prevention of Terrorism Act 2005. New Zealand enacted the Terrorism Suppression Act 2002.

In the United States, the Department of Homeland Security was created by the Homeland Security Act to coordinate domestic anti-terrorism efforts.

The USA Patriot Act gave the federal government greater powers, including the authority to detain foreign terror suspects for a week without charge, to monitor telephone communications, e-mail, and Internet use by terror suspects, and to prosecute suspected terrorists without time restrictions.

The FAA ordered that airplane cockpits be reinforced to prevent terrorists gaining control of planes, and assigned sky marshals to flights. Further, the Aviation and Transportation Security Act made the federal government, rather than airports, responsible for airport security. The law created the Transportation Security Administration to inspect passengers and luggage, causing long delays and concern over passenger privacy.

INVESTIGATIONS—FBI

Immediately after the attacks, the Federal Bureau of Investigation started PENTTBOM, the largest criminal inquiry in the history of the United States. At its height, more than half of the FBI's agents worked on the investigation and followed a half-million leads. The FBI concluded that there was "clear and irrefutable" evidence linking al-Qaeda and bin Laden to the attacks.

The FBI was quickly able to identify the hijackers, including leader Mohamed Atta, when his luggage was discovered at Boston's Logan Airport. Atta had been forced to check two of his three bags due to space limitations on the 19-seat commuter flight he took to Boston. Due to a new policy instituted to prevent flight delays, the luggage failed to make it aboard American Airlines Flight 11 as planned.

The luggage contained the hijackers' names, assignments and al-Qaeda connections. "It had all these Arab-language (sic) papers that amounted to the Rosetta stone of the investigation", said one FBI agent.

Within hours of the attacks, the FBI released the names and in many cases the personal details of the suspected pilots and hijackers. On September 27, 2001, they released photos of all 19 hijackers, along with information about possible nationalities and aliases. Fifteen of the men were from Saudi Arabia, two from the United Arab Emirates, one from Egypt, and one from Lebanon.

By midday, the U.S. National Security Agency and German intelligence agencies had intercepted communications pointing to Osama bin Laden.

Two of the hijackers were known to have travelled with a bin Laden associate to Malaysia in 2000 and hijacker Mohammed Atta had previously gone to Afghanistan. He and others were part of a terrorist cell in Hamburg. One of the members of theHamburg cell was discovered to have been in communication with Khalid Sheik Mohammed who was identified as a member of al-Qaeda.

Authorities in the United States and Britain also obtained electronic intercepts, including telephone conversations and electronic bank transfers, which indicate that Mohammed Atef, a bin Laden deputy, was a key figure in the planning of the 9/11 attacks.

Intercepts were also obtained that revealed conversations that took place days before September 11 between bin Laden and an associate in Pakistan. In those conversations, the two referred to "an incident that would take place in America on, or around, September 11" and they discussed potential repercussions. In another conversation with an associate in Afghanistan, bin Laden discussed the "scale and effects of a forthcoming operation." These conversations did not specifically mention the World Trade Center or Pentagon, or other specifics.

CIA Performance

The Inspector General of the Central Intelligence Agency (CIA) conducted an internal review of the agency's pre-9/11 performance and was harshly critical of senior CIA officials for not doing everything possible to confront terrorism.

He criticized their failure to stop two of the 9/11 hijackers, Nawaf al-Hazmi and Khalid al-Mihdhar, as they entered the United States and their failure to share information on the two men with the FBI. In May 2007, senators from both major U.S. political parties drafted legislation to make the review public. One of the backers, Senator Ron Wyden said, "The American people have a right to know what the Central Intelligence Agency was doing in those critical months before 9/11."

Congressional Inquiry

In February 2002 the Senate Select Committee on Intelligence and the House Permanent Select Committee on Intelligence formed a joint inquiry into the performance of the U.S. Intelligence Community. Their 832 page report released in December 2002 detailed failings of the FBI and CIA to use available information, including about terrorists the CIA knew were in the United States, in order to disrupt the plots.

The joint inquiry developed its information about possible involvement of Saudi Arabian government officials from non-classified sources. Nevertheless, the Bush administration demanded 28 related pages remain classified.

In December 2002 the inquiry's chairBob Graham (D-FL) revealed in an interview that there was "evidence that there were foreign governments involved in facilitating the activities of at least some of the terrorists in the United States." September 11th victim families were frustrated by the unanswered questions and redacted material from the Congressional inquiry and demanded an independent commission. September 11th victim families,members of congress and the Saudi Arabian government are still seeking release of the documents.

9/11 Commission

The *National Commission on Terrorist Attacks Upon the United States* (9/11 Commission), chaired by Thomas Kean and Lee H. Hamilton, was formed in late 2002 to prepare a thorough account of the circumstances surrounding the attacks, including preparedness for and the immediate response to the attacks. On July 22, 2004, the Commission issued the 9/11 Commission Report. The report detailed the events of 9/11, found the attacks were carried out by members of al-Qaeda, and examined how security and intelligence agencies were inadequately coordinated to prevent the attacks. Formed from an independent bipartisan group of mostly former Senators, Representatives, and Governors, the commissioners explained, "We believe the 9/11 attacks revealed four kinds of failures: in imagination, policy, capabilities, and management".

The Commission made numerous recommendations on how to prevent future attacks, and in 2011 was dismayed that several of its recommendations had yet to be implemented.

Collapse of the World Trade Center

The U.S. National Institute of Standards and Technology (NIST) investigated the collapses of the Twin Towers and 7 WTC. The investigations examined why the buildings collapsed and what fire protection measures were in place, and evaluated how fire protection systems might be improved in future construction. The investigation into the collapse of 1 WTC and 2 WTC was concluded in October 2005 and that of 7 WTC was completed in August 2008.

NIST found that the fireproofing on the Twin Towers' steel infrastructures was blown off by the initial impact of the planes and that, had this not occurred, the towers likely would have remained standing. A 2007 study of the north tower's collapse published by researchers of Purdue University determined that, since the plane's impact had stripped off much of the structure's thermal insulation, the heat from a typical office fire would have softened and weakened the exposed girders and columns enough to initiate the collapse regardless of the number of columns cut or damaged by the impact.

The director of the original investigation stated that, "the towers really did amazingly well. The terrorist aircraft didn't bring the buildings down; it was the fire which followed. It was proven that you could take out two thirds of the columns in a tower and the building would still stand." The fires weakened the trusses supporting the floors, making the floors sag. The sagging floors pulled on the exterior steel columns causing the exterior columns to bow inward.

With the damage to the core columns, the buckling exterior columns could no longer support the buildings, causing them to collapse. Additionally, the report found the towers' stairwells were not adequately reinforced to provide adequate emergency escape for people above the impact zones. NIST concluded that uncontrolled fires in 7 WTC caused floor beams and girders to heat and subsequently "caused a critical support column to fail, initiating a fire-induced progressive collapse that brought the building down".

REBUILDING

On the day of the attacks, New York City mayor Rudy Giuliani stated: "We will rebuild. We're going to come out of this stronger than before, politically stronger, economically stronger. The skyline will be made whole again."

The damaged section of the Pentagon was rebuilt and occupied within a year of the attacks. The temporary World Trade Center PATH station opened in late 2003 and construction of the new 7 World Trade Center was completed in 2006. Work on rebuilding the main World Trade Center site was delayed until late 2006 when leaseholder Larry Silverstein and the Port Authority of New York and New Jersey agreed on financing. The construction of One World Trade Center began on April 27, 2006, and reached its full height on May 20, 2013. The spire was installed atop the building at that date, putting 1 WTC's height at 1,776 feet (541 m) and thus claiming the title of the tallest building in the Western Hemisphere. One WTC finished construction and opened on November 3, 2014. On the World Trade Center site, three more office towers are expected to be built one block east of where the original towers stood. Construction has begun on all three of these towers.

Memorials

In the days immediately following the attacks, many memorials and vigils were held around the world, and photographs of the dead and missing were posted around Ground Zero. A witness described being unable to "get away from faces of innocent victims who were killed. Their pictures are everywhere, on phone booths, street lights, walls of subway stations. Everything reminded me of a huge funeral, people quiet and sad, but also very nice. Before, New York gave me a cold feeling; now people were reaching out to help each other."

One of the first memorials was the Tribute in Light, an installation of 88 searchlights at the footprints of the World Trade Center towers. In New York, the World Trade Center Site Memorial Competition was held to design an appropriate memorial on the site. The winning design,*Reflecting Absence,* was selected in August 2006, and consists of a pair of reflecting pools in the footprints of the towers, surrounded by a list of the victims' names in an underground memorial space.

The Pentagon Memorial was completed and opened to the public on the seventh anniversary of the attacks in 2008. It consists of a landscaped park with 184 benches facing the Pentagon. When the Pentagon was repaired in 2001–2002, a private chapel and indoor memorial were included, located at the spot where Flight 77 crashed into the building.

In Shanksville, a permanent Flight 93 National Memorial is planned to include a sculpted grove of trees forming a circle around the crash site, bisected by the plane's path, while wind chimes will bear the names of the victims. A temporary memorial is located 500 yards (457 m) from the crash site. New York City firefighters donated a cross made of steel from the World Trade

Center and mounted on top of a platform shaped like the Pentagon. It was installed outside the firehouse on August 25, 2008. Many other permanent memorials are elsewhere. Scholarships and charities have been established by the victims' families, and by many other organizations and private figures.

On every anniversary, in New York City, the names of the victims who died there are read out against a background of somber music. The President of the United States attends a memorial service at the Pentagon, and asks Americans to observe Patriot Day with a moment of silence. Smaller services are held in Shanksville, Pennsylvania, which are usually attended by the President's spouse.

4

War against Terrorism in Afghanistan

The Afghan government has sent army reinforcements to Sangin in an attempt to push back Taliban militants, who in the last two days have appeared close to taking control of the strategically important town. Deputy governor of the Helmand district Mohammad Jan Rasoulyar said the army was "now taking the fight to the Taliban". He also said military planes had dropped food supplies to bolster government positions.

There are conflicting claims as to who is getting the upper hand. The Taliban insist that their siege of the town is not over "and the government will soon announce their defeat".

On Tuesday Taliban forces had reportedly taken much of the town with fighting centred on the police headquarters where Afghan regulars were holding out. The resurgence of rebel activity in Sangin district poses a major security threat to the struggling Afghan government, a year after the withdrawal of the bulk of US and allied combat forces.

The loss of Sangin would be a serious reverse for the government in a province that has been a major centre of the Taliban insurgency with important supply routes for the opium trade. Its proximity to Pakistan also serves to give the area a broader strategic significance. The fighting has seen British forces drawn back into the conflict with the UK Ministry of Defence ordering a small deployment of military advisers to Helmand to support the besieged Afghan troops in the town.

Sangin came to symbolise the UK army's more than decade-long campaign against the Taliban, with more than 100 British troops killed in the struggle to hold the district before responsibility for the area was handed over to the Americans in 2010. The MoD on Tuesday said a small number of British personnel had been sent to Camp Shorabak in Helmand in an "advisory role". But a spokesman insisted they would not be engaged in combat and are part of a larger Nato team.

Security analysts say Taliban forces are determined to regain control of Helmand, a region with which many Taliban leaders have close ties, and where they enjoy considerable popular support. "Helmand is a base area for many of the Taliban leaders," said Ahmed Rashid, the author of several books on Afghanistan, Pakistan and central Asia. "It is dear and important to them."

He also said the Taliban were likely to try to declare an alternative governing council once they gained full control over Helmand, which would be a further blow to the Afghan government in Kabul. "There is very strong speculation that the Taliban — perhaps pushed by Pakistan — are wanting to set up an alternative council on Afghan soil," Mr Rashid said. "If they could achieve that in one of their base areas, or heartlands, it would be a huge coup d'état."

The UK ended combat operations in Afghanistan last year, but around 450 troops remain in mentoring and support roles, defence officials say. Analysts say the allied effort to support the Afghan government is facing a new threat, with elements linked to Isis fighters in Syria and Iraq establishing a presence in the region. The MoD said the UK deployment was part of its "ongoing contribution" to Nato's Resolute Support mission. "These personnel are part of a larger Nato team which is providing advice to the Afghan National Army. They are not deployed in a combat role and will not deploy outside the camp," it said.

The central government in Kabul is facing instability across the region, with a Taliban suicide bombing near Bagram in the east of the country killing six US soldiers on Monday in one of the deadliest attacks on foreign forces in Afghanistan this year. Although Nato's combat role in Afghanistan ended in 2014, the battle for Sangin highlights how stretched the Afghan security forces have become in holding back the Taliban advance.

However, Lord Dannatt, a former chief of the general staff, told the BBC that instability in Helmand should not lead to British forces being redeployed in a combat role. "My own view is Afghanistan is a lesser priority than thinking about Libya and thinking about Syria," he told BBC's *Today* programme. The losses in Helmand and the pressure on Sangin are just the latest reversals for the Afghan government of President Ashraf Ghani.

In September, Taliban forces took control of the northern town of Kunduz, though Afghan forces eventually regained control, with the support of US Special Forces. But the earlier capture of Kunduz, and losses in Helmand, underscore the limitations of the Afghan security forces, which suffers poor logistics and a lack of vital air power.

Defence analysts say they are badly stretched trying to hold back the Taliban advance on multiple fronts, with fears the militants will capture further swaths of territory. "There are a series of provinces that are in extreme danger," Mr Rashid says. Mr Ghani's government is also facing mounting tensions with the former Afghani president Hamid Karzai and his loyalists. He is also wrestling with serious economic problems stemming from the lack of jobs.

At the height of the international military intervention in Afghanistan, tens of thousands of educated Afghans were employed in service jobs, supporting the international forces, but most of these jobs disappeared with the drawdown of foreign troops, with nothing to take their place. Afghans fleeing their country's grim situation have been a significant component of the wave of migrants that have sought refuge in Europe this year.

AFGHANISTAN WAR MUST END BUT NOT AT ANY COST

Afghanistan must now reconcile with the groups that have wreaked havoc in the country's villages and cities for the past 10 years. That is what the United States, the United Kingdom and the rest of NATO states want. Even China is on board. The already staggering Afghan casualty figures have soared to new heights after the international combat mission ended a year ago. The country suffered almost 5,000 civilian casualties only during the first half of 2015; nearly 30,000 Afghan soldiers and policemen were killed from 2009 to mid-2015. December saw a 57 percent rise in civilian casualties.

Obviously Afghans, more than anyone else, want an end to the conflict. But, unlike their international partners, they do not want peace at any cost. They are not willing to forsake the gains of the past 15 years. After many ups and downs, the troubled peace process was resuscitated recently through the creation of the Quadrilateral Coordination Group (QCG) comprising Afghanistan, Pakistan, the US and China. The first QCG meeting was held last week in Islamabad, and the group is due to meet again in Kabul on Monday.

Pakistan Wants Peace or Powersharing

The initial meeting's modest outcome was praised in Pakistani and Western media, but failed to generate confidence among Afghans. On the same day that Islamabad was hosting the QCG talks, three students were killed and eight wounded in a rocket attack on an elementary girls' school in Afghanistan's Khost province, and a complex suicide attack on Jalalabad city was thwarted. Meanwhile in Islamabad, Sartaj Aziz, the Pakistani representative at the talks, urged the Afghan government to create an "environment conducive to reconciliation", take "confidence-building measures" and "offer incentives" to the Taliban.

President Ashraf Ghani wants to frame the talks with a focus on "the drivers of conflict" and on ways to end the use of non-state actors as instruments of foreign policy. In other words, he wants Pakistan to stop its proxy war in Afghanistan for achieving its strategic goals. Pakistan wishes to have a measure of control over the Afghan state. It wants to use Afghanistan to create a "strategic depth" vis-a-vis its arch-nemesis, India.

A sovereign Afghanistan is also an obstacle to Pakistan's desire to have free access to Central Asian natural resources and markets. At the same time, Islamabad wants Kabul to recognise the Durand Line as the official border between the two countries. Pakistan's change of terminology from "peace" to "reconciliation" reflects its push for Kabul to agree to a power-sharing arrangement with Islamabad's proxies. Amending the constitution to reflect the Taliban's ideology is another demand on Islamabad's list.

Neither this nor any future Afghan government can make a unilateral decision on the Durand Line. The artificial border is a remnant of the British Raj and was imposed in 1884 after the second Anglo-Afghan war. Afghans maintain that since the agreement was with the British colonial power, it became null and void after India's independence and the creation of Pakistan in 1947. This is a matter of national pride for the Afghans.

Afghanistan and its relationship with India

Pakistan's demand to control Afghanistan's relations with India - its opposition to the Indian consular offices in Afghan provinces being one manifestation of this - is a clear infringement of Afghan sovereignty. Ghani has made it abundantly clear that such an intrusion is not acceptable. He has repeatedly said that Afghanistan's independence, sovereignty and constitution are non-negotiable and that "peace is not equivalent to reconciliation". Ghani has also assured Afghans, time and again, that the first two chapters of the constitution, containing the nature and structure of the state and the fundamental rights and obligations of citizens, are not negotiable.

Women's equal rights, freedom of expression, inviolability of human life and dignity, the right to form political parties and associations and the right to education are among values that the Taliban do not share, if its rule in the 1990s and its current behaviour are any indication. While Pakistan was pushing for a "conducive environment" for Taliban groups at the QCG meeting, Afghan media headlines were about the completion of 63 new school buildings in Sar-e-Pul province, the graduation of 300 young women from USAID's women's leadership development programme, the launch of the Afghanistan National Institute of Music's sixth winter season, and the thousands of fans welcoming the triumphant national cricket team at Kabul airport.

Under the Taliban rule, girls were prohibited from attending school; women were entirely shunned from public life; boys were forbidden to play sports; music was banned. Afghans don't want to return to that life. The QCG statement underscored "Afghan-owned" and "Afghan-led" talks. In reality, peace has so far been a US-driven agenda.

Parallel to the decision to end its Afghanistan war, the US initiated a push for the peace process as a means to leave behind a semblance of stability. The process has not been successful, mainly because Pakistan believes that it is through patience and sustained pounding of the Afghan state and people - especially after the international troops' exit - that it will eventually attain its objectives. Attending meetings in the name of peace or reconciliation since 2010 is but a stalling tactic.

Will Taliban Renounce Power?

Perhaps Islamabad is also counting on the collapse or weakening of the National Unity Government of Ghani and his Chief Executive Officer Abdullah Abdullah. The Afghan president is already paying a heavy political price domestically for his initial conciliatory gestures, as they have not borne results. The fragile political environment in Kabul has no room for more concessions. Afghanistan is not prepared to make further compromises. Pakistan has certainly no reason to make compromises. The majority and stronger Taliban groups, including the Haqqani Network, are not likely to renounce violence. Therefore, prospects for Washington's Pax Afghana are not bright.

To end the conflict in Afghanistan and prevent the country from becoming a springboard for a multitude of terrorist groups requires a bold shift of paradigm. First, the balance of power on the ground must be tilted. The US should revert back to full combat missions with clear strategic objectives. After 15 years of experience, US generals can surely devise effective combat strategies that won't require a dramatic surge of troops.

Simultaneously, the US must abandon its ambiguous policy towards Pakistan and - along with China, other key allies, and the UN - apply pressure on Islamabad through sanctions, a comprehensive suspension of aid, and the threat of isolation. US President Barack Obama still has a chance to initiate a true end to America's longest war before leaving office.

WAR IN AFGHANISTAN

The War in Afghanistan (2015–present) refers to the period of the war in Afghanistan following the 2001–2014 phase led by the United States. The U.S.-led war followed the September 11 attacks, aiming to dismantle al-Qaeda and deny it a safe-haven in Afghanistan by removing the Taliban from power.

After 2001, theNorth Atlantic Treaty Organization (NATO) became increasingly involved, eventually running combat operations, under the direction of a U.S. commander. On 28 December 2014, NATO formally ended combat operations in Afghanistan and transferred full security responsibility to the Afghan government via a ceremony inKabul, marking the beginning of the new phase of the conflict.

The planned partial withdrawal of U.S. troops from Afghanistan, as well as NATO troops, and the transfer of many combat roles from NATO forces to the Afghan security forces occurred between 2011 and 2014. A bilateral security agreementwas signed between the US and Afghanistan that would allow NATO troops to remain after the withdrawal date in an advisory and counter-terrorism capacity.The NATO troop presence would amount to approximately 13,000 troops including 9,800 Americans.

Background

As early as November 2012, the U.S. was considering the precise configuration of their post-2014 presence in Afghanistan. On 27 May 2014, President Barack Obama announced that U.S. combat operations in Afghanistan would end in December 2014. A residual force of 9,800 troops would remain in the country, training Afghan security forces and supporting counterterrorism operations against remnants of al-Qaeda.

This force would be halved by the end of 2015, and consolidated at Bagram Air Base and in Kabul. Obama also announced all U.S. forces, with the exception of a "normal embassy presence," would be removed from Afghanistan by the end of 2016. These plans were confirmed with the signing of the Bilateral Security Agreement between the United States and Afghanistan on 30 September 2014.

The Special Operations Joint Task Force – Afghanistan, the remnant U.S./NATO special forces organisation, includes a counter-terrorism task force. In the words of the U.S. Special Operations Command Factbook for 2015, this task force '..[c]onducts offensive operations in Afghanistan to degrade the Taliban, Al-Qaeda, and the Haqqani Networks in order to prevent them from establishing operationally significant safe havens which threaten the stability and sovereignty of Government of the Islamic Republic of Afghanistan and the United States.' This task force is similar to previous forces such as Task Force 373.

The Taliban began a resurgence due to several factors. At the end of 2014, the US and NATO combat mission ended and the withdrawal of most foreign forces from Afghanistan reduced the risk the Taliban faced of being bombed and raided. In June 2014, the Pakistani military's Operation Zarb-e-Azb, launched in the North Waziristan tribal area in June 2014, dislodged thousands of mainly Uzbek, Arab and Pakistani militants, who flooded into Afghanistan and swelled the Taliban's ranks.

The group was further emboldened by the comparative lack of interest from the international community and the diversion of its attention to crisis in other parts of the world, such as Syria, Iraq and Ukraine. Afghan security forces also lack certain capabilities and equipment, especially air power and reconnaissance. There is also the political infighting in the central government in Kabul and the apparent weakness in governance at different levels is also exploited by the Taliban.

2015: AFGHAN FORCES TAKE THE LEAD

On 5 January, a suicide car bomber attacked the HQ of EUPOL Afghanistan inKabul, killing 1 person and injuring 5. The Taliban claimed responsibility. On January 15, Afghan security officials arrested five men in Kabul in relation to their suspected involvement in the 2014 Peshawar school massacre in Pakistan. In mid-January 2015, the Islamic State of Iraq and the Levant established a branch in Afghanistan called Wilayah Khorasan and began recruiting fighters and clashing with the Taliban. However, an Afghan military officer stated that he believed the Afghan military could handle any threat that the group presented in the country.

American forces have increased raids against "Islamist militants", moving beyond counter-terrorism missions. This is partially due to improved relations with the United States due to the Ghani presidency.

Reasoning used for these raids include protecting American forces, which has been broadly interpreted. One raid, a joint raid by American and Afghan forces arrested six Taliban connected to the 2014 Peshawar school massacre. American Secretary of Defense Ash Carter traveled to Afghanistan in February 2015; during a period when it was discussed that the U.S. would slow down its withdrawal from Afghanistan.

In February 2015, the headquarters element of the U.S. 7th Infantry Division began to deploy to Afghanistan.

It will serve as the Resolute Support Mission's Train Advise Assist Command - South headquarters. It will be joined by 10th Mountain Division's 2nd Brigade Combat Team, and 101st Combat Aviation Brigade.

On 18 March 2015, Hafiz Wahidi, ISIL's replacement deputy Emir in Afghanistan, was killed by the Afghan Armed Forces, along with 9 other ISIL militants who were accompanying him.

On 19 March 2015, it was reported by Reuters that the U.S. military bases in Kandahar and Jalalabad are likely to remain open beyond the end of 2015, a senior U.S. official said, as the Federal Government of the United States considers slowing its military withdrawal to help the new government fight the Taliban.

The anticipated policy reversal reflects U.S. support of Afghanistan's new and more cooperative president, Ashraf Ghani, and a desire to avoid the collapse of local security forces that occurred in Iraq after the U.S. withdrawal there.

On 25 March, the Afghan National Army killed twenty-nine insurgents and injured twenty-one others in a series of operations in theDaikundi, Ghazni, and Parwan provinces. Eleven people, including one U.S. service member, died in a Taliban attack on Camp Integrity in Kabul in August.

Kabul Parliament Attack

On June 22, 2015, the Taliban detonated a car bomb outside the National Assembly in Kabul, and Taliban fighters attacked the building with assault rifles and RPGs. A Taliban fighter driving a car loaded with explosives managed to get though security checkpoints before detonating the vehicle outside the parliament's gates. Six Taliban insurgents with AK-47 rifles and RPGs took up positions in a construction site nearby. Members of Parliament were evacuated to safety, while security forces battled the insurgents in a two-hour gun battle. Afghan Interior Ministry spokesman Sediq Sediqqi said all seven attackers were killed by police and no MPs were wounded. The UN mission in Afghanistan said a woman and a child were killed in the attack, and forty civilians were injured.

Taliban Negotiations

Chinese officials have declared that Afghan stability affects separatist movements in the region, including in China's West as well as the security of the China–Pakistan Economic Corridor. China and Pakistan have been involved in negotiations between the Afghan government and the Taliban. The bombing of the Kabul parliament has highlighted fractures within the Taliban in their approach to peace talks.

Kunduz Offensive

Heavy fighting has occurred in the Kunduz province, which was the site of clashes from 2009 onwards. In May, flights into the Northern city of Kunduz were suspended due to weeks of clashes between the Afghan security forces and the Taliban outside the city.The intensifying conflict in the Northern Char Dara District within the Kunduz province led the Afghan government to enlist local militia fighters to bolster opposition to the Taliban insurgency. In June, the Taliban intensified attacks around the Northern city of Kunduz as part of a major offensive in an attempt to capture the city. Tens of thousands of inhabitants have been displaced internally in Afghanistan by the fighting. The government recaptured the Char Dara district after roughly a month of fighting.

In late September, Taliban forces launched an attack on Kunduz, seizing several outlying villages and entering the city. The Taliban stormed the regional hospital and clashed with security forces at the nearby university. The fighting saw the Taliban attack from four different districts: Chardara to the west, Aliabad to the south-west, Khanabad to the east and Imam Saheb to the north. According to the Guardian the Taliban had taken the Zakhel and Ali Khel villages on the highway leading south, which connects the city to Kabul and Mazar-e Sharif through Aliabad district. The Taliban reportedly made their largest gains in the south-west of Kunduz, where some local communities had picked up weapons and supported the Taliban. Taliban fighters had allegedly blocked the route to the Airport to prevent civilians fleeing the city. One witness reported that the headquarters of the National Directorate of Security was set on fire.

Taliban Infighting

On 11 November 2015 it was reported that infighting had broken out between different Taliban factions in Zabul province. Fighters loyal to the new Taliban leader Mullah Akhtar Mansoor fought a Pro-ISIS splinter faction led by Mullah Mansoor Dadullah. Even though Dadullah's faction enjoyed the support of foreign ISIS fighters including Uzbeks and Chechens it was reported that Mansoor's Taliban loyalists had the upper hand. According to Ghulam Jilani Farahi, provincial director of security in Zabul, more than 100 militants from both sides were killed since the fighting broke out.

Taliban Offensive in Helmand Province

In 2015 the Taliban began an offensive in Helmand Province, taking over parts of the Province. By June 2015, they had seized control ofDishu and Bagharm killing 5,588 Afghan government security forces (3,720 of them were police officers). By the end of July, the Taliban had overrun Nawzad District and on August 26, the Taliban took control of Musa Qala. the status of the remaining districts, by December 18, 2015, is that Taliban and Afghan security forces are contesting Nahr-i-Sarraj, Sangin, Kajaki, Nad Ali and Khanashin (Afghan security forces claim to have previously "ejected" the Taliban from the Khanashin district center, with 42

Taliban fighters were killed) whilstGarmsir, Washir, and Nawa-i-Barak are believed to be contested.

In October 2015, Taliban forces had attempted to take Lashkar Gah; the capital of Helmand province. Whilst the assault was repelled, Taliban forces remained dug into the city's suburbs as of December 2015. December 2015 saw a renewed Taliban offensive in Helmand focused on the town of Sangin, Sangin district fell to the Taliban on December 21, after fierce clashes that killed more than 90 soldiers in two days.

It was reported that 30 members of the SAS alongside 60 US special forces operators joined the Afghan Army in the Battle to retake parts of Sangin from Taliban insurgents. On or around 23 December, approximately 200 Afghan Police and Army forces were besieged inside the towns police headquarters, with ammunition, military equipment and food having to be airdropped to their positions, with the rest of Sangin being under Taliban control, and an attempted relief mission failing.

AFGHAN SECURITY FORCES AND ALLIED MILITIAS

Afghan National Army

U.S. policy called for boosting the Afghan National Army to 134,000 soldiers by October 2010. By May 2010 the Afghan Army had accomplished this interim goal and was on track to reach its ultimate number of 171,000 by 2011. This increase in Afghan troops allowed the U.S. to begin withdrawing its forces in July 2011.

In 2010, the Afghan National Army had limited fighting capacity. Even the best Afghan units lacked training, discipline and adequate reinforcements. In one new unit in Baghlan Province, soldiers had been found cowering in ditches rather than fighting. Some were suspected of collaborating with the Taliban. "They don't have the basics, so they lay down," said Capt. Michael Bell, who was one of a team of U.S. and Hungarian mentors tasked with training Afghan soldiers. "I ran around for an hour trying to get them to shoot, getting fired on. I couldn't get them to shoot their weapons." In addition, 9 out of 10 soldiers in the Afghan National Army were illiterate.

In early 2015, Philip Munch of the Afghanistan Analysts' Network wrote that '..the available evidence suggests that many senior ANSF members, in particular, use their positions to enrich themselves.

Within the ANSF there are also strong external loyalties to factions who themselves compete for influence and access to resources.

All this means that the ANSF may not work as they officially should. Rather it appears that the political economy of the ANSF prevents them from working like modern organisations – the very prerequisite' of theResolute Support Mission. Formal and informal income, Munch said, which can be generated through state positions, is rent-seeking – income without a corresponding investment of labour or capital.

'Reportedly, ANA appointees also often maintain clients, so that patron-client networks, structured into competing factions, can be traced within the ANA down to the lowest levels... There is evidence that Afghan officers and officials, especially in the higher echelons, appropriate large parts of the vast resource flows which are directed by international donors into the ANA.

Afghan National Police

The Afghan National Police provides support to the Afghan army. Police officers in Afghanistan are also largely illiterate. Approximately 17 percent of them tested positive for illegal drugs in 2010.

They were widely accused of demanding bribes. Attempts to build a credible Afghan police force were faltering badly, according to NATO officials. A quarter of the officers quit every year, making the Afghan government's goals of substantially building up the police force even harder to achieve.

A report from the Pentagon said Afghan national defence and security forces had 27 percent more casualties from the beginning of 2015 up to mid-November compared with the same period last year.

Allied anti-Taliban Militias

The two largest anti-Taliban militias are the mainly Tajik-led Jamiat-e Islami and the Uzbek-led Junbish-i-Milli. Jamiat-e Islami was active during the Soviet war in Afghanistan and the following civil war in Afghanistan. Junbish-i-Milli was also involved in the civil war in Afghanistan. Both groups were members of the anti-Taliban Northern Alliance.

Junbish-i-Milli is led by former General and current Vice President, Abdul Rashid Dostum. Atta Muhammad Nur, the Governor of Balkh province in Afghanistan serves as a prominent leader within Jamiat-e Islami, and has been responsible for mobilizing Jamiat forces against the Taliban in northern Afghanistan. He has been joined by Dostum to form a coalition to fight the Taliban in the north.

TALIBAN AND ALLIED FORCES

As of mid-2015, the Taliban are "directly or indirectly" supported in Afghanistan by "about a dozen" militant groups, having "different goals and agendas" according to the BBC. The groups include many headquartered elsewhere in Pakistan (Lashkar-e-Taiba and Lashkar-e-Jhangvi) or other countries (East Turkestan Islamic Movement). Among the groups are:

- Islamic Emirate of Afghanistan—Afghan Taliban led by Mullah Akhtar Mohammad Mansour
- High Council of Afghanistan Islamic Emirate—Taliban splinter group led Mullah Muhammad Rasool
- Hezbi Islami (HIG) or Islamic Party—a comparatively minor Afghan insurgent group led by Gulbuddin Hekmatyar
- Tehrik-i-Taliban Pakistan (TTP) — Pakistani Taliban
- Al-Qaeda—supports the Afghan Taliban and has renewed its allegiance to the Taliban leader, Mullah Mansour
- Lashkar-e-Taiba (LeT) — Pakistani militant group traditionally focused on India
- Lashkar-e-Jhangvi (LeJ) — Pakistani sectarian militant group targeting Shias

- Islamic Movement of Uzbekistan (IMU) — linked to ISIL since August 2015
- Islamic Jihad Union (IJU) — a splinter faction of IMU now loyal to Afghan Taliban
- East Turkistan Islamic Party (ETIM) — China-focused Uighur separatist group

Opposing the Taliban and the Afghan government are

- ISIL's Khorasan Province—challenges the Taliban's legitimacy and supremacy.

5

Iraq War and the War on Terror

Before the United States invaded Iraq, *Al Qa'ida* was on the ropes. The United States and its coalition partners had rousted it from Afghanistan and toppled the Taliban, while a global manhunt was steadily shutting down jihadist cells from Morocco to Malaysia. Perhaps equally important, many Islamists, including fellow jihadists, harshly criticized bin Ladin for having rashly attacked a super power and, in so doing, causing the defeat of the Taliban, the only "true" Islamic regime in the eyes of many radicals.

The invasion of Iraq breathed new life into the organization. On an operational level, the United States diverted troops to Iraq rather than consolidate its victory in Afghanistan and increase its chances of hunting down Bin Ladin.

Today, *Al Qa'ida* is reconstituting itself in the tribal areas of Pakistan. Politically, Iraq vindicated bin Ladin's argument that the primary enemy of the Muslim world was not the local Muslim autocrats, but the "faraway enemy," the United States. Today, *Al Qa'ida* is again on the march.

It was not supposed to be this way. Toppling Saddam Husayn's regime was meant to usher in an era of prosperity for Iraq and put Osama bin Ladin and his followers on the run. Instead, the tables have turned. Today, Iraq is torn by crime, plagued by a vicious insurgency, and devoid of competent government and basic services. Strife in Iraq continues without end in sight, while the human and financial costs to the United States and its allies mount. With each car bomb and kidnapping, critics urging the withdrawal of troops grow more and more vociferous.

Every additional day that the United States remains in Iraq is a boon for *Al Qa'ida* and the broader jihadist movement. On the other hand, *Al Qa'ida* and its allies would also exploit a U.S. withdrawal that left Iraq in chaos.

How then should the United States solve this conundrum? Victory in Iraq cannot be judged entirely or even primarily in light of U.S. efforts against *Al Qa'ida*. Added to the mix are the importance of a stable oil-rich region, the human costs of a massive civil war, and the moral burden that the United States must bear in the eyes of the world for the carnage it unleashed. But just as counter terrorism was an important justification for the war, so too is it an important criterion for judging the next steps with regard to this bloody challenge.

Iraq, as President Bush has declared, has indeed become a "central front" in the war on terrorism. This "central front" exists in no small part to administration policies, which have created a jihadist problem in Iraq where none existed. But that oft-repeated criticism does not solve the problem of where to go next in Iraq.

Developing a long-term Iraq policy is vital. From a counterterrorism point of view, the problem of Iraq does not go away if the United States abandons the country to strife. Indeed, in many ways it would get worse. By early 2007, the conflict had already generated over two million refugees who could spread instability and terrorism to neighboring states. In Iraq, jihadists from around the world are learning new skills, forging new networks, and otherwise training to fight the next war as well as defeat America and its Iraqi allies.

THE INVASION OF IRAQ WAS AN ENGINE OF TERRORIST GROWTH

By attacking Iraq rather than focusing on al-Qaida, we fell into our enemies' trap. The al-Qaida manual, "The Management of Savagery," prescribed forcing America "to abandon its war against Islam by proxy" by provoking it into a feckless military confrontation with a Muslim country with the goal of overextending

America militarily, bleeding us financially, and exposing the hollowness of American values.

Many defense intellectuals who supported the war at the time now call the invasion a distraction from the war on terrorism. But the occupation of Iraq was much more than a distraction: it was an engine of terrorist growth. By going to war in Iraq, we set the stage for the emergence for an entirely new branch of al-Qaida—al-Qaida in Iraq. We thought we had mitigated its strength with the surge, and to some extent, we did. But now that US troops have left Iraq, the group that emerged in direct response to our occupation is resurgent, not just inside Iraq but as a regional movement, rebuilding its networks in Syria, Jordan, and Libya.

The United States invaded Iraq with three stated goals: to disarm Iraq of weapons of mass destruction, to end Saddam Hussein's support for terrorism, and to free the Iraqi people. Within six weeks, Saddam's regime was deposed, no functional WMD had been found, and President Bush announced "mission accomplished." Like many leaders before him preparing to go to war, President Bush was optimistic about the prospect of victory. He persuaded himself and the U.S. Congress that the war in Iraq would be quick and cheap: approximately $50 to $60 billion to overthrow Saddam, reinstate order, and install a new government.

The actual costs of the war in Iraq include the deaths of 4488 U.S. military personnel and hundreds of thousands of Iraqi civilians. According to Brown University's Costs of War project, financial costs, including the cost to service the debt, will likely total nearly $4 trillion.

VIEWS OF U.S. CONGRESS, PUBLIC, AND TROOPS

Calls for Withdrawal from Iraq

First, was this war necessary or did it actually divert important resources from al Qaeda and the true war on terror? The withdrawal of American military forces from Iraq has been a contentious issue within the United States since the beginning of the Iraq War. As the war has progressed from its initial invasion phase to the more than four-year occupation, U.S. public opinion has turned in favor of troop withdrawal. As of May 2007, 55 percent of Americans believe that the Iraq war was a mistake, and 51 percent of registered voters favor troop withdrawal. In late April 2007, the U.S. Congress passed a supplementary spending bill for Iraq that sets a deadline for troop withdrawal, but President Bush vetoed this bill soon afterwards. In the wake of the veto, proponents of withdrawal appear to be shifting towards establishing benchmarks that the Iraqi government will need to meet, a plan that may be more palatable to President Bush and his advisers. Journalist Pepe Escobar points to the destiny of the Iraq oil law as the crucial point determining the will of the American administrations to withdraw.

Opinion from 2003 to 2005

At the outset of the war, the U.S. Congress and public opinion supported the notion that the Iraq War was part of the global war on terror. The 2002 Congressional resolution authorising military force against Iraq cited the U.S. determination to "prosecute the war on terrorism", and in April 2003, one month after the invasion, a poll found that 77% of Americans agreed that the Iraq War was part of the War on Terror. Much of the organized violence encountered by the U.S. military was framed by the metaphor of a crusade, or total conflict, that was taken up by the terrorists. In 2004, an Army War College report said the war diverts attention and resources from the threat posed by Al Qaeda and called for downsizing the war on terror and focusing instead on the threat from Al Qaeda.

Opinion from 2006 to Date

The military and civilian death toll has mounted, the Iraqi insurgency has shifted to what many observers have labeled a civil war, and thepolitics of Iraq have remained unstable, many politicians and citizens from the United States and across the world have begun pushing for the U.S. to withdraw from Iraq. Significant American calls for withdrawal include the Iraq Study Group Report and the Center for American Progress's proposal for strategic reset.

As of spring 2007, surveys showed a majority of Americans in support of a timetable for withdrawal. While up to 70 percent of Americans in one survey favored withdrawal, most prefer to leave gradually over 12 months, and 60 percent say the U.S. has a moral obligation to the Iraqi people. In addition to voicing concerns over the human and financial costs of the war, supporters of withdrawal argue that the U.S. presence fosters ongoing violence by providing a target for al-Qaeda. It also allows Iraqi political leaders to avoid reaching a power-sharing agreement. The withdrawal will induce Iraq's neighbors to become more involved in quelling violence in the country and will relieve the strain on the U.S. military. The withdrawal debate has brought comparison of Iraq and Vietnam wars.

After the 2006 midterm Congressional elections, Congress has pushed to begin withdrawing troops from Iraq, in part based on the argument that Iraq is a distraction, as opposed to a part of, the war on terror. Likewise, a January 2007 poll found that 57% of Americans feel that the Iraq War is not part of the War on Terror. By June 2007, polls revealed that only 30% of Americans support the war. On July 12, 2007 the House passed a resolution by 223 to 201, for redeployment [or withdrawal] of U.S. armed forces out of Iraq. The resolution requires most troops to withdraw from Iraq by April 1, 2008.

Increase in Terrorism

According to the Israel Intelligence Heritage & Commemoration Center, Saddam Hussein had a long history before the invasion of giving money to families of suicide bombers in Palestine. And, as part of the justification for the war, the Bush Administration argued that Saddam Hussein also had ties to al-Qaeda, and that his overthrow would lead to democratisation in the Middle East, decreasing terrorism overall. However, reports from the CIA, the U.S. State Department, the FBI, and the Senate Select Committee on Intelligence, as well as the investigations of foreign intelligence agencies found no evidence of an operational connection between Saddam and al-Qaeda. Some intelligence experts have a contrary view - that the Iraq war has increased terrorism. Counterterrorism expert Rohan Gunaratna frequently refers to the invasion of Iraq as a "fatal mistake." London's conservative International Institute for Strategic Studies concluded in 2004 that the occupation of Iraq had become "a potent global recruitment pretext" for jihadists and that the invasion "galvanised" al-Qaeda and "perversely inspired insurgent violence" there. The U.S.National Intelligence Council concluded in a January 2005 report that the war in Iraq had become a breeding ground for a new generation of terrorists; David B. Low, the national intelligence officer for transnational threats, indicated that the report concluded that the war in Iraq provided terrorists with "a training ground, a recruitment ground, the opportunity for enhancing technical skills... There is even, under the best scenario, over time, the likelihood that some of the jihadists who are not killed there will, in a sense, go home, wherever home is, and will therefore disperse to various other countries." The Council's Chairman Robert L. Hutchings said, "At the moment, Iraq is a magnet for international terrorist activity." And the 2006 National Intelligence Estimate, which outlined the considered judgment of all 16 U.S. intelligence agencies, held that "The Iraq conflict has become the 'cause celebre' for jihadists, breeding a deep resentment of US involvement in the Muslim world and cultivating supporters for the global jihadist movement." According to Mohammed Hafez, "Since 2003, the number of suicide bombings in Iraq has surpassed all those of Hamas in Israel, Hezbollah in Lebanon, and the Tamil Tigers in Sri Lanka combined."

Al-Qaeda leaders have seen the Iraq war as a boon to their recruiting and operational efforts, providing evidence to jihadists worldwide that America is at war with Islam, and the training ground for a new generation of jihadists to practice attacks on American forces. In October 2003, Osama bin Laden announced: "Be glad of the good news: America is mired in the swamps of the Tigris and Euphrates. Bush is, through Iraq and its oil, easy prey. Here is he now, thank God, in an embarrassing situation and here is America today being ruined before the eyes of the whole world." Al-Qaeda commander Seif al-Adl gloated about the war in Iraq, indicating, "The Americans took the bait and fell into our trap." A letter thought to be from al-Qaeda leader Atiyah Abd al-Rahman found in Iraq among the rubble where al-Zarqawi was killed and released by the U.S. military in October 2006, indicated that al-Qaeda perceived the war as beneficial to its goals: "The most important thing is that the jihad continues with steadfastness... indeed, prolonging the war is in our interest.".

INTERNATIONAL OPINION OF THE WAR ON TERROR

The declaration of a global war on terror in the aftermath of the attacks of in September 2001 constituted the single most ambitious reordering of America's foreign policy objectives since the Second World War.

Alongside this re-evaluation of foreign policy priorities came a stark warning to the rest of the world. At the joint session of the United States Congress following the attacks, President Bush said that 'every nation, in every region, now has a decision to make. Either you are with us, or you are with the terrorists.' This ultimatum deepened America's relations with states that had a strong interest in destroying Al-Qaeda, and strained those with states that had mixed records in combating terrorism, such as Saudi Arabia.

While September 11 did not change everything-the unipolar structure of the international system remained intact, for example-it nevertheless profoundly altered American grand strategy, reshuffling the alliance system that had served as the foundation of US foreign policy since 1945 and making the defeat of terrorism the chief object of American power. For a brief time the 'war on terror' appeared to chart a new, even revolutionary, direction for America's grand strategy.

After the United States was attacked by terrorists on September 11, 2001, its European allies were among the first nations to express sympathy and pledge their aid in the war to come. The fact that many European countries have long experienced terrorism themselves helped ensure a great deal of transatlantic empathy and cooperation- at least at first. France, Germany, Italy, Spain, and the United Kingdom have suffered political violence over the past 30 years and were thus predisposed to help the United States its new struggle against al-Qaeda. But the kind of terrorism these European countries have suffered-"old" terrorism-differs substantially from that suddenly faced by the United States. As time passed, these differences started to erode the through going unity that had flourished right after September 11.

Starting in the 1970S and 198os, however, a rise of violent activity in Europe by international terrorist groups (such as the Palestine Liberation Organization and Hezbollah) began to prove these traditional European responses to terror inadequate. Governments reacted with more robust and effective-cooperative measures. Still, unlike the enemies the United States faces today, few terrorists in those days sought to debilitate European governments or recruit large numbers of members. And even those that did harbor global religious and ideological objectives (such as the Algerian Islamist Group, or GIA) still tended to employ "old" terrorist techniques.

Al Qaeda, on the other hand, represents a transnational threat-one very different in kind from that posed by the IRA or even newer groups such as Hamas. Al Qaeda has potentially thousands of members and no interest in bargaining with the United States or its allies. Instead, it seeks to cripple them, by inflicting mass casualties if p possible, potentially with weapons of mass destruction (WMDI).

To understand Europe's approach to counterterrorism, it helps to remember that its attitude has been informed by the region's experience with the old form of terrorism-not the new transnational kind. Because of the limited form that most of European terrorism has taken in the past, European governments remain more inclined than Washington to distinguish the political wings of terrorist groups from their military elements. This in turn helps explain why, although European governments have generally been very effective in stopping terrorists financially-they have frozen about $35 million in suspected al Qaeda assets since September 11 (compared to about $34 million in the United States and $124.5 million worldwide)-as of December 2002,they still had not frozen the assets of Hamas' political wing.

Before September 11, only six European countries-France, Germany, Italy, Portugal, Spain, and the United Kingdom-had specific counter terrorism laws (as distinct from ordinary criminal codes). Some of these six have since strengthened their laws still further or improved enforcement. Other countries such as the Netherlands, which did not have such laws or counterterrorism programs, have enacted and implemented them. Spanish magistrates, seasoned by long-standing Basque terrorism and equipped with tough statutes, have been among the most dogged pursuers of al Qaeda suspects. Germany has substantially increased funding for its border guard, prosecutor's office, and intelligence agencies, and has increased law enforcement's access to personal financial data. Berlin has also authorized the prosecution of foreigners associated with terrorist groups based outside Germany, and the deportation of those perpetrating political violence or otherwise threatening Germany's "basic order of democratic freedom." Italy, for its part, has similarly broadened its statutory authority for apprehending terrorists.

Other countries, however-such as Belgium-have done little, and even in European countries that have taken action, the measures have been largely remedial. Both Germany and Italy have long been plagued by bureaucratic in efficiencies and significant statutory gaps in their law-enforcement regimes. Prior to September 11, for instance, Germany had no provision outlawing foreign-based terrorist organizations, and Italy had not authorized surveillance of those suspected of belonging to such groups.

Still, there is no doubt that European leaders are aware that their countries were infiltrated by al Qaeda prior to September 11. This fact, along with more recent developments showing that al Qaeda has reconstituted itself and expanded its list of targets has energized EU law enforcement. This is not surprising, given that al Qaeda or its affiliates have attacked German tourists in Tunisia; French submarine engineers in Pakistan; a French oil tanker in the Gulf of Aden; U.S. marines in Kuwait; Australian, European, and American tourists in Bali; and Israelis in Kenya. As this list indicates, until it is ready to stage another mass-casualty attack in America, al Qaeda will content itself with soft targets over a wider geographical range. Confirming the point, in an audiotape that surfaced in November 2002, Osama bin Laden expressly cited Australia, Canada, France, Germany, Israel, Italy, and the United Kingdom as targets.

In response, several European governments departed from their relatively circumspect, low-key approach to terrorism alerts and issued stark warnings about planned attacks in Europe.

Nevertheless, these incentives off or improving territorial security in Europe remain subject to countervailing attitudes and political forces. Germany, the United Kingdom, and France all have large Muslim populations. And whereas the roughly1 5million Muslims living in the EU'S 15 current member states constitute about four percent of the total EU population, the 6 million Muslims (a liberal estimate) living in the United States compose only slightly higher than two percent of the U.S. population-a significant difference. European Muslims, however, are only half-accepted socially and are politically underrepresented. This marginal status makes them susceptible to radicalization-one factor that has helped prevent governments from taking steps that might seem anti-Muslim.

Concern about terrorism varies significantly around the world, with the highest levels found in the Middle East, South Asia, and Western Europe—all regions that have suffered significant terrorist attacks. Despite 9/11, Americans are only average in their level of concern. Asked how big a problem terrorism is in their country, in sixteen out of forty-seven nations a majority or plurality said it was a very big problem; in fifteen nations a majority or plurality said it was at least a moderately big problem; and in thirteen nations a majority or plurality said it was a small problem or not a problem at all. An average of 41 percent of respondents across all countries polled said that terrorism is a very big problem in their country, while 23 percent said it was a moderately big problem, 19 percent said it is a small problem, and 14 percent said it is not a problem at all.

All of the countries that show the highest levels of concern are ones where there have been significant terrorist attacks. The highest levels of concern are found in the Middle East and South Asia, led by Morocco (81 percent calling it a very big problem), Bangladesh (77 percent),Lebanon (76 percent), Pakistan (76 percent), India (72 percent), and Turkey (72 percent). But concern is also strong in European countries that have experienced terrorist attacks over the years, including Italy (73 percent), Spain (66 percent), France (54 percent), and in other countries around the world with such experiences—for instance Peru (70 percent) and Japan (59 percent).

Despite September 11, though, Americans are only average in their level of concern, with 44 percent saying it is a very big problem and 38 percent saying it is a somewhat big problem. In fourteen countries a majority or plurality said terrorism was only a small problem or not a problem at all. These include most of the African countries polled, some Eastern European countries, as well as several Asian countries (including China).

IRAQ WAR

The Iraq War was a protracted armed conflict that began with the 2003 invasion of Iraq by a United States-led coalition. The invasion regime toppled the government ofSaddam Hussein. However, the conflict continued for much of the next decade as aninsurgency emerged to oppose the occupying forces and the post-invasion Iraqi government. An estimated 151,000 to 600,000 or more Iraqis were killed in the first 3–4 years of conflict. The United States officially withdrew from the country in 2011 but became re-involved in 2014 at the head of a new coalition; the insurgency and many dimensions of the civil armed conflict continue.

The invasion began on 20 March 2003, with the U.S., joined by the United Kingdom and several coalition allies, launching a "shock and awe" bombing campaign. Iraqi forces were quickly overwhelmed as U.S. forces swept through the country. The invasion led to the collapse of the Ba'athist government; Saddam was captured in December 2003 and executed by a military court three years later. However, the power vacuum following Saddam's demise and the mismanagement of the occupationled to widespread sectarian violence between Shias and Sunnis as well as a lengthy insurgency against U.S. and coalition forces. The United States responded with atroop surge in 2007 to attempt to reduce the violence. The U.S. began withdrawing its troops in the winter of 2007–08. The winding down of U.S. involvement in Iraq accelerated under President Barack Obama. The U.S. formally withdrew all combat troops from Iraq by December 2011.

The Bush administration based its rationale for war principally on the assertion that Iraq possessed weapons of mass destruction (WMDs) and that Saddam's government posed an immediate threat to the United States and its coalition allies. Select U.S. officials accused Saddam of harboring and supporting al-Qaeda, while others cited the desire to end a repressive dictatorship and bring democracy to the people of Iraq. After the invasion, no substantial evidence was found to verify the initial claims about WMDs. The rationale and misrepresentation of pre-war intelligence faced heavy criticism within the U.S. and internationally.

As a result of the war, Iraq held multi-party elections in 2005. Nouri al-Maliki became Prime Minister in 2006 and remained in office until 2014. The Maliki government enacted policies that were widely seen as having the effect of alienating the country's Sunni minority and worsening sectarian tensions. In the summer of 2014, the Islamic State of Iraq and the Levant (ISIL) launched a military offensive in Northern Iraq and declared a worldwide Islamic caliphate, eliciting another military response from the United States and its allies. The Iraq War caused hundreds of thousands of civilian, and thousands of military casualties. The majority of casualties occurred as a result of the insurgency and civil conflicts between 2004 and 2007.

Iraq Disarmament and Pre-war Intelligence

Prior to September 2002, the CIA was the Bush administration's main provider of intelligence on Iraq. In September, a Pentagon unit called Office of Special Plans(OSP), was created by Paul Wolfowitz and Douglas Feith, and headed by Feith, as charged by then-United States Secretary of Defense Donald Rumsfeld, to supply senior George W. Bush administration officials with raw intelligence pertaining toIraq. Seymour Hersh writes that, according to a Pentagon adviser, "[OSP] was created in order to find evidence of what Wolfowitz and his boss, Defense Secretary Donald Rumsfeld, wanted to be true—that Saddam Hussein had close ties to Al Qaeda, and that Iraq had an enormous arsenal of chemical, biological, and possibly even nuclear weapons (WMD) that threatened the region and, potentially, the United States. [...] 'The agency [CIA] was out to *disprove* linkage between Iraq andterrorism,' the Pentagon adviser told me."

U.N. Weapons Inspections Resume

The issue of Iraq's disarmament reached a turning point in 2002–03, when President Bush demanded a complete end to alleged Iraqi production of weapons of mass destruction and full compliance with U.N. Security Council Resolutions requiring U.N. weapons inspectors unfettered access to suspected weapons production facilities. The U.N. had prohibited Iraq from developing or possessing such weapons after the Persian Gulf War and required Iraq to permit inspections confirming compliance. During inspections in 1999, U.S. intelligence agents supplied the United States with a direct feed of conversations between Iraqi security agencies as well as other information. This was confirmed by *The New York Times* and *The Wall Street Journal.*

During 2002, U.S. President George Bush repeatedly warned of military action against Iraq unless inspections were allowed to progress unfettered. In accordance with U.N. Security Council Resolution 1441 Iraq agreed to new inspections in late 2002. With the cooperation of the Iraqis, a third weapons inspection team in 2003 led by David Kelly viewed and photographed two alleged mobile weapons laboratories, which were actually facilities for the production of hydrogen gas to fill balloons.

As part of its weapons inspection obligations, Iraq was required to supply a full declaration of its current weapons capabilities and manufacturing. On 3 November 2002, Iraq supplied an 11,800-page report to the UN Security Council and the IAEA, stating that it had no WMDs. Copies of the report were also unofficially supplied to several European journalists. Colombia, chair of the Security Council, allowed U.S. officials to secretly remove 8,000 pages from the report before it was viewed by the full security council, and on the basis of this the report was declared incomplete and Iraq in breach of its obligations. The removed pages contained details of U.S. and European companies and government agencies who had historically assisted Iraq in developing its chemical and biological weapons capabilities.

Shortly before the invasion, Hans Blix, the lead weapons inspector, advised the U.N. Security Council that Iraq was cooperating with inspections and the confirmation of disarmament through inspections could be achieved quickly if Iraq remained cooperative.

WEAPONS OF MASS DESTRUCTION

Yellowcake Uranium

In 1990, before the Persian Gulf War, Iraq had stockpiled 550 short tons (500 t) of yellowcakeuranium at the Tuwaitha nuclear complex about 20 kilometres (12 mi) south of Baghdad. In late February 2002, the CIA sent former Ambassador Joseph C. Wilson to investigate reports(later found to be forgeries) that Iraq was attempting to purchase additional yellowcake fromNiger. Wilson returned and informed the CIA that reports of yellowcake sales to Iraq were "unequivocally wrong." The Bush administration, however, continued to allege Iraq's attempts to obtain additional yellowcake were a justification for military action, most prominently in the January 2003, State of the Union address, in which President Bush declared that Iraq had sought uranium, citing British intelligence sources.

In response, Wilson wrote a critical *New York Times* op-ed piece in June 2003 stating that he had personally investigated claims of yellowcake purchases and believed them to be fraudulent. After Wilson's op-ed, Wilson's wife Valerie Plame was publicly identified as an undercover CIA analyst by the columnist Robert Novak. This led to a Justice Department investigation into the source of the leak. The federal investigation led to the conviction of I. Lewis (Scooter) Libby, Vice President Dick Cheney's chief of staff, on charges of perjury and obstruction of justice.

On 1 May 2005, the "Downing Street memo" was published in *The Sunday Times*. It contained an overview of a secret 23 July 2002, meeting among British government, Ministry of Defence, andBritish intelligence figures who discussed the build-up to the Iraq war—including direct references to classified U.S. policy of the time. The memo stated that "Bush wanted to remove Saddam, through military action, justified by the conjunction of terrorism and WMD. But the intelligence and facts were being fixed around the policy".

In September 2002, the Bush administration, the CIA and the DIA (Defense Intelligence Agency) said attempts by Iraq to acquire high-strength aluminum tubes that were prohibited under the UN monitoring program and which they said pointed to a clandestine effort to make centrifuges to enrich uranium for nuclear bombs. This analysis was opposed by the United States Department of Energy (DOE) and INR, which was significant because of DOE's expertise in such gas centrifuges and nuclear weapons programs. The DOE and INR argued that the Iraqi tubes were poorly suited for centrifuges and that while it was technically possible with additional modification, conventional military uses were more plausible. A report released by the Institute for Science and International Security in 2002 reported that it was highly unlikely that the tubes could be used to enrich uranium.

An effort by the DOE to correct this detail in comments prepared for United States Secretary of State Colin Powell's UN appearance was rebuffed by the administration and Powell, in his address to the UN Security Council just before the war, referenced the aluminum tubes, stating that while experts disagreed on whether or not the tubes were destined for a centrifuge program, the specifications of the tubes were unusually tight. Powell later admitted he had presented what turned out to be an inaccurate case to the UN on Iraqi weapons, and the intelligence he was relying on was, in some cases, "deliberately misleading." After the 2008 U.S. presidential election, and the election of Democratic party nominee Barack Obama, President Bush stated that "[my] biggest regret of all the presidency has to have been the intelligence failure in Iraq".

Poison Gas

The CIA had contacted Iraq's foreign minister, Naji Sabri, who was being paid by the French as an agent. Sabri informed them that Saddam had hidden poison gas among Sunni tribesmen, had ambitions for a nuclear program but that it was not active, and that no biological weapons were being produced or stockpiled, although research was underway. According to Sidney Blumenthal, George Tenet briefed Bush on 18 September 2002, that Sabri had informed them that Iraq did not have WMD.

On 21 June 2006, the U.S. House of Representatives Permanent Select Committee on Intelligence released key points from a classified report from the National Ground Intelligence Center on the recovery of a small number of degraded chemical munitions in Iraq. The report stated, "Coalition forces have recovered approximately 500 weapons munitions which contain potentially lethal mustard and pure sarin nerve agent." However, all are thought to be pre-Gulf War munitions. According to the commander of the National Ground Intelligence Center "These are chemical weapons as defined under the Chemical Weapons Convention, and yes... they do constitute weapons of mass destruction,". In 2006, 2,400 nerve-agent rockets were found in a single compound.

In October 2014, the New York Times reported that U.S. servicemen had been exposed and injured during the disposal and destruction of abandoned 4,990 chemical weapons that had been discovered in Iraq. CBS News reported that the U.S. government had concealed the injuries to the troops by chemical weapons. US soldiers reporting exposure to mustard gas and sarin allege they were required to keep their exposure secret, sometimes declined admission to hospital and evacuation home despite the request of their commanders."We were absolutely told not to talk about it" by a colonel, the former sergeant said.

In November 2014, the Organization for the Prohibition of Chemical Weapons reported the recovery and destruction of 4,530 aging chemical weapons by American forces.

In February 2015, The New York Times revealed that following the recovery of 17 Borak in 2004 and early 2005, the United States began acquiring and destroying Borak rockets. The "extraordinary arms purchase plan", known as Operation Avarice, continued into 2006 and led to the destroying of more then 400 Borak rockets filled with sarin. The sarin purity level was higher then the Iraq's sarin production in the 1980s.

Biological Weapons

Based on reports obtained by the German intelligence service from an Iraqi defector codenamed "Curveball", Colin Powell presented evidence to the United Nations security council that Iraq had an active biological weapons programs. On 15 February 2011, the defector—a scientist identified as Rafid Ahmed Alwan al-Janabi—admitted to journalists working for *The Guardian* newspaper that he lied to the*Bundesnachrichtendienst* in order to strengthen the case against Saddam Hussein, whom he wished to see removed from power.

Post-invasion Views on WMD

In December 2009, the former British prime minister, Tony Blair, stated that he "would still have thought it right to remove [Saddam Hussein]" regardless of whether Iraq possessed weapons of mass destruction or not.

Preparations

In the days immediately following 9/11, the Bush Administration national security team actively debated an invasion of Iraq. A memo written by Sec. Rumsfeld dated 27 November 2001 considers a U.S.–Iraq war. One section of the memo questions "How start?", listing multiple possible justifications for a U.S.–Iraq War.

During 2002, the amount of ordnance used by British and American aircraft patrolling the no-fly zones of Iraq increased compared to the previous years and by August had "become a full air offensive". Tommy Franks, the allied commander, later stated that the bombing was designed to "degrade" the Iraqi air defense system before an invasion.

In October 2002, a few days before the United States Senate voted on the Joint Resolution to Authorize the Use of United States Armed Forces Against Iraq, about 75 senators were told inclosed session that Iraq had the means of attacking the Eastern Seaboard of the U.S. with biological or chemical weapons delivered by unmanned aerial vehicles (UAVs.) On 5 February 2003, Colin Powell presented further evidence in his Iraqi WMD program presentation to the UN Security Council that UAVs were ready to be launched against the United States. At the time, there was a vigorous dispute within the U.S. military and intelligence communities as to whether CIA conclusions about Iraqi UAVs were accurate and other intelligence agencies suggested that Iraq did not possess any offensive UAV capability, saying the few they had were designed for surveillance and intended for reconnaissance. The Senate voted to approve the Joint Resolution with the support of large bipartisan majorities on 11 October 2002, providing the Bush administration with alegal basis for the U.S. invasion under U.S. law.

The resolution granted the authorization by the Constitution of the United States and the United States Congress for the President to command the military to fight anti-United States violence. Citing the Iraq Liberation Act of 1998, the resolution reiterated that it should be the policy of the United States to remove the Saddam regime and promote a democratic replacement. The authorization was signed by President George W. Bush on 16 October 2002.

Chief UN weapons inspector Hans Blix remarked in January 2003 that "Iraq appears not to have come to a genuine acceptance—not even today—of the disarmament, which was demanded of it and which it needs to carry out to win the confidence of the world and to live in peace." Among other things he noted that 1,000 short tons (910 t) of chemical agent were unaccounted for, information on Iraq's VX nerve agent program was missing, and that "no convincing evidence" was presented for the destruction of 8,500 litres (1,900 imp gal; 2,200 US gal) of anthrax that had been declared.

In the 2003 State of the Union address, President Bush said "we know that Iraq, in the late 1990s, had several mobile biological weapons labs". On 5 February 2003, Secretary of State Colin Powell appeared before the UN to present evidence that Iraq was hiding unconventional weapons. The French government also believed that Saddam had stockpiles of anthrax and botulism toxin, and the ability to produce VX. In March, Blix said progress had been made in inspections, and no evidence of WMD had been found. Iraqi scientist Rafid Ahmed Alwan al-Janabi codenamed "Curveball", admitted in February 2011, that he lied to the CIA about biological weapons in order to get the U.S. to attack and remove Saddam from power.

In early 2003, the U.S., British, and Spanish governments proposed the so-called "eighteenth resolution" to give Iraq a deadline for compliance with previous resolutions enforced by the threat of military action. This proposed resolution was subsequently withdrawn due to lack of support on the UN Security Council. In particular, North Atlantic Treaty Organization(NATO) members France, Germany and Canada and non-NATO member Russia were opposed to military intervention in Iraq, due to the high level of risk to the international community's security, and defended disarmament through diplomacy.

A meeting between George W. Bush and Tony Blair took place on 31 January 2003, in theWhite House. A secret memo of this meeting purportedly showed that the Bush administration had already decided on the invasion of Iraq at that point. Bush was allegedly floating the idea of painting a U 2 spyplane in UN colors and letting it fly low over Iraq to provoke Iraqi forces into shooting it down, thereby providing a pretext for the United States and Britain to invade. Bush and Blair made a secret deal to carry out the invasion regardless of whether WMD were discovered by UN weapons inspectors, in direct contradiction with statements Blair made to the British House of Commons afterwards that the Iraqi regime would be given a final chance to disarm. In the memo, Bush is paraphrased as saying, "The start date for the military campaign was now pencilled in for 10 March. This was when the bombing would begin." Bush said to Blair that he "thought it unlikely that there would be internecine warfare between the different religious and ethnic groups" in Iraq after the war.

Opposition to Invasion

In October 2002, former U.S. President Bill Clinton warned about possible dangers of pre-emptive military action against Iraq. Speaking in the UK on a Labour Party conference he said: "As a preemptive action today, however well-justified, may come back with unwelcome consequences in the future.... I don't care how precise your bombs and your weapons are, when you set them off, innocent people will die." Hillary Clinton while serving as senator voted in favor for military action, though she now says it was a mistake. The majority of Democrats in Congress voted for the Authorization for Use of Military Force Against Iraq Resolution of 2002. Sen. Jim Webbwrote shortly before the vote "Those who are pushing for a unilateral war in Iraq know full well that there is no exit strategy if we invade."

On 20 January 2003, French Foreign Minister Dominique de Villepin declared "we believe that military intervention would be the worst solution". Meanwhile anti-war groups across the world organised public protests. According to French academic Dominique Reynié, between 3 January and 12 April 2003,36 million people across the globe took part in almost 3,000 protests against war in Iraq, with demonstrations on 15 February 2003, being the largest and most prolific. Nelson Mandela voiced his opposition in late January, stating "All that (Mr. Bush) wants is Iraqi oil," and questioning if Bush deliberately undermined the U.N. "because the secretary-general of the United Nations [was] a black man".

In February 2003, the U.S. Army's top general, Eric Shinseki, told the Senate Armed Services Committee that it would take "several hundred thousand soldiers" to secure Iraq. Two days later, U.S. Defense Secretary Donald Rumsfeld said the post-war troop commitment would be less than the number of troops required to win the war, and that "the idea that it would take several hundred thousand U.S. forces is far from the mark." Deputy Defense Secretary Paul Wolfowitz said Shinseki's estimate was "way off the mark," because other countries would take part in an occupying force.

In March 2003, Hans Blix reported that "No evidence of proscribed activities have so far been found" in Iraq, saying that progress was made in inspections, which would continue. He estimated the time remaining for disarmament being verified through inspections to be "months". But the U.S. government announced that "diplomacy has failed", and that it would proceed with a coalition of allied countries—named the "coalition of the willing"—to rid Iraq of its alleged WMD. The U.S. government abruptly advised UN weapons inspectors to leave Baghdad immediately.

There were serious legal questions surrounding the launching of the war against Iraq and the Bush Doctrine of preemptive war in general.

On 16 September 2004, Kofi Annan, the Secretary General of the United Nations, said of the invasion, "I have indicated it was not in conformity with the UN Charter. From our point of view, from the Charter point of view, it was illegal."

In November 2008 Lord Bingham, the former British Law Lord, described the war a serious violation of international law, and accused Britain and the United States of acting like a "world vigilante". He also criticized the post-invasion record of Britain as "an occupying power in Iraq".

Regarding the treatment of Iraqi detainees in Abu Ghraib, Bingham said: "Particularly disturbing to proponents of the rule of law is the cynical lack of concern for international legality among some top officials in the Bush administration." In July 2010, Deputy Prime Minister of the UK Nick Clegg, in an official PMQs session in Parliament, condemned the invasion of Iraq as illegal. Theorist Francis Fukuyama has argued that "the Iraq war and the close association it created between military invasion and democracy promotion tarnished the latter".

THE INVASION

The first Central Intelligence Agency team entered Iraq on 10 July 2002. This team was composed of members of the CIA's Special Activities Division and was later joined by members of the U.S. military's elite Joint Special Operations Command (JSOC).

Together, they prepared for the invasion of conventional forces. These efforts consisted of persuading the commanders of several Iraqi military divisions to surrender rather than oppose the invasion, and to identify all of the initial leadership targets during very high risk reconnaissance missions.

Most importantly, their efforts organized the Kurdish Peshmerga to become the northern front of the invasion. Together this force defeated Ansar al-Islam in Iraqi Kurdistan before the invasion and then defeated the Iraqi army in the north. The battle against Ansar al-Islam led to the death of a substantial number of militants and the uncovering of a chemical weapons facility at Sargat.

At 5:34 a.m. Baghdad time on 20 March 2003 (9:34 p.m., 19 March EST) the surprise military invasion of Iraq began. There was no declaration of war. The 2003 invasion of Iraq, led by U.S. Army General Tommy Franks, under the codename "Operation Iraqi Freedom", the UK codename Operation Telic, and the Australian codenameOperation Falconer. Coalition forces also cooperated with Kurdish Peshmerga forces in the north. Approximately forty other governments, the "Coalition of the Willing," participated by providing troops, equipment, services, security, and special forces, with 248,000 soldiers from the United States, 45,000 British soldiers, 2,000 Australian soldiers and 194 Polish soldiers from Special Forces unit GROM sent to Kuwait for the invasion. The invasion force was also supported by Iraqi Kurdish militia troops, estimated to number upwards of 70,000.

According to General Tommy Franks, the objectives of the invasion were, "First, end the regime of Saddam Hussein. Second, to identify, isolate and eliminate Iraq's weapons of mass destruction. Third, to search for, to capture and to drive out terrorists from that country. Fourth, to collect such intelligence as we can related to terrorist networks. Fifth, to collect such intelligence as we can related to the global network of illicit weapons of mass destruction. Sixth, to end sanctions and to immediately deliver humanitarian support to the displaced and to many needy Iraqi citizens. Seventh, to secure Iraq's oil fields and resources, which belong to the Iraqi people. And last, to help the Iraqi people create conditions for a transition to a representative self-government."

The invasion was a quick and decisive operation encountering major resistance, though not what the U.S., British and other forces expected. The Iraqi regime had prepared to fight both a conventional and irregular war at the same time, conceding territory when faced with superior conventional forces, largely armored, but launching smaller scale attacks in the rear using fighters dressed in civilian and paramilitary clothes. Since the initiation of the war in Iraq, numerous programs were created to "enhance psychological resilience and prevent psychological morbidity in troops."

Coalition troops launched air and amphibious assault on the Al-Faw peninsula to secure the oil fields there and the important ports, supported by warships of the Royal Navy,Polish Navy, and Royal Australian Navy. The United States Marine Corps' 15th Marine Expeditionary Unit, attached to 3 Commando Brigade and the Polish Special Forces unitGROM attacked the port of Umm Qasr, while the British Army's 16 Air Assault Brigadesecured the oil fields in southern Iraq.

The heavy armor of the U.S. 3rd Infantry Divisionmoved westward and then northward through the western desert toward Baghdad, while the1st Marine Expeditionary Force moved more easterly along Highway 1 through the center of the country, and 1 (UK) Armoured Division moved northward through the eastern marshland. The U.S. 1st Marine Division fought through Nasiriyah in a battle to seize the major road junction and nearby Talil Airfield. The United States Army 3rd Infantry Division defeated Iraqi forces entrenched in and around the airfield.

With the Nasiriyah and Talil Airfields secured in its rear, the 3rd Infantry Division supported by 101st Airborne Division continued its attack north toward Najaf and Karbala, but a severe sand storm slowed the coalition advance and there was a halt to consolidate and make sure the supply lines were secure. When they started again they secured the Karbala Gap, a key approach to Baghdad, then secured the bridges over theEuphrates River, and U.S. forces poured through the gap on to Baghdad. In the middle of Iraq, the 1st Marine Division fought its way to the eastern side of Baghdad, and prepared for the attack into Baghdad to seize it.

In the north, OIF 1 used the largest special operations force since the successful attack on the Taliban government of Afghanistan just over a year earlier.

On 9 April, Baghdad fell, ending Saddam's 24 year rule. U.S. forces seized the deserted Ba'ath Party ministries and stage-managedthe tearing down of a huge iron statue of Saddam, photos and video of which became symbolic of the event, although later controversial. Not seen in the photos or heard on the videos, shot with a zoom lens, was the chant of the inflamed crowd for Muqtada al-Sadr, the radical Shiite cleric. In November 2008, Iraqi protesters staged a similar stomping on and burning of an effigy of George W. Bush. The abrupt fall of Baghdad was accompanied by a widespread outpouring of gratitude toward the invaders, but also massive civil disorder, including the looting of public and government buildings and drastically increased crime.

According to the Pentagon, 250,000 short tons (230,000 t) (of 650,000 short tons (590,000 t) total) of ordnance was looted, providing a significant source of ammunition for the Iraqi insurgency. The invasion phase concluded when Tikrit, Saddam's home town, fell with little resistance to the U.S. Marines of Task Force Tripoli.

In the invasion phase of the war (19 March–30 April), an estimated 9,200 Iraqi combatants were killed by coalition forces along with an estimated 3,750 non-combatants, i.e. civilians who did not take up arms. Coalition forces reported the death in combat of 139 U.S. military personnel and 33 UK military personnel.

POST-INVASION PHASE

2003: Beginnings of Insurgency

On 1 May 2003, President Bush visited the aircraft carrier USS *Abraham Lincoln* operating a few miles west of San Diego, California. At sunset Bush held his nationally televised "Mission Accomplished" speech, delivered before the sailors and airmen on the flight deck: Bush declared victory due to the defeat of Iraq's conventional forces.

Nevertheless, Saddam remained at large and significant pockets of resistance remained. After President Bush's speech, coalition forces noticed a gradually increasing flurry of attacks on its troops in various regions, especially in the "Sunni Triangle". The initial Iraqi insurgents were supplied by hundreds of weapons caches created before the invasion by the Iraqi army andRepublican Guard.

Initially, Iraqi resistance (described by the coalition as "Anti-Iraqi Forces") largely stemmed fromfedayeen and Saddam/Ba'ath Party loyalists, but soon religious radicals and Iraqis angered by the occupation contributed to the insurgency. The three provinces with the highest number of attacks were Baghdad, Al Anbar, and Salah Ad Din. Those three provinces account for 35% of the population, but as of 5 December 2006, were responsible for 73% of U.S. military deaths and an even higher percentage of recent U.S. military deaths (about 80%.)

Insurgents used guerrilla tactics including: mortars, missiles, suicide attacks, snipers, improvised explosive devices (IEDs), car bombs, small arms fire (usually with assault rifles), and RPGs (rocket propelled grenades), as well as sabotage against the petroleum, water, and electrical infrastructure.

Post-invasion Iraq coalition efforts commenced after the fall of Saddam's regime. The coalition nations, together with the United Nations, began to work to establish a stable, compliant democraticstate capable of defending itself from non-coalition forces, as well as overcoming internal divisions.

Meanwhile, coalition military forces launched several operations around the Tigris River peninsula and in the Sunni Triangle. A series of similar operations were launched throughout the summer in the Sunni Triangle. Toward the end of 2003, the intensity and pace of insurgent attacks began to increase. A sharp surge in guerrilla attacks ushered in an insurgent effort that was termed the "Ramadan Offensive", as it coincided with the beginning of the Muslim holy month of Ramadan.

To counter this offensive, coalition forces begin to use air power and artillery again for the first time since the end of the invasion by striking suspected ambush sites and mortar launching positions. Surveillance of major routes, patrols, and raids on suspected insurgents were stepped up. In addition, two villages, including Saddam's birthplace of al-Auja and the small town of Abu Hishmawere surrounded by barbed wire and carefully monitored.

Coalition Provisional Authority and the Iraq Survey Group

Shortly after the invasion, the multinational coalition created the Coalition Provisional Authority (CPA; Arabic: ÓáØÉ ÇáÇÆÊáÇÝ ÇáãæÞÊÉý), based in the Green Zone, as a transitional government of Iraq until the establishment of a democratic government. Citing United Nations Security Council Resolution 1483 (22 May 2003) and the laws of war, the CPA vested itself with executive, legislative, and judicial authority over the Iraqi government from the period of the CPA's inception on 21 April 2003, until its dissolution on 28 June 2004.

The CPA was originally headed by Jay Garner, a former U.S. military officer, but his appointment lasted only until 11 May 2003, when President Bush appointed L. Paul Bremer. On 16 May 2003 on his first day on the job Paul Bremer issued CPA executive order No1 to exclude from the new Iraqi government and administration members of the Baathist party. This eventually led to the removal of 85,000 to 100,000 Iraqi people from their job. including 40,000 school teachers who had joined the Baath Party simply to keep their jobs. U.S. army general Sanchez called the decision a "catastrophic failure" Bremer served until the CPA's dissolution in July 2004.

Another group created by the multinational force in Iraq post-invasion was the 1,400-member international Iraq Survey Group who conducted a fact-finding mission to find Iraqi weapons of mass destruction (WMD) programmes. In 2004 the ISG's Duelfer Report stated that Iraq did not have a viable WMD program.

Capturing Former Government Leaders

In the summer of 2003, the multinational forces focused on capturing the remaining leaders of the former government. On 22 July, a raid by the U.S. 101st Airborne Division and soldiers from Task Force 20 killed Saddam's sons (Uday and Qusay) along with one of his grandsons. In all, over 300 top leaders of the former government were killed or captured, as well as numerous lesser functionaries and military personnel.

Most significantly, Saddam Hussein himself was captured on 13 December 2003, on a farm nearTikrit in Operation Red Dawn. The operation was conducted by the United States Army's 4th Infantry Division and members of Task Force 121. Intelligence on Saddam's whereabouts came from his family members and former bodyguards.

With the capture of Saddam and a drop in the number of insurgent attacks, some concluded the multinational forces were prevailing in the fight against the insurgency. The provisional government began training the new Iraqi security forces intended to police the country, and the United States promised over $20 billion in reconstruction money in the form of credit against Iraq's future oil revenues. Oil revenue was also used for rebuilding schools and for work on the electrical and refining infrastructure.

Shortly after the capture of Saddam, elements left out of the Coalition Provisional Authority began to agitate for elections and the formation of an Iraqi Interim Government. Most prominent among these was the Shia cleric Grand Ayatollah Ali al-Sistani. The Coalition Provisional Authority opposed allowing democratic elections at this time. The insurgents stepped up their activities. The two most turbulent centers were the area around Fallujah and the poor Shia sections of cities fromBaghdad (Sadr City) to Basra in the south.

2004: Insurgency Expands

The start of 2004 was marked by a relative lull in violence. Insurgent forces reorganised during this time, studying the multinational forces' tactics and planning a renewed offensive. However, violence did increase during the Iraq Spring Fighting of 2004 with foreign fighters from around the Middle East as well as al-Qaeda in Iraq (an affiliated al-Qaeda group), led by Abu Musab al-Zarqawi helping to drive the insurgency.

As the insurgency grew there was a distinct change in targeting from the coalition forces towards the new Iraqi Security Forces, as hundreds of Iraqi civilians and police were killed over the next few months in a series of massive bombings. An organized Sunni insurgency, with deep roots and both nationalist and Islamist motivations, was becoming more powerful throughout Iraq. The Shia Mahdi Army also began launching attacks on coalition targets in an attempt to seize control from Iraqi security forces. The southern and central portions of Iraq were beginning to erupt in urban guerrilla combat as multinational forces attempted to keep control and prepared for a counteroffensive.

The most serious fighting of the war so far began on 31 March 2004, when Iraqi insurgents inFallujah ambushed a Blackwater USA convoy led by four U.S. private military contractors who were providing security for food caterers Eurest Support Services. The four armed contractors, Scott Helvenston, Jerko Zovko, Wesley Batalona, and Michael Teague, were killed with grenades and small arms fire. Subsequently, their bodies were dragged from their vehicles by local people, beaten, set ablaze, and their burned corpses hung over a bridge crossing the Euphrates. Photos of the event were released to news agencies worldwide, causing a great deal of indignation and moral outrage in the United States, and prompting an unsuccessful "pacification" of the city: the First Battle of Fallujah in April 2004.

The offensive was resumed in November 2004 in the bloodiest battle of the war so far: the Second Battle of Fallujah, described by the U.S. military as "the heaviest urban combat (that they had been involved in) since the battle of Hue City in Vietnam." During the assault, U.S. forces used white phosphorus as an incendiary weapon against insurgent personnel, attracting controversy. The 46 day battle resulted in a victory for the coalition, with 95 U.S. soldiers killed along with approximately 1,350 insurgents. Fallujah was totally devastated during the fighting, though civilian casualties were low, as they had mostly fled before the battle.

Another major event of that year was the revelation of widespread prisoner abuse at Abu Ghraib, which received international media attention in April 2004. First reports of the Abu Ghraib prisoner abuse, as well as graphic pictures showing U.S. military personnel taunting and abusing Iraqi prisoners, came to public attention from a *60 Minutes II* news report (28 April) and a Seymour M. Hersh article in *The New Yorker* (posted online on 30 April.) Military correspondent Thomas Ricks claimed that these revelations dealt a blow to the moral justifications for the occupation in the eyes of many people, especially Iraqis, and was a turning point in the war.

2004 also marked the beginning of Military Transition Teams in Iraq, which were teams of U.S. military advisors assigned directly to New Iraqi Army units.

2005: Elections and Transitional Government

On 31 January, Iraqis elected the Iraqi Transitional Government in order to draft a permanent constitution. Although some violence and a widespread Sunni boycott marred the event, most of the eligible Kurd and Shia populace participated. On 4 February, Paul Wolfowitz announced that 15,000 U.S. troops whose tours of duty had been extended in order to provide election security would be pulled out of Iraq by the next month. February to April proved to be relatively peaceful months compared to the carnage of November and January, with insurgent attacks averaging 30 a day from the prior average of 70.

The Battle of Abu Ghraib on 2 April 2005 was an attack on United States forces at Abu Ghraib prison, which consisted of heavy mortar and rocket fire, under which armed insurgents attacked with grenades, small arms, and two vehicle-borne improvised explosive devices (VBIED). The U.S. force's munitions ran so low that orders to fix bayonets were given in preparation for hand-to-hand fighting. An estimated 80–120 armed insurgents launched a massive coordinated assault on the U.S. military facility and internment camp at Abu Ghraib, Iraq. It was considered to be the largest coordinated assault on a U.S. base since the Vietnam War.

Hopes for a quick end to the insurgency and a withdrawal of U.S. troops were dashed in May, Iraq's bloodiest month since the invasion. Suicide bombers, believed to be mainly disheartened Iraqi Sunni Arabs, Syrians and Saudis, tore through Iraq. Their targets were often Shia gatherings or civilian concentrations of Shias. As a result, over 700 Iraqi civilians died in that month, as well as 79 U.S. soldiers.

The summer of 2005 saw fighting around Baghdad and at Tall Afar in northwestern Iraq as U.S. forces tried to seal off the Syrian border. This led to fighting in the autumn in the small towns of the Euphrates valley between the capital and that border.

A referendum was held on 15 October in which the new Iraqi constitution was ratified. An Iraqi national assembly was elected in December, with participation from the Sunnis as well as the Kurds and Shia.

Insurgent attacks increased in 2005 with 34,131 recorded incidents, compared to a total 26,496 for the previous year.

2006: Civil War and Permanent Iraqi Government

The beginning of 2006 was marked by government creation talks, growing sectarian violence, and continuous anti-coalition attacks. Sectarian violence expanded to a new level of intensity following the al-Askari Mosque bombing in the Iraqi city of Samarra, on 22 February 2006. The explosion at the mosque, one of the holiest sites in Shi'a Islam, is believed to have been caused by a bomb planted by al-Qaeda.

Although no injuries occurred in the blast, the mosque was severely damaged and the bombing resulted in violence over the following days. Over 100 dead bodies with bullet holes were found on 23 February, and at least 165 people are thought to have been killed. In the aftermath of this attack the U.S. military calculated that the average homicide rate in Baghdad tripled from 11 to 33 deaths per day. In 2006 the UN described the environment in Iraq as a "civil war-like situation".

On March 12, five United States Army soldiers of the 502nd Infantry Regiment, raped the 14-year-old Iraqi girl Abeer Qassim Hamza al Janabi, and then murdered her, her father, her mother Fakhriya Taha Muhasen and her six-year-old sister Hadeel Qassim Hamza al-Janabi. The soldiers then set fire to the girl's body to conceal evidence of the crime. Four of the soldiers were convicted of rape and murder and the fifth was convicted of lesser crimes for the involvement in the war crime, that became known as theMahmudiyah killings.

On 6 June 2006, the United States was successful in tracking Abu Musab al-Zarqawi, the leader of al-Qaeda in Iraq who was killed in a targeted killing, while attending a meeting in an isolated safehouse approximately 8 km (5.0 mi) north of Baqubah. Having been tracked by a British UAV, radio contact was made between the controller and two United States Air Force F-16C jets, which identified the house and at 14:15 GMT, the lead jet dropped two 500 pound (230 kg) guided bombs, a laser-guided GBU 12 and GPS-guided GBU 38 on the building where he was located at. Six others—three male and three female individuals—were also reported killed. Among those killed were one of his wives and their child.

The current government of Iraq took office on 20 May 2006, following approval by the members of the Iraqi National Assembly. This followed the general election in December 2005. The government succeeded the Iraqi Transitional Government, which had continued in office in a caretaker capacity until the formation of the permanent government.

Iraq Study Group report and Saddam's Execution

The Iraq Study Group Report was released on 6 December 2006. Iraq Study Group, made up of people from both of the major U.S. parties, was led by co-chairs James Baker, a former Secretary of State (Republican), and Lee H. Hamilton, a former U.S. Representative (Democrat). It concluded that "the situation in Iraq is grave and deteriorating" and "U.S. forces seem to be caught in a mission that has no foreseeable end." The report's 79 recommendations include increasing diplomatic measures with Iran and Syria and intensifying efforts to train Iraqi troops. On 18 December, a Pentagon report found that insurgent attacks were averaging about 960 attacks per week, the highest since the reports had begun in 2005.

Coalition forces formally transferred control of a province to the Iraqi government, the first since the war. Military prosecutors charged eight U.S. Marines with the murders of 24 Iraqi civilians in Haditha in November 2005, 10 of them women and children. Four officers were also charged with dereliction of duty in relation to the event.

Saddam Hussein was hanged on 30 December 2006, after being found guilty of crimes against humanity by an Iraqi court after a year-long trial.

2007: U.S. Troops Surge

In a 10 January 2007, televised address to the U.S. public, Bush proposed 21,500 more troops for Iraq, a job program for Iraqis, more reconstruction proposals, and $1.2 billion for these programs. On 23 January 2007, in the 2007 State of the Union Address, Bush announced "deploying reinforcements of more than 20,000 additional soldiers and Marines to Iraq".

On 10 February 2007, David Petraeus was made commander of Multi-National Force – Iraq (MNF-I), the four-star post that oversees all coalition forces in country, replacing General George Casey. In his new position, Petraeus oversaw all coalition forces in Iraq and employed them in the new "Surge" strategy outlined by the Bush administration. 2007 also saw a sharp increase in insurgent chlorine bombings.

On 10 May 2007, 144 Iraqi Parliamentary lawmakers signed onto a legislative petition calling on the United States to set a timetable for withdrawal. On 3 June 2007, the Iraqi Parliament voted 85 to 59 to require the Iraqi government to consult with Parliament before requesting additional extensions of the UN Security Council Mandate for Coalition operations in Iraq. Despite this, the mandate was renewed on 18 December 2007, without the approval of the Iraqi parliament.

Pressures on U.S. troops were compounded by the continuing withdrawal of coalition forces. In early 2007, British Prime Minister Blair announced that following Operation Sinbad British troops would begin to withdraw from Basra Governorate, handing security over to the Iraqis. In July Danish Prime Minister Anders Fogh Rasmussen also announced the withdrawal of 441 Danish troops from Iraq, leaving only a unit of nine soldiers manning four observational helicopters.

Planned Troop Reduction

In a speech made to Congress on 10 September 2007, Petraeus "envisioned the withdrawal of roughly 30,000 U.S. troops by next summer, beginning with a Marine contingent [in September]." On 13 September, Bush backed a limited withdrawal of troops from Iraq. Bush said 5,700 personnel would be home by Christmas 2007, and expected thousands more to return by July 2008. The plan would take troop numbers back to their level before the surge at the beginning of 2007.

Effects of the Surge on Security

By March 2008, violence in Iraq was reported curtailed by 40–80%, according to a Pentagon report. Independent reports raised questions about those assessments. An Iraqi military spokesman claimed that civilian deaths since the start of the troop surge plan were 265 in Baghdad, down from 1,440 in the four previous weeks. *The New York Times* counted more than 450 Iraqi civilians killed during the same 28 day period, based on initial daily reports from Iraqi Interior Ministryand hospital officials.

Historically, the daily counts tallied by *The New York Times* have underestimated the total death toll by 50% or more when compared to studies by the United Nations, which rely upon figures from theIraqi Health Ministry and morgue figures.

The rate of U.S. combat deaths in Baghdad nearly doubled to 3.14 per day in the first seven weeks of the "surge" in security activity, compared to previous period. Across the rest of Iraq it decreased slightly.

On 14 August 2007, the deadliest single attack of the whole war occurred. Nearly 800 civilians were killed by a series of coordinated suicide bomb attacks on the northern Iraqi settlement of Kahtaniya. More than 100 homes and shops were destroyed in the blasts. U.S. officials blamed al Qaeda. The targeted villagers belonged to the non-Muslim Yazidi ethnic minority. The attack may have represented the latest in a feud that erupted earlier that year when members of the Yazidi community stoned to death a teenage girl called Du'a Khalil Aswad accused of dating a Sunni Arab man and converting to Islam. The killing of the girl was recorded on camera-mobiles and the video was uploaded onto the internet.

On 13 September 2007, Abdul Sattar Abu Risha was killed in a bomb attack in the city of Ramadi. He was an important U.S. ally because he led the "Anbar Awakening", an alliance of Sunni Arab tribes that opposed al-Qaeda. The latter organisation claimed responsibility for the attack. A statement posted on the Internet by the shadowy Islamic State of Iraq called Abu Risha "one of the dogs of Bush" and described Thursday's killing as a "heroic operation that took over a month to prepare".

There was a reported trend of decreasing U.S. troop deaths after May 2007, and violence against coalition troops had fallen to the "lowest levels since the first year of the American invasion".

These, and several other positive developments, were attributed to the surge by many analysts.

Data from the Pentagon and other U.S. agencies such as the Government Accountability Office (GAO) found that daily attacks against civilians in Iraq remained "about the same" since February. The GAO also stated that there was no discernible trend in sectarian violence. However, this report ran counter to reports to Congress, which showed a general downward trend in civilian deaths and ethno-sectarian violence since December 2006. By late 2007, as the U.S. troop surge began to wind down, violence in Iraq had begun to decrease from its 2006 highs.

Entire neighborhoods in Baghdad were ethnically cleansed by Shia and Sunni militias and sectarian violence has broken out in every Iraqi city where there is a mixed population. Investigative reporter Bob Woodward cites U.S. government sources according to which the U.S. "surge" was not the primary reason for the drop in violence in 2007–08. Instead, according to that view, the reduction of violence was due to newer covert techniques by U.S. military and intelligence officials to find, target and kill insurgents, including working closely with former insurgents.

In the Shia region near Basra, British forces turned over security for the region to Iraqi Security Forces. Basra is the ninth province of Iraq's 18 provinces to be returned to local security forces' control since the beginning of the occupation.

Political Developments

More than half of the members of Iraq's parliament rejected the continuing occupation of their country for the first time. 144 of the 275 lawmakers signed onto a legislative petition that would require the Iraqi government to seek approval from Parliament before it requests an extension of the UN mandate for foreign forces to be in Iraq, which expires at the end of 2008. It also calls for a timetable for troop withdrawal and a freeze on the size of foreign forces. The UN Security Council mandate for U.S. led forces in Iraq will terminate "if requested by the government of Iraq." Under Iraqi law, the speaker must present a resolution called for by a majority of lawmakers. 59% of those polled in the U.S. support a timetable for withdrawal.

In mid-2007, the Coalition began a controversial program to recruit Iraqi Sunnis (often former insurgents) for the formation of "Guardian" militias. These Guardian militias are intended to support and secure various Sunni neighborhoods against the Islamists.

Tensions with Iran

In 2007, tensions increased greatly between Iran and Iraqi Kurdistan due to the latter's giving sanctuary to the militant Kurdish secessionist group Party for a Free Life in Kurdistan (PEJAK.) According to reports, Iran had been shelling PEJAK positions in Iraqi Kurdistan since 16 August. These tensions further increased with an alleged border incursion on 23 August by Iranian troops who attacked several Kurdish villages killing an unknown number of civilians and militants.

Coalition forces also began to target alleged Iranian Quds force operatives in Iraq, either arresting or killing suspected members. The Bush administration and coalition leaders began to publicly state that Iran was supplying weapons, particularly EFP devices, to Iraqi insurgents and militias although to date have failed to provide any proof for these allegations. Further sanctions on Iranian organizations were also announced by the Bush administration in the autumn of 2007. On 21 November 2007, Lieutenant General James Dubik, who is in charge of training Iraqi security forces, praised Iran for its "contribution to the reduction of violence" in Iraq by upholding its pledge to stop the flow of weapons, explosives and training of extremists in Iraq.

Tensions with Turkey

Border incursions by PKK militants based in Northern Iraq have continued to harass Turkish forces, with casualties on both sides. In the fall of 2007, the Turkish military stated their right to cross the Iraqi Kurdistan border in "hot pursuit" of PKK militants and began shelling Kurdish areas in Iraq and attacking PKK bases in the Mount Cudi region with aircraft. The Turkish parliament approved a resolution permitting the military to pursue the PKK in Iraqi Kurdistan. In November, Turkish gunships attacked parts of northern Iraq in the first such attack by Turkish aircraft since the border tensions escalated. Another series of attacks in mid-December hit PKK targets in the Qandil, Zap, Avashin and Hakurk regions. The latest series of attacks involved at least 50 aircraft and artillery and Kurdish officials reported one civilian killed and two wounded.

Additionally, weapons that were given to Iraqi security forces by the U.S. military were being recovered by authorities in Turkey after being used by PKK in that state.

Blackwater Private Security Controversy

On 17 September 2007, the Iraqi government announced that it was revoking the license of the U.S. security firm Blackwater USA over the firm's involvement in the killing of eight civilians, including a woman and an infant, in a firefight that followed a car bomb explosion near a State Department motorcade.

2008: Civil War Continues

Throughout 2008, U.S. officials and independent think tanks began to point to improvements in the security situation, as measured by key statistics. According to the U.S. Defense Department, in December 2008 the "overall level of violence" in the country had dropped 80% since before the surgebegan in January 2007, and the country's murder rate had dropped to prewar levels. They also pointed out that the casualty figure for U.S. forces in 2008 was 314 against a figure of 904 in 2007.

According to the Brookings Institution, Iraqi civilian fatalities numbered 490 in November 2008 as against 3,500 in January 2007, whereas attacks against the coalition numbered somewhere between 200 and 300 per week in the latter half of 2008, as opposed to a peak of nearly 1,600 in summer 2007. The number of Iraqi security forces killed was under 100 per month in the second half of 2008, from a high of 200 to 300 in summer 2007.

Meanwhile, the proficiency of the Iraqi military increased as it launched a spring offensive against Shia militias, which Prime Minister Nouri al-Maliki had previously been criticized for allowing to operate. This began with a March operation against the Mehdi Army in Basra, which led to fighting in Shia areas up and down the country, especially in the Sadr City district of

Baghdad. By October, the British officer in charge of Basra said that since the operation the town had become "secure" and had a murder rate comparable to Manchester in England. The U.S. military also said there had been a decrease of about a quarter in the quantity of Iranian-made explosives found in Iraq in 2008, possibly indicating a change in Iranian policy.

Progress in Sunni areas continued after members of the Awakening movement were transferred from U.S. military to Iraqi control. In May, the Iraqi army – backed by coalition support – launched an offensive in Mosul, the last major Iraqi stronghold of al-Qaeda. Despite detaining thousands of individuals, the offensive failed to lead to major long-term security improvements in Mosul. At the end of the year, the city remained a major flashpoint.

In the regional dimension, the ongoing conflict between Turkey and PKK intensified on 21 February, when Turkey launched a ground attack into the Quandeel Mountains of Northern Iraq. In the nine-day-long operation, around 10,000 Turkish troops advanced up to 25 km into Northern Iraq. This was the first substantial ground incursion by Turkish forces since 1995.

Shortly after the incursion began, both the Iraqi cabinet and the Kurdistan regional government condemned Turkey's actions and called for the immediate withdrawal of Turkish troops from the region.

Turkish troops withdrew on 29 February. The fate of the Kurds and the future of the ethnically diverse city of Kirkuk remained a contentious issue in Iraqi politics.

U.S. military officials met these trends with cautious optimism as they approached what they described as the "transition" embodied in the U.S.–Iraq Status of Forces Agreement, which was negotiated throughout 2008. The commander of the coalition, U.S. General Raymond T. Odierno, noted that "in military terms, transitions are the most dangerous time" in December 2008.

Spring Offensives on Shia Militias

At the end of March, the Iraqi Army, with Coalition air support, launched an offensive, dubbed "Charge of the Knights", in Basra to secure the area from militias. This was the first major operation where the Iraqi Army did not have direct combat support from conventional coalition ground troops. The offensive was opposed by the Mahdi Army, one of the militias, which controlled much of the region. Fighting quickly spread to other parts of Iraq: including Sadr City, Al Kut, Al Hillahand others. During the fighting Iraqi forces met stiff resistance from militiamen in Basra to the point that the Iraqi military offensive slowed to a crawl, with the high attrition rates finally forcing the Sadrists to the negotiating table.

Following talks with Brig. Gen. Qassem Suleimani, commander of the Qods brigades of Iran'sRevolutionary Guard Corps, and the intercession of the Iranian government, on 31 March 2008, al Sadr ordered his followers to ceasefire. The militiamen kept their weapons.

By 12 May 2008, Basra "residents overwhelmingly reported a substantial improvement in their everyday lives" according to *The New York Times*. "Government forces have now taken over Islamic militants' headquarters and halted the death squads and 'vice enforcers' who attacked women, Christians, musicians, alcohol sellers and anyone suspected of collaborating with Westerners", according to the report; however, when asked how long it would take for lawlessness to resume if the Iraqi army left, one resident replied, "one day".

In late April roadside bombings continued to rise from a low in January—from 114 bombings to more than 250, surpassing the May 2007 high.

Congressional Testimony

Speaking before the Congress on 8 April 2008, General David Petraeus urged delaying troop withdrawals, saying, "I've repeatedly noted that we haven't turned any corners, we haven't seen any lights at the end of the tunnel," referencing the comments of then President Bush and former Vietnam-era General William Westmoreland. When asked by the Senate if reasonable people could disagree on the way forward, Petraeus said, "We fight for the right of people to have other opinions."

Upon questioning by then Senate committee chair Joe Biden, Ambassador Crocker admitted that Al Qaedain Iraq was less important than the Al Qaeda organization led by Osama bin Laden along the Afghan-Pakistani border. Lawmakers from both parties complained that U.S. taxpayers are carrying Iraq's burden as it earns billions of dollars in oil revenues.

Iraqi Security Forces Rearm

Iraq became one of the top current purchasers of U.S. military equipment with their army trading its AK 47 assault rifles for the U.S. M 16 and M 4 rifles, among other equipment. In 2008 alone, Iraq accounted for more than $12.5 billion of the $34 billion U.S. weapon sales to foreign countries (not including the potential F-16 fighter planes.).

Iraq sought 36 F 16s, the most sophisticated weapons system Iraq has attempted to purchase. The Pentagon notified Congress that it had approved the sale of 24 American attack helicopters to Iraq, valued at as much as $2.4 billion.

Including the helicopters, Iraq announced plans to purchase at least $10 billion in U.S. tanks and armored vehicles, transport planes and other battlefield equipment and services.

Over the summer, the Defense Department announced that the Iraqi government wanted to order more than 400 armored vehicles and other equipment worth up to $3 billion, and six C-130J transport planes, worth up to $1.5 billion. From 2005 to 2008, the United States had completed approximately $20 billion in arms sales agreements with Iraq.

Status of Forces Agreement

The U.S.–Iraq Status of Forces Agreement was approved by the Iraqi government on 4 December 2008. It established that U.S. combat forces would withdraw from Iraqi cities by 30 June 2009, and that all U.S.

forces would be completely out of Iraq by 31 December 2011. The pact was subject to possible negotiations which could have delayed withdrawal and a referendum scheduled for mid-2009 in Iraq, which might have required all U.S. forces to completely leave by the middle of 2010. The pact required criminal charges for holding prisoners over 24 hours, and required a warrant for searches of homes and buildings that are not related to combat. U.S. contractors working for U.S. forces will be subject to Iraqi criminal law, while contractors working for the State Department and other U.S. agencies may retain their immunity.

If U.S. forces commit still undecided "major premeditated felonies" while off-duty and off-base, they will be subject to the still undecided procedures laid out by a joint U.S. Iraq committee if the United States certifies the forces were off-duty.

Some Americans have discussed "loopholes" and some Iraqis have said they believe parts of the pact remain a "mystery".U.S. Secretary of Defense Robert Gates has predicted that after 2011 he would expect to see "perhaps several tens of thousands of American troops" as part of a residual force in Iraq.

Several groups of Iraqis protested the passing of the SOFA accord as prolonging and legitimizing the occupation. Tens of thousands of Iraqis burned an effigy of George W. Bush in a central Baghdad square where U.S. troops five years previously organized a tearing down of a statue of Saddam Hussein.

Some Iraqis expressed skeptical optimism that the U.S. would completely end its presence by 2011. On 4 December 2008, Iraq's presidential council approved the security pact.

A representative of Grand Ayatollah Ali Husseini al Sistani's expressed concern with the ratified version of the pact and noted that the government of Iraq has no authority to control the transfer of occupier forces into and out of Iraq, no control of shipments, and that the pact grants the occupiers immunity from prosecution in Iraqi courts.

He said that Iraqi rule in the country is not complete while the occupiers are present, but that ultimately the Iraqi people would judge the pact in a referendum.

Thousands of Iraqi have gathered weekly after Friday prayers and shouted anti U.S. and anti-Israeli slogans protesting the security pact between Baghdad and Washington. A protester said that despite the approval of the Interim Security pact, the Iraqi people would break it in a referendum next year.

2009: COALITION REDEPLOYMENT

Transfer of Green Zone

On 1 January 2009, the United States handed control of the Green Zone and Saddam Hussein's presidential palace to the Iraqi government in a ceremonial move described by the country's prime minister as a restoration of Iraq's sovereignty. Iraqi Prime Minister Nouri al-Maliki said he would propose 1 January be declared national "Sovereignty Day". "This palace is the symbol of Iraqi sovereignty and by restoring it, a real message is directed to all Iraqi people that Iraqi sovereignty has returned to its natural status", al Maliki said.

The U.S. military attributed a decline in reported civilians deaths to several factors including the U.S. led "troop surge", the growth of U.S.-funded Awakening Councils, and Shiite cleric Muqtada al-Sadr's call for his militia to abide by a cease fire.

Provincial Elections

On 31 January, Iraq held provincial elections. Provincial candidates and those close to them faced some political assassinations and attempted assassinations, and there was also some other violence related to the election.

Iraqi voter turnout failed to meet the original expectations which were set and was the lowest on record in Iraq, but U.S. Ambassador Ryan Crocker characterized the turnout as "large". Of those who turned out to vote, some groups complained of disenfranchisement and fraud.After the post-election curfew was lifted, some groups made threats about what would happen if they were unhappy with the results.

Exit Strategy Announcement

On 27 February, United States President Barack Obama gave a speech at Marine Corps Base Camp Lejeune in the U.S. state of North Carolina announcing that the U.S. combat mission in Iraq would end by 31 August 2010. A "transitional force" of up to 50,000 troops tasked with training theIraqi Security Forces, conducting counterterrorism operations, and providing general support may remain until the end of 2011, the president added.

The day before Obama's speech, Prime Minister of Iraq Nuri al Maliki said at a press conference that the government of Iraq had "no worries" over the impending departure of U.S. forces and expressed confidence in the ability of the Iraqi Security Forces and police to maintain order without U.S. military support.

Sixth Anniversary Protests

On 9 April, the 6th anniversary of Baghdad's fall to coalition forces, tens of thousands of Iraqis thronged Baghdad to mark the anniversary and demand the immediate departure of coalition forces. The crowds of Iraqis stretched from the Sadr City slum in northeast Baghdad to the square around 5 km (3.1 mi) away, where protesters burned an effigy featuring the face of U.S. President George W. Bush.

There were also Sunni Muslims in the crowd. Police said many Sunnis, including prominent leaders such as a founding sheikh from the Sons of Iraq, took part.

Coalition Forces Withdraw

On 30 April, the United Kingdom formally ended combat operations. Prime Minister Gordon Brown characterized the operation in Iraq as a "success story" because of UK troops' efforts. Britain handed control of Basra to the United States Armed Forces.

On 28 July, Australia withdrew its combat forces as the Australian military presence in Iraq ended, per an agreement with the Iraqi government.

The withdrawal of U.S. forces began at the end of June, with 38 bases to be handed over to Iraqi forces. On 29 June 2009, U.S. forces withdrew from Baghdad. On 30 November 2009, Iraqi Interior Ministry officials reported that the civilian death toll in Iraq fell to its lowest level in November since the 2003 invasion.

Iraq Awards Oil Contracts

On 30 June and again on 11 December, the Iraqi ministry of oil awarded contracts to international oil companies for some of Iraq's many oil fields. The winning oil companies enter joint ventures with the Iraqi ministry of oil, and the terms of the awarded contracts include extraction of oil for a fixed fee of approximately

$1.40 per barrel. The fees will only be paid once a production threshold set by the Iraqi ministry of oil is reached.

2010: U.S. DRAWDOWN AND OPERATION NEW DAWN

On 17 February 2010, U.S. Secretary of Defense Robert Gates announced that as of 1 September, the name "Operation Iraqi Freedom" would be replaced by "Operation New Dawn".

On 18 April, U.S. and Iraqi forces killed Abu Ayyub al-Masri the leader of al-Qaeda in Iraq in a joint American and Iraqi operation near Tikrit,Iraq. The coalition forces believed al-Masri to be wearing a suicide vest and proceeded cautiously. After the lengthy exchange of fire and bombing of the house, the Iraqi troops stormed inside and found two women still alive, one of whom was al-Masri's wife, and four dead men, identified as al-Masri, Abu Abdullah al-Rashid al-Baghdadi, an assistant to al-Masri, and al-Baghdadi's son. A suicide vest was indeed found on al-Masri's corpse, as the Iraqi Army subsequently stated. Iraqi Prime Minister Nouri al-Maliki announced the killings of Abu Omar al-Baghdadi and Abu Ayyub al-Masri at a news conference in Baghdad and showed reporters photographs of their bloody corpses. "The attack was carried out by ground forces which surrounded the house, and also through the use of missiles," Mr Maliki said. "During the operation computers were seized with e-mails and messages to the two biggest terrorists, Osama bin Laden and [his deputy] Ayman al-Zawahiri", Maliki added. U.S. forces commander Gen. Raymond Odierno praised the operation. "The death of these terrorists is potentially the most significant blow to al Qaeda in Iraq since the beginning of the insurgency", he said. "There is still work to do but this is a significant step forward in ridding Iraq of terrorists."

U.S. Vice President Joe Biden stated that the deaths of the top two al Qaeda figures in Iraq are "potentially devastating" blows to the terror network there and proof that Iraqi security forces are gaining ground.

On 20 June, Iraq's Central Bank was bombed in an attack that left 15 people dead and brought much of downtown Baghdad to a standstill. The attack was claimed to have been carried out by the Islamic State of Iraq. This attack was followed by another attack on Iraq's Bank of Trade building that killed 26 and wounded 52 people.

In late August 2010, insurgents conducted a major attack with at least 12 car bombs simultaneously detonating from Mosul to Basra and killing at least 51. These attacks coincided with the U.S. plans for a withdrawal of combat troops.

From the end of August 2010, the United States attempted to dramatically cut its combat role in Iraq, with the withdrawal of all U.S. ground forces designated for active combat operations. The last U.S. combat brigades departed Iraq in the early morning of 19 August. Convoys of U.S. troops had been moving out of Iraq to Kuwait for several days, and NBC News broadcast live from Iraq as the last convoy crossed the border. While all combat brigades left the country, an additional 50,000 personnel (including Advise and Assist Brigades) remained in the country to provide support for the Iraqi military. These troops are required to leave Iraq by 31 December 2011 under anagreement between the U.S. and Iraqi governments.

The desire to step back from an active counter-insurgency role did not however mean that the Advise and Assist Brigades and other remaining U.S. forces would not be caught up in combat. A standards memo from the Associated Press reiterated "combat in Iraq is not over, and we should not uncritically repeat suggestions that it is, even if they come from senior officials".

State Department spokesman P. J. Crowley stated "... we are not ending our work in Iraq, We have a long-term commitment to Iraq."On 31 August, Obama announced the end of Operation Iraqi Freedom from the Oval Office. In his address, he covered the role of the United States' soft power, the effect the war had on the United States economy, and the legacy of the Afghanistan and Iraq wars.

On the same day in Iraq, at a ceremony at one of Saddam Hussein's former residences at Al Faw Palace in Baghdad, a number of U.S. dignitaries spoke in a ceremony for television cameras, avoiding overtones of the triumphalism present in U.S.

announcements made earlier in the war. Vice President Joe Biden expressed concerns regarding the ongoing lack of progress in forming a new Iraqi government, saying of the Iraqi people that "they expect a government that reflects the results of the votes they cast".

Gen. Ray Odierno stated that the new era "in no way signals the end of our commitment to the people of Iraq". Speaking in Ramadi earlier in the day, Gates said that U.S. forces "have accomplished something really quite extraordinary here, [but] how it all weighs in the balance over time I think remains to be seen".

When asked by reporters if the seven-year war was worth doing, Gates commented that "It really requires a historian's perspective in terms of what happens here in the long run". He noted the Iraq War "will always be clouded by how it began" in regards Saddam Hussein's supposed weapons of mass destruction, which were never confirmed to have existed. Gates continued, "This is one of the reasons that this war remains so controversial at home".

On the same day Gen. Ray Odierno was replaced by Lloyd Austin as Commander of U.S. forces in Iraq.

On 7 September, two U.S. troops were killed and nine wounded in an incident at an Iraqi military base. The incident is under investigation by Iraqi and U.S. forces, but it is believed that an Iraqi soldier opened fire on U.S. forces.

On 8 September, the U.S. Army announced the arrival in Iraq of the first specifically-designated Advise and Assist Brigade, the 3d Armored Cavalry Regiment. It was announced that the unit would assume responsibilities in five southern provinces. From 10–13 September, Second Advise and Assist Brigade, 25th Infantry Division fought Iraqi insurgents near Diyala.

According to reports from Iraq, hundreds of members of the Sunni Awakening Councils may have switched allegiance back to the Iraqi insurgency or al Qaeda.

Wikileaks disclosed 391,832 classified U.S. military documents on the Iraq War.Approximately, 58 people were killed with another 40 wounded in an attack on the Sayidat al Nejat church, a Chaldean

Catholic church in Baghdad. Responsibility for the attack was claimed by the Islamic State in Iraq organization.

Coordinated attacks in primarily Shia areas struck throughout Baghdad on 2 November, killing approximately 113 and wounding 250 with around 17 bombs.

Iraqi Security Forces Transition Towards Self-reliance

Preparing to buy $13 billion worth of American arms, the Iraq Defense Ministry intends to transform the country's degraded conventional forces into a state-of-the-art military and become among the world's biggest customers for American military arms and equipment. Part of the planned purchase includes 140 M1 Abrams main battle tanks. Iraqi crews have already begun training on them. In addition to the $13 billion purchase, the Iraqis have requested 18 F-16 Fighting Falcons as part of a $4.2 billion program that also includes aircraft training and maintenance, AIM 9 Sidewinder air-to-air missiles, laser-guided bombs and reconnaissance equipment. If approved by Congress, the first aircraft could arrive in spring 2013. Under the plan, the first 10 pilots would be trained in the United States.

The Iraqi navy also inaugurated U.S. built Swift Class patrol boat at Umm Qasr, Iraq's main port at the northern end of the gulf. Iraq is to take delivery of 14 more of these $20 million, 50 foot craft before U.S. forces depart. The high-speed vessels' main mission will be to protect the oil terminals at al Basra and Khor al-Amiya through which some 1.7 million barrels a day are loaded into tankers for export. Two U.S. built offshore support vessels, each costing $70 million, were expected to be delivered in 2011.

The United States Department of Defense had issued notification of an additional $100 million proposed sales of arms from the U.S. to Iraq. General Dynamics is to be the prime contractor on a $36 million deal for the supply of ammunition for Iraq's Abrams M1 A1 tanks. The sale consists of: 14,010 TP-T M831A1 120mm Cartridges; 16,110 TPCSDS-T M865 120mm Cartridges; and 3,510 HEAT-MP-T M830A1 120mm Cartridges. Raytheon is proposed as the prime contractor for a $68 million package of "Command, Control, Communications, Computers, Intelligence, Surveillance and Reconnaissance (C4ISR) Systems".

UN Lifts Restrictions on Iraq

In a move to legitimize the existing Iraqi government, the United Nations lifted the Saddam Hussein-era UN restrictions on Iraq. These included allowing Iraq to have a civilian nuclear program, permitting the participation of Iraq in international nuclear and chemical weapons treaties, as well as returning control of Iraq's oil and gas revenue to the government and ending the Oil-for-Food Programme.

2011: U.S. WITHDRAWAL

Muqtada al-Sadr returned to Iraq in the holy city of Najaf to lead the Sadrist movement after being in exile since 2007. On 15 January 2011, three U.S. troops were killed in Iraq. One of the troops was killed on a military operation in central Iraq, while the other two troops were deliberately shot by one or two Iraqi soldiers during a training exercise.

On 6 June, five U.S. troops were killed in an apparent rocket attack on JSS Loyalty.A sixth soldier, who was wounded in the attack, died 10 days later of his wounds.

On 29 June, three U.S. troops were killed in a rocket attack on a U.S. base located near the border with Iran. It was speculated that the militant group responsible for the attack was the same one which attacked JSS Loyalty just over three weeks before.With the three deaths, June 2011, became the bloodiest month in Iraq for the U.S. military since June 2009, with 15 U.S. soldiers killed, only one of them outside combat.

In September, Iraq signed a contract to buy 18 Lockheed Martin F-16 warplanes, becoming the 26th nation to operate the F-16. Because of windfall profits from oil, the Iraqi government is planning to double this originally planned 18, to 36 F-16s. Iraq is relying on the U.S. military for air support as it rebuilds its forces and battles a stubborn Islamist insurgency.

With the collapse of the discussions about extending the stay of any U.S. troops beyond 2011, where they would not be granted any immunity from the Iraqi government, on 21 October 2011, President Obama announced at a White House press conference that all remaining U.S. troops and trainers would leave Iraq by the end of the year as previously scheduled, bringing the U.S. mission in Iraq to an end. The last American soldier to die in Iraq before the withdrawal was killed by a roadside bomb in Baghdad on 14 November.

In November 2011, the U.S. Senate voted down a resolution to formally end the war by bringing its authorization by Congress to an end.

The last U.S. troops withdrew from Iraq on 18 December, although the U.S. embassy and consulates continue to maintain a staff of more than 20,000 including U.S. Marine Embassy Guardsand between 4,000 and 5,000 private military contractors. The next day, Iraqi officials issued an arrest warrant for the Sunni Vice-President Tariq al-Hashimi. He has been accused of involvement in assassinations and fled to the Kurdish part of Iraq.

AFTERMATH - POST U.S. WITHDRAWAL

The invasion and occupation led to sectarian violence which caused widespread displacement among Iraqi civilians. The Iraqi Red Crescent organization estimated the total internal displacement was around 2.3 million in 2008, and as many as 2 million Iraqis leaving the country. Poverty led many Iraqi women to turn to prostitution to support themselves and their families, attracting sex tourists from regional lands. The invasion led to a constitution which supported democracy as long as laws did not violate traditional Islamic principles, and a parliamentary election was held in 2005. In addition the invasion preserved the autonomy of the Kurdish region, and stability brought new economic prosperity. Because the Kurdish region is historically the most democratic area of Iraq, many Iraqi refugees from other territories fled into the Kurdish land.

Iraqi insurgency surged in the aftermath of the U.S. withdrawal. The terror campaigns have since been engaged by Iraqi, primarily radical Sunni, insurgent groups against the central government and the warfare between various factions within Iraq. The events of post U.S. withdrawal violence succeeded the previous insurgency in Iraq (prior to 18 December 2011), but have showed different patterns, raising concerns that the surging violence might slide into another civil war. Some 1,000 people were killed across Iraq within the first two months after U.S. withdrawal.

Sectarian violence continued in the first half of 2013— at least 56 people died in April when a Sunni protest in Hawija was interrupted by a government-supported helicopter raid and a series of violent incidents occurred in May. On 20 May 2013, at least 95 people died in a wave of car bomb attacks that was preceded by a car bombing on 15 May that led to 33 deaths; also, on 18 May, 76 people were killed in the Sunni areas of Baghdad. Some experts have stated that Iraq could return to the brutal sectarian conflict of 2006.

On 22 July 2013, at least five hundred convicts, most of whom were senior members of al-Qaida who had received death sentences, broke out of Iraq's Abu Ghraib jail when comrades launched a military-style assault to free them. The attack began when a suicide bomber drove a car packed with explosives into prison gates. James F. Jeffrey, the United States ambassador in Baghdad when the last American troops exited, said the assault and resulting escape "will provide seasoned leadership and a morale boost to Al Qaeda and its allies in both Iraq and Syria... it is likely to have an electrifying impact on the Sunni population in Iraq, which has been sitting on the fence."

By mid-2014 the country was in chaos with a new government yet to be formed following national elections, and the insurgency reaching new heights. In early June 2014 the Islamic State in Iraq and the Levant (ISIS) took over the cities of Mosul and Tikrit and said it was ready to march on Baghdad, while Iraqi Kurdish forces took control of key military installations in the major oil city of Kirkuk. Prime Minister Nouri al-Maliki asked his parliament to declare a state of emergency that would give him increased powers, but the lawmakers refused.

In the summer of 2014 President Obama announced the return of U.S. Forces to Iraq, but only in the form of aerial support, in an effort to halt the advance of ISIS forces, render humanitarian aid to stranded refugees and stabilize the political situation. On 14 August 2014, Prime Minister Nouri al-Maliki succumbed to pressure at home and abroad to step down. This paved the way for Haidar al-Abadi to take over On 19 August 2014. In what was claimed to be revenge for the aerial bombing ordered by President Obama, ISIS, which by this time had changed their name to the Islamic State, beheaded an American journalist, James Foley, who had been kidnapped two years previously. Despite U.S. bombings and breakthroughs on the political front, Iraq remained in chaos with the Islamic State consolidating its gains, and sectarian violence continuing unabated. On 22 August 2014, suspected Shia militants opened fire on a Sunni mosque during Friday prayers, killing 70 worshippers. Separately, Iraqi forces in helicopters killed 30 Sunni fighters in the town of Dhuluiya. A day later, apparently in retaliation for the attack on the mosque, three bombings across Iraq killed 35 people.

CASUALTY ESTIMATES

For coalition death totals see the infobox at the top right. See also Casualties of the Iraq War, which has casualty numbers for coalition nations, contractors, non-Iraqi civilians, journalists, media helpers, aid workers, and the wounded. Casualty figures, especially Iraqi ones, are highly disputed.

Criticism and Cost

The Bush Administration's rationale for the Iraq War has faced heavy criticism from an array of popular and official sources both inside and outside the United States, with many U.S. citizens finding many parallels with the Vietnam War. For example, a former CIA officer described theOffice of Special Plans as a group of ideologues who were dangerous to U.S. national security and a threat to world peace, and stated that the group lied and manipulated intelligence to further its agenda of removing Saddam. The Center for Public Integrity alleges that the Bush administrationmade a total of 935 false statements between 2001 and 2003 about Iraq's alleged threat to the United States.

Both proponents and opponents of the invasion have also criticized the prosecution of the war effort along a number of other lines. Most significantly, critics have assailed the United States and its allies for not devoting enough troops to the mission, not adequately planning for post-invasion Iraq, and for permitting and perpetrating human rights abuses. As the war has progressed, critics have also railed against the high human and financial costs.

Criticisms include:

- Legality of the invasion
- Human casualties
- Human rights violations such as the Iraq prison abuse scandals
- Insufficient post-invasion plans, in particular inadequate troop levels (a RAND Corporation study stated that 500,000 troops would be required for success)
- Financial costs with approximately $612 billion spent as of 4/09 the CBO has estimated the total cost of the war in Iraq to the United States will be around $1.9 trillion.
- Adverse effect on U.S.-led global "war on terror"
- Damage to U.S.' traditional alliances and influence in the region, especially Israel and Saudi Arabia.
- Endangerment and ethnic cleansing of religious and ethnic minorities by insurgents
- Disruption of Iraqi oil production and related energy security concerns (the price of oil has quadrupled since 2002)

After President Barack Obama was inaugurated in 2009, some anti-war groups decided to stop protesting even though the war was still going on. Some of them decided to stop because they felt they should give the new President time to establish his administration, and others stopped because they believed that Obama would end the war.

Financial Cost

The financial cost of the war has been more than £4.55 billion ($9 billion) to the UK, and over $845 billion to the U.S. government. According to Nobel Prize-winning economist Joseph E. Stiglitz and Harvard public finance professor Linda Bilmes it costs the United States $720 million a day to wage the Iraq war. This number takes into account the long-term health care for veterans, interest on debt and replacement of military hardware.

In March 2013, the total cost of the Iraq War was estimated to have been $1.7 trillion by the Watson Institute of International Studies atBrown University. Critics have argued that the total cost of the war to the U.S. economy is estimated to be from $3 trillion to$6 trillion, including interest rates, by 2053. The upper ranges of these estimates include long-term veterans costs and economic impacts. For example Harvard's public finance expert Linda J. Bilmes has estimated that the long-term cost of providing disability compensation and medical care to U.S. troops injured in the Iraq conflict will reach nearly $1 trillion over the next 40 years.

A CNN report noted that the United States-led interim government, the Coalition Provisional Authority lasting until 2004 in Iraq had lost $8.8 billion in the Development Fund for Iraq. In June 2011, it was reported by CBS News that $6 billion in neatly packaged blocks of $100 bills was air-lifted into Iraq by the George W. Bush administration, which flew it into Baghdad aboard C 130 military cargo planes. In total, the *Times* says $12 billion in cash was flown into Iraq in 21 separate flights by May 2004, all of which has disappeared. An inspector general's report mentioned that "'Severe inefficiencies and poor management' by the Coalition Provisional Authority would leave no guarantee that the money was properly used", said Stuart W. Bowen, Jr., director of the Office of the Special Inspector General for Iraq Reconstruction. "The CPA did not establish or implement sufficient managerial, financial and contractual controls to ensure that funds were used in a transparent manner." Bowen told the Times the missing money may represent "the largest theft of funds in national history."

HUMANITARIAN CRISES

The child malnutrition rate rose to 28%. Some 60–70% of Iraqi children were reported to be suffering from psychological problems in 2007. Most Iraqis had no access to safe drinking water. A cholera outbreak in northern Iraq was thought to be the result of poor water quality. As many as half of Iraqi doctors left the country between 2003 and 2006. The use of depleted uranium and white phosphorus by the U.S. military has been blamed for birth defects and cancers in the Iraqi city of Fallujah. A study entitled "Birth defects in Iraq and the plausibility of environmental exposure: A review" was completed to review the impact of other war-related environmental factors on birth defects in Iraq.

As of 2011, nearly 3 million Iraqis have been displaced, with 1.3 million within the Iraq and 1.6 million in neighboring countries, mainly Jordan and Syria. More than half of Iraqi Christians have fled to neighboring countries since the start of the war.

The Foreign Policy Association reported that "Perhaps the most perplexing component of the Iraq refugee crisis... has been the inability for the United States to absorb more Iraqis following the 2003 invasion of the country. To date, the United States has granted around 84,000 Iraqis refugee status, of the more than two million global Iraqi refugees. By contrast, the United States granted asylum to more than 100,000 Vietnamese refugees during the Vietnam War."

HUMAN RIGHTS ABUSES

Throughout the entire Iraq war, there have been human rights abuses on all sides of the conflict.

Iraqi Government

- The use of torture by Iraqi security forces.
- Iraqi police from the Interior Ministry accused of forming Death Squads and committing numerous massacres and tortures of Sunni Arabs and the police collusion with militias in Iraq have compounded the problems.

Coalition Forces and Private Contractors

- Deaths of civilians as a result of bombing and missile strikes.
- Abu Ghraib torture and prisoner abuse by U.S. Army personnel.
- Haditha killings of 24 civilians (ongoing with some charges dropped)
- White phosphorus use in Iraq

- Rape and murder of an Iraqi girl, and murder of her family.
- The torture and killing of prisoner of war, Iraqi Air Force commander, Abed Hamed Mowhoush
- The killing of Baha Mousa
- Mukaradeeb wedding party massacre where 42 civilians were allegedly killed by coalition forces.
- Planting weapons on noncombatant, unarmed Iraqis by three U.S. Marines after killing them.According to a report by *The Nation*, other similar acts have been witnessed by U.S. soldiers.Members of Iraq Veterans Against the War tell similar stories.
- Blackwater Baghdad shootings
- Allegations of beatings, electrocution, mock executions, and sexual assault by British troops were presented to the International Criminal Court (ICC) by Public Interest Lawyers (PIL) and the European Center for Constitutional and Human Rights (ECCHR) on 12 January 2014.

Insurgent Groups

- Killing over 12,000 Iraqis from January 2005 to June 2006, according to Iraqi Interior MinisterBayan Jabr, giving the first official count for the victims of bombings, ambushes and other deadly attacks. The insurgents have also conducted numerous suicide attacks on the Iraqi civilian population, mostly targeting the majority Shia community. An October 2005 report fromHuman Rights Watch examines the range of civilian attacks and their purported justification.
- Attacks against civilians including children through bombing of market places and other locations reachable by suicide bombers.
- Attacks against civilians by sectarian death squads primarily during the Iraqi Civil war.
- Attacks on diplomats and diplomatic facilities including; the bombing of the UN headquarters in Baghdad in August 2003 killing the top UN representative in Iraq and 21 other

UN staff members; beheading several diplomats: two Algerian diplomatic envoys Ali Belaroussi and Azzedine Belkadi, Egyptian diplomatic envoy al-Sherif, and four Russian diplomats.

- The February 2006 bombing of the al-Askari Mosque, destroying one of the holiest Shiite shrines, killing over 165 worshipers and igniting sectarian strife and reprisal killings.
- The publicised killing of several contractors; Eugene Armstrong, Jack Hensley, Kenneth Bigley, Ivaylo Kepov and Georgi Lazov (Bulgarian truck drivers.) Other non-military personnel murdered include: translator Kim Sun-il, Shosei Koda, Fabrizio Quattrocchi(Italian), charity worker Margaret Hassan, reconstruction engineer Nick Berg, photographer Salvatore Santoro (Italian) and supply worker Seif Adnan Kanaan (Iraqi.) Four private armed contractors, Scott Helvenston, Jerko Zovko, Wesley Batalona and Michael Teague, were killed with grenades and small arms fire, their bodies dragged from their vehicles, beaten and set ablaze. Their burned corpses were then dragged through the streets before being hung over a bridge crossing the Euphrates.
- Torture or killing of members of the New Iraqi Army, and assassination of civilians associated with the Coalition Provisional Authority, such as Fern Holland, or the Iraqi Governing Council, such as Aqila al-Hashimi and Ezzedine Salim, or other foreign civilians, such as those from Kenya.

PUBLIC OPINION ON THE WAR

International Opinion

According to a January 2007 BBC World Service poll of more than 26,000 people in 25 countries, 73% of the global population disapproved of U.S. handling of the Iraq War. A September 2007 poll conducted by the BBC found that two-thirds of the world's population believed the U.S. should withdraw its forces from Iraq. In 2006 it was found that majorities in the UK and Canada believed that the war in Iraq was "unjustified" and – in the UK – were critical of their government's support of U.S. policies in Iraq.

According to polls conducted by the Arab American Institute, four years after the invasion of Iraq, 83% of Egyptians had a negative view of the U.S. role in Iraq; 68% of Saudi Arabians had a negative view; 96% of the Jordanian population had a negative view; 70% of the population of the United Arab Emirates and 76% of the Lebanese population also described their view as negative. The Pew Global Attitudes Project reports that in 2006 majorities in the Netherlands, Germany, Jordan, France, Lebanon, Russia, China, Canada, Poland,Pakistan, Spain, Indonesia, Turkey, and Morocco believed the world was safer before the Iraq War and the toppling of Saddam, while pluralities in the United States and India believe the world is safer without Saddam Hussein.

Iraqi Opinion

Directly after the invasion, polling suggested that a slight majority supported the U.S. invasion.Polls conducted between 2005 and 2007 showed 31–37% of Iraqi's wanted U.S. and other Coalition forces to withdraw once security was restored and that 26–35% wanted immediate withdrawal instead. Despite a majority having previously been opposed to the U.S. presence, 60% of Iraqis opposed American troops leaving directly prior to withdrawal, with 51% saying withdrawal would have a negative effect. In 2006, a poll conducted on the Iraqi public revealed that 52% of the ones polled said Iraq was going in the right direction and 61% claimed it was worth ousting Saddam Hussein.

RELATION TO THE GLOBAL WAR ON TERRORISM

Though explicitly stating that Iraq had "nothing" to do with 9/11, erstwhile President George W. Bush consistently referred to the Iraq war as "the central front in the War on Terror", and argued that if the United States pulled out of Iraq, "terrorists will follow us here". While other proponents of the war have regularly echoed this assertion, as the conflict has dragged on, members of the U.S. Congress, the U.S. public, and even U.S. troops have questioned the connection between Iraq and the fight against anti-U.S.

terrorism. In particular, a consensus has developed among intelligence experts that the Iraq war has increased terrorism.Counterterrorism expert Rohan Gunaratna frequently refers to the invasion of Iraq as a "fatal mistake".

London's conservative International Institute for Strategic Studies concluded in 2004 that the occupation of Iraq had become "a potent global recruitment pretext" for Mujahideen and that the invasion "galvanised" al-Qaeda and "perversely inspired insurgent violence" there. The U.S. National Intelligence Council concluded in a January 2005 report that the war in Iraq had become a breeding ground for a new generation of terrorists; David Low, the national intelligence officer for transnational threats, indicated that the report concluded that the war in Iraq provided terrorists with "a training ground, a recruitment ground, the opportunity for enhancing technical skills ... There is even, under the best scenario, over time, the likelihood that some of the jihadists who are not killed there will, in a sense, go home, wherever home is, and will therefore disperse to various other countries." The Council's chairman Robert Hutchings said, "At the moment, Iraq is a magnet for international terrorist activity." And the 2006 National Intelligence Estimate, which outlined the considered judgment of all 16 U.S. intelligence agencies, held that "The Iraq conflict has become the 'cause celebre' for jihadists, breeding a deep resentment of U.S. involvement in the Muslim world and cultivating supporters for the global jihadist movement."

FOREIGN INVOLVEMENT

According to studies, most of the suicide bombers in Iraq are foreigners, especiallySaudis.

Iranian Involvement

Although some military intelligence analysts have concluded there is no concrete evidence, U.S. Major General Rick Lynch has claimed that Iran has provided training, weapons, money, and intelligence to Shiite insurgents in Iraq and that up to 150 Iranian intelligence agents, plus members of the Iranian Revolutionary Guard are believed to be active in Iraq at any given time. Lynch thinks that members of the Iranian Quds Force and the Iranian

Revolutionary Guard have trained members of the Qazali terror network in explosives technology and also provided the network with arms, munitions, and military advisors. Many explosive devices, including improvised explosives (IEDs) and explosively-formed projectiles (EFPs), used by insurgents are claimed by Lynch to be Iranian-made or designed.

According to two unnamed U.S. officials, the Pentagon is examining the possibility that the Karbala provincial headquarters raid, in which insurgents managed to infiltrate an American base, kill five U.S. soldiers, wound three, and destroy three humvees before fleeing, was supported by Iranians. In a speech on 31 January 2007, Iraqi Prime Minister Nouri al-Maliki stated that Iran was supporting attacks against Coalition forces in Iraq and some Iraqis suspect that the raid may have been perpetrated by the Islamic Revolutionary Guards Corps'sQods Force in retaliation for the detention of five Iranian officials by U.S. forces in the northern Iraqi city of Irbil on 11 January.

Michael Weiss and Dexter Filkins have described the extensive involvement of Iranian Quds Force commander Qasem Suleimani in arming and training both Sunni and Shi'ite militias in Iraq. According to Weiss, Iranian strategy was designed to prevent the Iraqi government from functioning so that Iran could exert greater control over the country under the guise of providing stability. Weiss also traced the origins of al Qaeda in Iraq, which entered Iraqi Kurdistan through Iran, to covert Iranian operations to destabilize the Iraqi government of Saddam Hussein. According to a Western diplomat quoted by Filkins: "Suleimani wanted to bleed the Americans, so he invited in the jihadis, and things got out of control." In 2011, U.S. ambassador James Jeffrey stated that Iranian proxies were responsible for roughly one-fourth of U.S. casualties in Iraq.

6

Military Intervention against ISIS

In response to rapid territorial gains made by the Islamic State of Iraq and the Levant (ISIL or ISIS or Daesh, calling itself the Islamic State) militants during the first half of 2014, and internationally condemned brutality, reportedhuman rights abuses and the fear of further spillovers of the Syrian Civil War, many states began to intervene against ISIL in Syria and Iraq. Later, there were also minor interventions by some states against ISIL-affiliated groups in Nigeria and Libya.

In mid-June 2014, Iran, according to American and British information, started flying drones over Iraq, and, according to Reuters, Iranian soldiers were in Iraq fighting ISIL. Simultaneously, the United States ordered a small number of troops to Iraq and started flying manned aircraft over Iraq.

In July 2014, according to the International Institute for Strategic Studies, Iran sent Sukhoi Su-25 aircraft to Iraq, and Hezbollah purportedly sent trainers and advisers to Iraq to monitor ISIL's movements. In August 2014, the US and Iran separately began a campaign of airstrikes on ISIL targets in Iraq. Since then, fourteen countries in a US-led coalition have also executed airstrikes on ISIL in Iraq and in Syria.

In September 2015, Russian forces, at the request of the Syrian government, began hundreds of bombing raids against Syrian rebel groups, including theFSA and ISIL.

INTERNATIONAL COALITIONS AGAINST ISIL

US-led coalitions – 5 September 2014

On the margins of the 4/5 September 2014 NATO summit in Wales, U.S. Secretary of State John Kerry on 5 September invited Ministers of the United Kingdom, France, Germany, Canada, Australia, Turkey, Italy, Poland and Denmark for a separate meeting in which he pressed them to support the fight against ISIL militarily and financially. Those nine countries agreed to do so by supporting anti-ISIL forces in Iraq and Syria with supplies and air support, according to a statement that day of Kerry and U.S. Secretary of Defense Hagel.

3 December 2014

On 3 December 2014, at the NATO headquarters in Brussels, diplomats/(foreign) ministers from 59 countries gathered to plot a way forward against the threat of ISIL. U.S. Secretary of State John Kerrytold the gathering, that "defeating the ideology, the funding, the recruitment" of Daesh (ISIL) must be the primary focus of their discussion, more important than airstrikes and other military action.

The countries represented on 3 December were: the 10 countries of the above-mentioned 5 September coalition in Wales; the extra 18 countries of the 15 September France-led coalition in Paris except for China and Russia; and 33 additional countries: Albania, Austria, Bosnia-Herzegovina, Bulgaria, Croatia, Cyprus, Estonia, Finland, Georgia, Greece, Hungary, Iceland, Ireland, Kosovo, Latvia, Lithuania, Luxembourg, Macedonia, Moldova, Montenegro, Morocco, New Zealand, Portugal, South Korea, Romania, Serbia, Singapore, Slovakia, Slovenia, Somalia, Sweden, Taiwan and Ukraine.

They styled themselves as the *Global Coalition to Counter the Islamic State of Iraq and the Levant (ISIL)*, and agreed to a strategy that included:

- exposing ISIL's true nature;
- cutting off ISIL's financing and funding;
- supporting military operations.

France-led Coalition

On 15 September 2014, on the 'International Conference on Peace and Security in Iraq' hosted by the French President François Hollande in Paris, 26 countries were represented: the countries of a US-led coalition that on 5 September in Wales had agreed on a coalition against ISIL except Australia and Poland, and furthermore Bahrain, Egypt, Iraq, Jordan, Kuwait, Lebanon, Oman, Qatar, Saudi Arabia, United Arab Emirates, Belgium, China, Czech Republic, Japan, the Netherlands, Norway, Russia and Spain. They committed themselves to supporting the Iraqi government with military assistance in its fight against ISIL, and they reaffirmed their commitment to UNSC Resolution 2170 of 15 August (condemning all trade with ISIL and urging to prevent all financial donations and all payments of ransoms to ISIL), so reported the French government.

In retaliation for the November 2015 Paris attacks, the French Air Forcesignificantly intensified airstrikes against ISIL targets in Syria, hitting among other the Syrian city of Raqqa, the de facto capital of ISIL.

Russia-led Coalition

At the end of September 2015, Russia, Iraq, Iran and Syria set up a 'joint information center' in Baghdad to "gather, process and analyse current information about the situation in the Middle East – primarily for fighting IS." On 30 September 2015, Russia began its air campaign on the side and in support of the Syrian government.

Russia was also reported to have reached agreements on co-ordiantion of operations in Syria with Jordan and Israel.

Islamic Nations Coalition

On 14 December 2015, Saudi Deputy Crown Prince and Defense MinisterMohammed bin Salman Al Saud announced that 34 countries will partner in the fight against Islamic extremism, which Salman called a "disease." Based out of Riyadh, Saudi Arabia, the coalition will include Bahrain, Bangladesh, Benin, Chad, Comoros, Côte d'Ivoire, Djibouti, Egypt, Gabon, Guinea, Jordan, Kuwait,

Lebanon, Libya, Maldives, Mali, Malaysia, Morocco, Mauritania, Niger, Nigeria, Pakistan, Palestine, Qatar, Saudi Arabia, Senegal, Sierra Leone, Somalia, Sudan, Turkey, Togo, Tunisia the United Arab Emirates and Yemen.

TURKISH INTERVENTION

ISIL is suspected of involvement in or responsibility for terrorist attacks in Turkey in May 2013 in Reyhanlý and March 2014 on Turkish police,kidnapping 49 Turkish diplomats in June 2014, the 5 June 2015 Diyarbakýr rally bombing and the 20 July 2015 Suruç bombing killing 32 young activists. The Turkish government until July 2015 once attacked ISIL militarily, in January 2014. In September 2014 Turkey joined a US-led coalition 'to fight ISIL'.

On 23 July 2015, Turkey allowed the United States to use Ýncirlik and Diyarbakýr air bases in southern Turkey for airstrikes on ISIL. Also on 23 July, after an alleged ISIL attack on a Turkish border outpost in Kilis Province killing one Turkish soldier, the Turkish army with tanks shelled ISIL militants in Syria killing one militant and destroying several ISIL vehicles.

On 24 July 2015, an anonymous report appeared on a Turkish newspaper/website stating that the United States had agreed with Turkey on a 'partial no-fly zone' in northern Syria. While no official statement about the zone has been released, commentators still speculate about the real motives and objectives of Turkey and the US with the supposed 'buffer zone' or 'ISIL-free zone'.

On 24 and 25 July, in a military operation entitled 'Operation Martyr Yalçýn' against both ISIL and the Kurdistan Workers' Party (PKK) deploying at least 70 F-16 fighter jets, Turkey reportedly bombarded at least eight ISIL positions in northern Syria, killing 35 ISIL militants.

IRANIAN INTERVENTION

In mid-June 2014, according to American and British sources Iran sentQasem Soleimani, major general of the Army of the Guardians of the Islamic Revolution (IRGC), to Iraq help it organize against ISIL, Iran started flying drones over Iraq, and, according to sources like Reuters, Iranian soldiers were in Iraq fighting ISIL.

One war correspondent suggested that Iran on 21 June "joined the air war" of Iraq against ISIL.

In July, according to the International Institute for Strategic Studies, Iran sent several Su-25 aircraft to Iraq, supported by Iranian/Iraqi ground crews trained in Iran. In early August, those Su-25 began combat against ISIL, according to *Business Insider*. By September, according to *Business Insider*, Iranian Quds Force personnel were deployed to Samarra, Baghdad, Karbala, and the abandoned U.S. military post formerly known as Camp Speicher. At the end of November 2014, an Israeli website claimed to have seen Iranian F-4 Phantom II jet-fighters bombing ISIL in northeastern Iraq; the U.S. army vaguely confirmed this.

In March and May 2015, American commentators indicated Iranian generalQasem Soleimani as 'leading Iraq's military strategy against ISIL'.

HEZBOLLAH INTERVENTION

Iraq

Already 'for a long time' before June 2014, Hezbollah had some presence in Iraq of advisers offering guidance to Shia fighters, according to a Hezbollah commander interviewed by newspaper *The National*. In June 2014, Hezbollah reportedly set up a dedicated command center in Lebanon to monitor developments in Iraq. Hezbollah leader Hassan Nasrallah on 17 June said that the party was "ready to sacrifice martyrs in Iraq five times more than what we sacrificed in Syria in order to protect shrines."

In July 2014, Hezbollah sent more technical trainers and advisers to Iraq, to monitor ISIL's movements, according to a Hezbollah commander interviewed by newspaper *The National* in the United Arab Emirates. Shortly thereafter, Hezbollah commander Ibrahim al-Hajj was reported killed in action near Mosul. An August Reuters story reported there were "dozens" of Hezbollah "battle-hardened veterans" in Iraq, while the *Christian Science Monitor* reported the party had deployed a 250-man unit "responsible for advising, training, and coordinating the Iraqi Shiite militias." In February 2015, Nasrallah admitted that he had sent troops to fight in Iraq.

Lebanon

In June 2015, Hezbollah leader Hassan Nasrallah claimed that ISIL and Nusra had taken a foothold in Lebanon and that fierce battles were raging between them and Hezbollah, as well as each other.

AMERICAN-LED INTERVENTION IN IRAQ

After having started flying manned aircraft over Iraq and sent some troops to Iraq in June, the U.S. in August 2014 began supplying Iraqi KurdishPeshmerga with weapons, humanitarian droppings of food for refugees fleeing from ISIL, and airstrikes against ISIL in Iraq.

On 9 August, speaking about U.S. airstrikes in Iraq, President Barack Obama said "this is going to be a long-term project." Since then, nine countries, allied with the US, have also executed airstrikes on ISIL in Iraq and various countries contributed military aid to Iraqi and Kurdish ground forces, and humanitarian aid.

16–19 August, according to the U.S., Kurdish and Iraqi forces with the help of U.S. airstrikes took back the Mosul Dam, the largest dam in Iraq. (For further wins and losses of Iraq against ISIL, see Iraq War (2014–present).)

President Obama announced on 10 September 2014 that the number of airstrikes in Iraq would increase and that he dispatched 500 more US troops to Iraq.

Military Aid to Kurds and Iraqis

On 5 August 2014, Zalmay Khalilzad, the former US ambassador to Iraq and the UN, wrote in the *Washington Post* that the United States is involved in "the direct supply of munitions to the Kurds and, with Baghdad's agreement, the shipment of some Foreign Military Sales (FMS) program weapons to the Kurds." The United States moved from indirectly supplying Kurdistan with small arms through the CIA to directly giving them weapons such asman-portable anti-tank systems.

In a coordinated effort led by the United States, many allied countries including NATO members and Middle Eastern partners have supplied or plan to supply Iraqi and/or Kurdish forces with heavy military equipment, small arms, ammunition, non-lethal military gear, and training support.

Building Partner Capacity (BPC)

The Building Partner Capacity (BPC) program is meant to help the Iraqi government to prepare forces for the counter-attack against ISIL and the regaining of its territory. According to the US Department of Defense, by May 2015 a dozen countries had committed themselves to the BPC program: Australia, Belgium, Denmark, France, Germany, Italy, Netherlands, New Zealand, Norway, Spain, United Kingdom and United States, and 6,500 Iraqi forces had been trained by BPC.

Humanitarian Efforts

The United States, the United Kingdom, and Australia, supported by international partners, launched a large humanitarian effort to support refugees stranded in northern Iraq. This included air-dropping tens of thousands of meals and thousands of gallons of drinking water to Yazidirefugees stranded in the Sinjar Mountains and threatened by advancing ISIL forces, between 7–14 August 2014, in what was later described as "the first mass air delivery of humanitarian cargo since the outbreak of violence in East Timor in 1999."

Thousands of Yazidis and other Iraqi civilians fled to the area following attacks on their villages and the town of Sinjar throughout late July and early August 2014.

Several human rights and observer organizations in the region reported that those who fled to the mountains were subjected to starvation, and lacked clean drinking water and medical care for several months as ISIL militantssurrounded them. Hundreds of men, women, and children were abducted and killed.

In response to the immediate threat to the approximately 30,000 people trapped on the mountain, coalition aircraft commenced humanitarian aid drops. These air drops included basic supplies such as food, water, and shelter and were conducted at low flight levels by coalition transport aircraft under the threat of ISIL surface-to-air attacks.

In direct support of humanitarian aid drops, CF-18s provided top cover for aRoyal Australian Air Force (RAAF) C-130 Hercules transport aircraft on 20 November, ensuring the transport crew was able to safely parachute supplies to waiting refugees below. Canadian fighter jets remained in close proximity to the transport aircraft to protect it from ISIL surface-to-air threats or attacks.

AMERICAN MILITARY ACTIONS

American Airstrikes

On 7 August, President Obama gave a live address describing the worsening conditions in Iraq and that the plight of the Yazidis particular had convinced him that U.S. military action was necessary to protect American lives, protect minority groups in Iraq, and to stop a possible ISIL advance on Erbil, the capital of the Kurdish Autonomous Region. On 8 August, the United States started to bomb ISIL targets in Iraq. By 10 August, assisted by these air attacks, Kurdish forces claimed to have recaptured the towns of Mahmour and Gweyr from Islamic State control. Additional Iraqi airstrikes conducted in Sinjar were reported to have killed 45 ISIL militants and injured an additional 60 militants. On 11 August, a spokesman for The Pentagonsaid the airstrikes had slowed down ISIL's advance in northern Iraq, but were unlikely to degrade ISIL's capabilities or operations in other areas.Between 8 and 13 August, U.S. airstrikes and Kurdish ground forces enabled 35,000 to 45,000 of Yazidi refugees to escape or be evacuated from theSinjar Mountains.

On 16 August, U.S. air power began a close air campaign aimed at supporting the advance of Kurdish fighters moving toward the Mosul Dam. Kurdish sources commented that it was the "heaviest US bombing of militant positions since the start of air strikes". Obama on 17 August defended this usage of U.S. Forces as support of the Iraqi and Kurdish fight in general against ISIL—which indeed went beyond Obama's reasoning for launching airstrikes on 7 August.

On 8 September, the Iraqi Army, with close air support from the U.S., retook the key Haditha Dam, and recaptured the town of Barwana, killing 15 ISIL fighters. ISIL responded with the public execution of David Haines.By the end of September 2014, the United States had conducted 240 airstrikes in Iraq and Syria, as well as 1,300 tanker refueling missions, totaling 3,800 sorties by all types of aircraft. A tactical arrangement with Kurdish and Iraqi forces, and drone videos are being used to coordinate close air support without needing U.S. troops in ground combat.

On 19 December 2014, US General James Terry announced that the number of US airstrikes on ISIL had increased to 1,361.

On 25 December 2014, Hassan Saeed Al-Jabouri, the ISIL governor of Mosul, who was also known as Abu Taluut, was killed by a US-led Coalition airstrike in Mosul. It was also reported that the US planned to retake the city of Mosul in January 2015.

On 15 January 2015, it was reported that over 16,000 airstrikes had been carried out by the Coalition. The U.S. Air Force has carried out around 60 percent of all strikes. Among them, F-16s performed 41 percent of all sorties, followed by the F-15E at 37 percent, then the A-10 at 11 percent, the B-1bomber at eight percent, and the F-22 at 3 percent. The remaining 40 percent has been carried out by the US Navy and allied nations.

On 20 January 2015, the SOHR reported that al-Baghdadi, the leader of ISIL, had been wounded in an airstrike in Al-Qa'im, an Iraqi border town held by ISIL, and as a result, withdrew to Syria.

On 21 January 2015, the US began coordinating airstrikes with a Kurdish launched offensive, to help them begin the planned operation to retake the city of Mosul.

On 21 July 2015, it was reported that nearly 44,000 sorties have flown since August 2014.

American Ground Forces

In July, Obama announced that due to the continuing violence in Iraq and the growing influence of non-state organizations, such as the Islamic State of Iraq and the Levant, the United States would be elevating its security commitment in the region. Approximately 800 U.S. troops secured American installations like the Embassy in Baghdad and the Consulate in Erbil as well as taking control of strategic locations like the Baghdad airport in cooperation with

Iraqi troops. U.S. forces also undertook a mission to "assess and to advise [Iraqi security forces] as they confront [ISIL] and the complex security situation on the ground." Reports from these American units about the capabilities of the Iraqi military have been consistently grim, viewing them as "compromised" by sectarian interests.

On 13 August 2014, the U.S. deployed another 130 military advisers to Northern Iraq and up to 20 U.S. Marines and special forces servicemen landed on Mount Sinjar from V-22 aircraft to coordinate the evacuation of Yazidi refugees joining British SAS already in the area.

On 3 September 2014, Obama announced increase of U.S. forces in Iraq to 1,213. On 10 September, Obama gave a speech reiterating that U.S. troops will not fight in combat, but about 500 more troops will be sent to Iraq to help train Iraqi forces.

In early November 2014, Obama announced that he would be doubling the U.S. ground presence inside Iraq to around 3,000 men. By early December 2014, the number of U.S. ground troops in Iraq had increased to 3,100.

On 9 December 2014, the United States Senate Committee on Foreign Relations authorized U.S. Military force againstISIL. However, it limits military force to three years, requires the administration to report to Congress every 60 days, and prohibits the deployment of U.S. combat troops, except in specific cases, such as those involving the rescue or protection of U.S. soldiers, or for intelligence operations.

During the early morning hours of 14 December 2014, U.S. ground forces allegedly clashed with ISILalongside the Iraqi Army and Tribal Forces near the Ain al-Assad Airbase, west of Anbar, in an attempt to repel them from the base of which includes about 100 U.S. advisers in it, when ISIL attempted to overrun the base. According to a field commander of the Iraqi Army inAnbar province, said that "the U.S. force equipped with light and medium weapons, supported by F-18, was able to inflict casualties against fighters of ISIL organization, and forced them to retreat from the al-Dolab area, which lies 10 kilometers from Ain al-Assad base." Sheikh Mahmud Nimrawi, a prominent tribal leader in the region, added that "U.S. forces intervened because of ISIL started to come near the base, which they are stationed in so out of self-defense," he responded, welcoming the U.S. intervention, and saying "which I hope will not be the last." This was said to be the first encounter between the United States and the Islamic State, in four years. However, this claim has been stated to be "false" by The Pentagon.

On 5 January 2015, The Pentagon acknowledged that ISIL had been ineffectively mortaring the base. In late February 2015, another 1,300 US soldiers were deployed to Iraq, increasing the number of US ground troops in Iraq to 4,400.

The Late Naming of Operation Inherent Resolve

Unlike their coalition partners, and unlike previous American combat operations, no name was initially given to the 2014 intervention against ISIL by the U.S. government. The decision to keep the conflict nameless drew considerable media criticism. U.S. Service members remain ineligible for Campaign Medals and other service decorations due to the continuing ambiguous nature of the continuing U.S. involvement in Iraq.

On 15 October 2014, the United States Central Command announced that the U.S.-led air campaign against ISIL in Iraq and Syria was henceforth designated as *Operation Inherent Resolve*. The CENTCOM news release noted:

"According to CENTCOM officials, the name INHERENT RESOLVE is intended to reflect the unwavering resolve and deep commitment of the U.S. and partner nations in the region and around the globe to eliminate the terrorist group ISIL and the threat they pose to Iraq, the region and the wider international community. It also symbolizes the willingness and dedication of coalition members to work closely with our friends in the region and apply all available dimensions of national power necessary—diplomatic, informational, military, economic—to degrade and ultimately destroy ISIL."

Australian Airstrikes

On 3 October 2014, Prime Minister Tony Abbott and the Australian Cabinet approved for RAAF Boeing F/A-18F Super

Hornet fighter bombers to begin airstrikes against Islamic State militants. Abbott said "It is in our national interest that we do so, it is in the interests of civilisation that we do so. It is in everyone's best interests that the murderous rage of the ISIL death cult be checked and rolled back and that's what we're determined to do."

On 6 October, Air Chief Marshall Mark Binskin announced two Super Hornets had conducted armed combat missions over Iraq although no armaments were expended. An Australian Air task Group KC-30A and an E-7A Wedgetail Airborne Early Warning and Control aircraft have also been flying in support to fighter bombers belonging to coalition forces. The KC-30A performs airborne refueling for coalition aircraft.Binskin said "One of our Super Hornet packages on the first night... had an identified target which it was tracking and that particular target moved into an urban area where the risks of conducting a strike on that target increased to a point where it exceeded our expectations of collateral damage, so they discontinued the attack at that point."

On 9 October, Prime Minister Tony Abbott confirmed that RAAF Super Hornets had been involved in a "strike missions on an ISIL position in Iraq". The aircraft dropped two bombs onto an isolated building which ISIL was using as a command and control center.

As of 17 October, the Royal Australian Air Force had conducted 43 combat sorties over Iraq. Recent strikes had targeted equipment facilities, with "at least two" resulting in ISIL casualties after Australian aircraft had increased the number of missions flown to allow U.S. and coalition forces to assist Kurdish fighters around Kobanî, in northern Syria.

British Airstrikes

On 12 August 2014, the United Kingdom deployed six Tornado GR4 strike aircraft to RAF Akrotiri inCyprus to help coordinate its humanitarian aid airdrops in Northern Iraq. On 16 August 2014, following the completion of humanitarian aid airdrops, the Tornado GR4s, along with an RC-135 Rivet Joint signals intelligence aircraft, were re-tasked to provide aerial surveillance to coalition forces.

In early September 2014, British Prime Minister David Cameron began voicing his support for British airstrikes against ISIL in Iraq. Weeks later, Parliament was recalled and Members debated whether or not to authorise airstrikes. The seven-hour debate resulted in overwhelming support for airstrikes, with 524 votes in favour and 43 votes against.

On 27 September 2014, the first armed sortie took place over Iraq. A pair of Tornado GR4s left Cyprus armed with laser-guided bombs, supported by a Voyager aerial refueling tanker. Ultimately, the aircraft did not locate any targets requiring immediate air attack and so gathered intelligence for coalition forces instead. The Royal Air Force (RAF) conducted its first airstrike on 30 September 2014. A pair of Tornado GR4s engaged an ISIL heavy weapon position and an armed pickup truck using a laser-guided bomb and air-to-surface missile.

On 3 October 2014, the RAF deployed two additional Tornado aircraft to bring its deployed fleet up to eight aircraft. During the same month, it was also confirmed that the Royal Navy was involved in anti-ISIL operations in a support role, with air defence destroyerHMS *Defender* providing escort to U.S. Navy aircraft carrier USS *George H.W. Bush* as she launched aircraft into Iraq and Syria. Nick Clegg, then Deputy Prime Minister, also disclosed during an interview that there was a nuclear attack submarine armed with Tomahawk cruise missiles deployed to the region.

On 16 October 2014, the Ministry of Defence announced it would deploy MQ-9 Reaper drones to assist with surveillance, although, Defence Secretary Michael Fallon stated that the drones could also conduct airstrikes if required. The first Reaper drone strike occurred weeks later in Bayji, north of Baghdad, against a group of ISIL militants which had been laying improvised explosive devices.

In addition to operations over Iraq, the United Kingdom had also intervened in Syria by 21 October 2014, making it the first Western country, other than the United States, to do so. However, British aircraft were not permitted to carrying out airstrikes until Parliament had voted to give its authorization. Despite this, the Royal Air Force carried out a drone strike in Syria on 21 August

2015, against two British-born ISIL fighters which had been plotting attacks against the United Kingdom. Prime Minister David Cameron insisted that it was a lawful act of self-defense.

Since the authorization of airstrikes in Iraq, Prime Minister David Cameron had made persistent calls for airstrikes in Syria, however, he acknowledged that no airstrikes would take place until after a vote in Parliament. On 2 December 2015, following the November 2015 Paris attacks and United Nations Security Council Resolution 2249, David Cameron opened a ten-hour debate in Parliament on Syrian airstrikes, which ended with a final vote. 397 MPs voted in favour of airstrikes, whilst 223 voted against. Airstrikes commenced two hours after the vote, taking place in eastern Syria against the ISIL-held Oman oilfield. Defence Secretary Michael Fallon also subsequently announced that the UK's "strike force" based in Cyprus would double, with the addition of six Eurofighter Typhoons and twoTornado GR4s.

As of September 2015, a year after operations first began, more than 330 ISIL fighters had been killed by British airstrikes in Iraq, without any civilian casualties.

In addition to airstrikes, the United Kingdom has also made significant contributions towards the coalition's ISTAR capabilities. The Royal Air Force has deployed Sentinel R1, Sentry AEW1, RC-135W Rivet Joint and Shadow R1 aircraft to gather surveillance, in addition to Tornado GR4 and MQ-9 Reaper strike aircraft. In September 2015, the United Kingdom was responsible for a third of all coalition surveillance flights over Iraq and Syria, with the Tornado GR4s RAPTOR reconnaissance pod accounting for 60% of the coalition's entire tactical reconnaissance in Iraq alone.

Canadian Airstrikes

The Canadian contribution has been code-named Operation Impact by the Canadian Department of National Defence. Canadian aircraft left for the Middle East to join in airstrikes on 21 October. In total, six CF-18 fighter jets, an Airbus CC-150 Polaris air-to-air refueling tanker and two CP-140 Aurora surveillance aircraft were sent, along with 700 military personnel.

Canadian CF-18 fighter jets completed their first operational flights departing from Kuwait on 31 October. The first Canadian airstrikes began on 2 November. Canada also flew an extra CF-18 to Kuwait to be used as a spare if the need arises, however a maximum of six are authorized to fly with the coalition missions.

On 4 November 2014, Royal Canadian Air Force CF-18s destroyed ISIL construction equipment using GBU-12 bombs. The construction equipment was being used to divert the Euphrates River to deny villages water, and to flood roads, diverting traffic to areas with IEDs.

On 12 November 2014, Canadian jets destroyed ISIL artillery just outside the Northern Iraqi town of Baiji. Airstrikes continued throughout December and into January 2015 totaling 28 strike missions. It was then reported that Canadian special forces troops, which had been highlighting targets for airstrikes, had engaged in fighting after coming under attack.

On 19 January 2015, Canadian special operations forces came under ISIL attack for the first time in Iraq over the last week, and returned sniper fire to "neutralize" the threat. Canadians are "enabling airstrikes from the ground," meaning they are actively finding targets for jets flying overhead.

On 29 January 2015, Canadian special forces in Iraq came under fire from ISIL forces, causing the Canadian troops to return fire, killing some ISIL militants. On 6 March, a Canadian soldier was killed in a friendly fire incident by Kurdish forces while returning to an observation post.

On 8 April 2015, two CF-18s carried out their first airstrike against ISIL in Syria, hitting one of the groups garrisons.

From 2 Nov 2014 to 13 May 2015 the Canadian armed forces struck 80 ISIL fighting positions, 19 ISIL Vehicles, and 10 storage facilities.

On 21 October 2015, Canadian Prime Minister-designate Justin Trudeau informed U.S. President Barack Obama that he intended to withdraw Canadian aircraft from operations over Iraq and Syria but increase training missions on the ground.

Dutch Airstrikes

On 24 September 2014, the Dutch government announced its participation in the operations against ISIL in Iraq. Since late 2014, eight F-16s (with two kept in reserve) were deployed to Jordan. Since then, numerous air attacks have been conducted on tactical facilities of ISIL, like camps and command posts. The F-16s also give air support to Iraqi and Kurdish ground forces. In June 2015 the Royal Netherlands Air Force flew its 1000th sortie above Iraq. During the first 9 months of the mission 575 strikes have been carried out.

French Airstrikes

On 19 September 2014, the French Air Force used its Rafale jets to conduct airstrikes on ISIL targets in Mosul. The airstrikes were approved by French President François Hollande, which indicated that France was committed to fighting ISIL using air power alongside the United States.

Hollande mentioned that no ground troops would be used in the conflict. To conduct its airstrikes, France deployed 9 Rafale fighters to the United Arab Emirates, 6 Dassault Mirage 2000 fighters to Jordan, in addition to a Atlantique 2 maritime patrol aircraft, a Boeing E-3 Sentry airborne early warning and control aircraft, and a Boeing KC-135 Stratotanker aerial refueling tanker.

On 23 February 2015, the French Navy also deployed its Task Forcẹ 473 carrier strike group to the Persian Gulf with the intent on conducting airstrikes from the aircraft carrier *Charles de Gaulle*. The *Charles de Gaulle* contributed 12 Rafale fighters, 9 Dassault-Breguet Super Étendard strike aircraft, and 2 E-2C Hawkeye airborne early warning and control aircraft.

The task force also included the French frigate *Chevalier Paul* (D621), a Rubis-class submarine, a Durance-class tanker, and the British frigate HMS *Kent*. After eight weeks of operations, the task force left the Persian Gulf on its way to India, heralding the end of its contribution to Operation Chammal.

On 5 November 2015, it was announced that the *Charles de Gaulle* would resume operations in Syria to fight ISIL.

On 15 November 2015, after the November 2015 Paris attacks, the French Air Force launched its largest airstrike of the bombing campaign sending 12 planes, including 10 fighters, that dropped

20 bombs in training camps and ammunition facilities in Raqqa, the de facto capital of ISIS.

Jordanian Airstrikes

After the downed Jordanian pilot, Muath al-Kasasbeh was executed by ISIL by being burned to death, King Abdullah II vowed revenge and temporarily took the lead in the bombing raids on ISIL during February 2015. On 8 February, Jordan claimed that during the course of 3 days, from 5–7 February, their airstrikes alone had killed 7,000 ISIL militants in Iraq and Syria, and also reportedly degraded 20% of the militant group's capability.

Morocco Airstrikes

In December 2014 Morocco sent 4 F-16s to bomb ISIL positions, initially in the outskirts of Baghdad and other undisclosed locations.The planes operated under the command of the UAE and suspended operations in February 2015.

AMERICAN-LED MILITARY INTERVENTION IN SYRIA

Hostage Rescue Attempt

On 4 July 2014, the U.S. bombed the "Osama bin Laden" ISIL military base in the village of Uqayrishah, Syria. Two dozen American Delta Force commandos then touched down in an effort to rescue hostages, including James Foley. In a series of videos, Foley,Steven Joel Sotloff, and several more hostages were murdered.

Aerial Surveillance

On 26 August 2014, the U.S. began sending surveillance flights, including drones, into Syria to gather intelligence. The Syrian Arab Republic was not asked for permission.

On 28 August, speaking about combatting ISIL in Syria, President Obama said "we don't have a strategy yet."

The British Royal Air Force has been operating over Syria in a surveillance role since 21 October 2014, making the UK the first Western country other than the United States to operate in both Iraq and Syria simultaneously.

Arming and Training Rebels

At the direction of President Obama, the U.S. Central Intelligence Agency played an active role since the early stages of the Syrian Civil War. The U.S. originally supplied the moderate rebels of the Free Syrian Army with non-lethal aid but soon escalated to providing training, cash, and intelligence to selected rebel commanders. On 17 September 2014, the House of Representatives voted to authorize spending to train and arm moderate Syrian rebels.

The United Kingdom announced in March 2015 that it would send 75 military personnel to help train moderate Syrian forces in the use of small arms, infantry tactics and basic medical skills. The training will take place in Turkey as part of the US-led effort.

According to the United States Department of Defense, Saudi Arabia has proposed that they would provide training to Syrian rebels so they could return to Syria and battle ISIL.

As of September 2015, the results have been limited, with only a small number trained and many captured, killed or not fighting.

Multi-national Airstrikes

U.S. President Obama announced on 10 September 2014 that he would begin to pursue airstrikes in Syria with or without congressional approval. Starting on 22 September 2014, the U.S., Bahrain,Jordan, Qatar, Saudi Arabia, and the United Arab Emirates began airstrikes against ISIL targets in Syria with fighters, bombers, and sea-based Tomahawk cruise missiles. Strikes continue to take place in Syria daily. Additionally, on the first night, U.S. forces launched eight cruise missile strikes against the al-Qaeda-affiliated Khorasan. In early November early December 2014, the U.S. launched additional airstrikes against the same group. In November 2014, Morocco sent 3 F-16s to be deployed in UAE, to fight ISIL in Iraq and Syria under U.S.-led operations.

On 24 December 2014, ISIL shot down a Jordanian fighter jet over Syria and captured and its pilot,Jordanian air force lieutenant Muath Al-Kasasbeh. Al-Kasabeh was offered in exchange for captured ISIL fighters. Jordan offered to make the exchange, but demanded "proof of life" first. However, Al-Kasabeh had already been executed by immolation. When video of the pilot's execution was released, a moratorium on executions inJordan was lifted and the Al-Qaida operatives, Sajida al-Rishawi and Ziad al-Karbouli were executed.

On 21 August 2015, three ISIL fighters, two with UK nationality, were targeted and killed in Raqqa, Syria by a British Royal Air Force MQ-9 Reaper strike. Prime Minister David Cameron gave a statement to Parliament that one of the British nationals targeted had been plotting attacks in the United Kingdom. Another British national was killed in a separate air strike by US forces in Raqqa on 24 August.

In October and November 2015, the U.S. intensified its airstrikes on ISIL-held oil facilities in an operation named "Tidal Wave II", after theWorld War II campaign against Axis oil targets in Romania. The U.S. strategy aimed "to knock out specific installations for six months to a year" by focusing on facilities near Deir el-Zour. The Omar oil field, which produced 30,000 barrels of oil per day and $1.7 million to $5.1 million in revenue per month at full capacity, was hit on October 21, reducing it to roughly a third of its capacity. French aircraft also participated in the strikes.

On 16 November 2015, a U.S. Operation Tidal Wave II sortie destroyed 116 IS fuel tankers clustered near Abu Kamal, a town on the Syrian border near Iraqi. Four A-10 Thunderbolt IIs and two AC-130 Spectre gunships participated in the raid. Before attacking the trucks the planes conducted several low-level, 'show of force' passes.

On 2 December, the Parliament of the United Kingdom voted in favour (397 to 223) to authorise air strikes in Syria. Within hours, RAF Tornado jets carried out their first air strikes, targeting the Omar oil fields in eastern Syria, which is under IS control. Tornado GR-4 jets are being used for surveillance and a further six Typhoons left RAF Lossiemouth, Scotland to join forces at RAF Akrotiri, Cyrpus.

RUSSIAN INTERVENTION

On 11 September 2015, a Syrian military source made mention of Russian troops present in Syria to help the Syrian government in its fight against ISIL (Daesh), as part of Operation Rescue.On 17 September, Syrian warplanes carried out a wave of airstrikes in the ISIL-held city of Raqqawith Russian weapons supplied by Russian Armed Forces. On the 20th of November, Russia claimed to have killed over 600 people using cruise-missiles in one mission.

INTERVENTION IN LIBYA

Egyptian Air Strikes

After ISIL killed 21 Egyptian Coptic Christians in Libya, Egypt conducted airstrikes on ISIL targets in Libya on 16 February 2015, killing a total of 64 ISIL militants (50 in Derna). Warplanes acting under orders from the "official" Libyan government also struck targets in Derna, reportedly in coordination with Egypt's airstrikes. A Libyan official stated that more joint airstrikes would follow.

US Surveillance Flights

Concern over ISIL activities in Derna District in Libya in December 2014 led to US drones and electronic surveillance planes making "constant flights" from Italian bases, over the district of Derna.

US Air Strike

On 13 November 2015, the United States launched an airstrike in Derna, Libya. Two U.S. F-15E fighter jets targeted a senior ISIL leaderAbu Nabil al-Anbari in the airstrike. The status of Abu Nabil is currently uncertain, but he is presumed dead.

US INTERVENTION IN AFGHANISTAN

A report says that, according to a Tehrik-i-Taliban Pakistan (TTP) spokesperson, in July 2015, a US drone strike killed Shahidullah Shadid, a senior leader of an ISIL group for the Khorasan region (parts of Iran, Turkmenistan and Afghanistan), and 24 other militants, in Nangarhar province in Afghanistan.

US INTERVENTION IN CAMEROON

In October 2015, with the approval of the Cameroonian

government, the U.S. military deployed 300 personnel to Cameroon, their primary missions will revolve around providing intelligence support to local forces as well as conducting reconnaissance flights.

CASUALTIES

ISIL

On 22 January 2015, U.S. Ambassador to Iraq Stuart Jones stated that the Coalition airstrikes had degraded ISIL, including killing off half of their leaders in Iraq and Syria.

In early February 2015, the Australian Defence Minister, Kevin Andrews, stated that more than 6,000 ISIL fighters had been killed in coalition airstrikes since they began, and that over 800 square kilometres (310 sq mi) had been recaptured; yet ISIL strength was estimated to have grown during this period to around 31,500 core fighters, including 3,000 fighters from Western nations.

On 23 February 2015, US General Lloyd Austin stated that over 8,500 ISIL militants had been killed by Coalition airstrikes in Iraq and Syria.

In early March 2015, General Lloyd repeated this statement, saying that "ISIS has assumed a defensive crouch" in Iraq, and that "We are where we said we would be," in relation to the airstrikes. This was in contrast to Jordan's claim that its airstrikes alone had killed 7,000 ISIL militants in Iraq and Syria over the course of 3 days, from 5 to 7 February 2015.

Civilians

According to *Airwars*, a team of independent journalists, by August 2015, 450 civilians had been killed by the U.S.-led coalition air campaign against ISIL in Iraq and Syria (of whom roughly 60% in Syria, 40% in Iraq). By that time, the US-led coalition officially acknowledged only two non-combatant deaths. According to *Airwars*, by January 2016, "between 815 and 1,149 civilian non-combatants appear likely to have been killed in 135 incidents where there is fair reporting publicly available of an event, and where Coalition strikes were confirmed in the near vicinity on that date."

Labeling

On 1 February 2015, Iraq's Foreign Minister Ibrahim al-Jaafari stated that the War on ISIL was effectively 'World War III', due to ISIL's proclamation of a worldwide caliphate, it also aims to conquer the world, and its success in spreading the conflict to multiple countries outside of the Levant region. Speaking of ISIL's destruction of pre-Islamic sites in the region, Syria's head of antiquities, Maamoun Abdul Karim, stated that "this is the entire world's battle."

7

American-led Intervention in Syria against ISIS

By taking the fight to Islamic State (Isis) militants in Syria, Barack Obama has opened up a broad new Middle East battlefront – and started something that, by his own admission, he cannot finish. The US president warned this month that his vow to "degrade and destroy" Isis would take years to achieve. Obama's successor in the White House is now likely to inherit, as did Obama in 2009, an ongoing, costly and intractable Middle East conflict.

The intervention is significant in other respects. Obama has stepped into the middle of Syria's civil war after three years of resolutely striving to keep out. The possible consequences of this volte-face are unfathomable. The scale of Tuesday's attack, involving fighter bombers, drones and sea-launched Tomahawk cruise missiles, was a big escalation compared with the more limited strikes on Isis in Iraq since August. Obama's action was triggered by fears of an imminent massacre of Syrian Kurds, who fled in large numbers across the Turkish border last weekend in the face of Isis attacks.

It is clear that joint military planning with Arab allies has been under way for some time. John Kerry, the US secretary of state, visited the Gulf earlier this month to coordinate preparations. The direct involvement of Sunni Muslim-led Saudi Arabia, Jordan, Bahrain, Qatar and the United Arab Emirates, in defiance of Shia Muslim Iran and its Syrian ally, potentially expands the Syria-Iraq conflict into a region-wide struggle. The US-led air strikes in Syria raise other key questions:

Legality

The legality of any western or foreign military action in Syria, present and future, is of paramount importance given the history of the 2003 Iraq intervention when the US and Britain acted without UN authorisation. Unlike the Iraqi government, Syria's president, Bashar al-Assad, has not requested outside assistance in fighting Isis. American officials admit Assad's permission was not sought, although the regime was informed of the air strikes in advance. The UN security council has not sanctioned military action, nor, given Russia's hostility, is it likely to.

On the other hand, under international law, UN members have a responsibility to protect groups of civilians such as the Syrian Kurds when their lives are imminently threatened. The US maintains Assad is no longer a legitimate leader following his alleged use of chemical weapons against civilians, a position echoed by Britain's David Cameron. But this view remains legally dubious.

Effectiveness

The Pentagon said it had attacked 22 targets in northern and eastern Syria in Tuesday's initial phase, principally command and control centres, weapons dumps, depots and barracks used by Isis and by an al-Qaida affiliate. A key target was the north-east Syrian town of Raqqa, which has become a safe haven for Isis cohorts fighting over the border in Iraq. Follow-up air strikes can be expected.

One potential problem is unintended civilian casualties, which became a big issue during Nato campaigns in Afghanistan. Another is whether air strikes have any lasting benefit. General Martin Dempsey, chairman of the US joint chiefs of staff, and other senior military figures in the US and Britain, have warned that air power alone cannot defeat Isis. Although the US has plans to train local ground forces, at present the Free Syrian Army and Kurdish peshmerga do not have the strength, resources or reach to occupy and hold territory freed of Isis control by air attacks. Thus any gains may prove to be temporary.

The Assad Regime

Like Britain, the Obama administration has repeatedly demanded the resignation of Assad and free elections to create an inclusive, democratic government in Syria. But the dramatic rise of Isis, with its extreme Islamist ideology and brutal methods, has come to be seen as a bigger threat to western interests than Assad. The Damascus regime, backed by its Russian ally, warned last month that unauthorised attacks on its sovereign territory would constitute aggression. But in truth Assad may quietly welcome Obama's action, since it in effect shores up his position with regard to a common enemy. The Isis threat is also having the effect of deflecting the hostility of neighbouring countries such as Turkey, which are now preoccupied with the security and refugee crisis along their shared border. Nevertheless, continued, sustained American and Arab bombing raids could bring the US and its allies into direct confrontation with Syrian government forces.

The Arab World

The participation of Saudi Arabia and four other Arab countries in the military attacks is a major development in the post-2003 Iraq-Syria story. The subsequent threat by an Isis spokesman to take unspecified, violent reprisals against them underlined the extent to which the Syrian civil war may be fuelling a region-wide conflict. The involvement of these "moderate" Sunni Muslim regimes in attacking Sunni extremists also underscores the supposedly widening schism with the Shia Muslim world, as represented by Iran and its Alawite allies in Damascus.

Tehran acquiesced in US attacks on Isis in Iraq, but is opposed to similar action inside Syria. What Iran does next may depend to some extent on the outcome of its long-running nuclear negotiations with the west. David Cameron, who willmeet the Iranian president, Hassan Rouhani, in New York this week, has a rare chance to influence Iranian thinking.

Britain's Role

Following his defeat in a House of Commons vote on Syria last year, Cameron has been ultra-cautious about offering direct British military support to the Americans in Iraq and Syria. France has been more engaged, launching air strikes against Isis in Iraq. But President François Hollande's government says it will not get involved in Syria. Now that Obama has thrown the dice and joined the fray in Syria, Britain will feel increasing pressure to do more to help. Given that Cameron has personally vowed to destroy Isis and that public opinion has hardened following the beheadings of British and American hostages, it seems likely he willseek parliamentary backing for military action in Iraq – but not in Syria.

U.S. Military Leaders: Strikes in Syria are just the Start of a Prolonged Campaign

U.S. military leaders said Tuesday their aerial bombardment of Syria was only the beginning of a prolonged campaign that will continue intermittently for months and will become more difficult as targeted militants seek refuge in populated areas.

The United States is now attacking two sets of enemies in the region: the Islamic State, a growing movement of jihadists seeking to create its own country in the Middle East, and the Khora-san group, a smaller network affiliated with al-Qaeda that officials say is plotting against Europe and the United States.

At the same time, as the U.S. military and its Arab partners prepare more airstrikes in Syria in the coming days, they will have to contend with another adversary: Syrian President Bashar al-Assad.

Although U.S. officials said they were not targeting Assad or his forces, many of the Sunni Muslim allies in President Obama's coalition would like to see Assad's government finally collapse after a devastating civil war. Whether the coalition's intervention in Syria will eventually help or hurt Assad represents one of the greatest unknowns in a military campaign filled with uncertainty.

Army Lt. Gen. William C. Mayville Jr., director of operations for the Joint Staff at the Pentagon, said the objectives set for the U.S.-led war in Iraq and now Syria could take years to complete. The attacks in Syria marked the start of a new phase, coming six weeks after the U.S. military began a similar campaign of airstrikes against Islamic State fighters in neighboring Iraq. The overarching goal, Mayville said at a news conference, is "to degrade and ultimately destroy" the Islamic State, first by directly attacking the group in both countries, severing its supply lines and disrupting its sources of arms and money. To succeed over the long term, Mayville added, the United States and its allies will have to train and equip three proxy forces: the Iraqi military, the Kurdish pesh merga fighters and moderate Syrian rebels. All have proved hapless in head-to-head battles with the Islamic State and will require U.S.-military backing to reclaim territory.

"The most important thing is to create some space for the Iraqi security forces to reorganize and replace leadership that needs to be replaced," Mayville said. "What we have been doing over these last couple of weeks and what last night's campaign was about was simply buying them some space so that they can get on the offensive." In confronting the Khorasan group, a network that had received scant public mention before this month, the Obama administration may find itself acting largely on its own.

The first wave of strikes, which took place on what was late Monday in Washington, primarily consisted of dozens of Tomahawk cruise missiles launched by U.S. warships against eight Khorasan group targets in northwestern Syria, near Aleppo. Military officials said they attacked Khorasan training camps, a munitions production center, a communications building and other sites.

Mayville justified the blitz by citing U.S. intelligence reports showing the Khorasan group "was in the final stages of plans to execute major attacks against Western targets and potentially the U.S. homeland." He did not elaborate on those reports and declined to comment when asked whether there was evidence that any plots had been set into motion. He also said the military was still assessing the overall damage it inflicted on the Khorasan group and whether its ability to carry out attacks beyond the region had been diminished.

SYRIAN CIVIL WAR

During the Syrian Civil War, which began in 2011, the United States first supplied the rebels of the Free Syrian Army with non-lethal aid (including food rations and pickup trucks), but quickly began providing training, cash, and intelligence to selected Syrian rebel commanders.

The United States began surveillance missions on ISIL positions in Syria in September 2014. On September 10, President Barack Obama gave a speech indicating his intent to "degrade and ultimately destroy" Islamic State of Iraq and the Levant (ISIL), saying, "I have made it clear that we will hunt down terrorists who threaten our country, wherever they are. That means I will not hesitate to take action against ISIL in Syria, as well as Iraq."

On September 22, 2014, the United States, Bahrain, Jordan, Qatar, Saudi Arabia, and the United Arab Emirates began to strike targets of the Islamic State of Iraq and the Levant (ISIL) inside Syria, as well as the Khorasan group in the Idlib Governorateto the west of Aleppo, and the al-Nusra Front around Ar-Raqqah, as part of theMilitary intervention against ISIL.

On November 2, in response to the intervention, representatives from Ahrar ash-Shamattended a meeting with the al-Nusra Front, the Khorasan Group, the ISIL, and Jund al-Aqsa, which sought to unite several hard-line groups against the US-led coalition and other moderate Syrian rebel groups. On November 6, a US airstrike struck Ahrar ash-Sham at its headquarters in Idlib. By 14 November 2014, it was revealed that the negotiations between al-Nusra, Jund al-Aqsa, ISIL and Ahrar ash-Sham had failed.

BACKGROUND

Following the start of the Arab Spring in 2011, protests in Syria against the Assad administration were suppressed and became violent. In 2012, the al-Nusra Front was established by the Islamic State of Iraq as the official branch of *al-Qaeda in Syria.* The al-Nusra Front was eclipsed by its own creator, and al-Qaeda severed its ties to the Islamic State of Iraq and the Levant in February 2014, after an eight-month power struggle.

Arming and Training the Syrian Opposition

At the direction of U.S. President Barack Obama, the Central Intelligence Agency (CIA) was put in charge of the operations, worth about $1 billion annually, to arm anti-government forces in

Syria at the early stages of the Syrian Civil War, which began in 2011. At first, the CIA only supplied the apparently moderate rebels of the Free Syrian Army with non-lethal aid, but quickly began providing training, cash, and intelligence to selected rebel commanders.

While the CIA-run programs to arm and train Syrian opposition factions began 2013,on September 17, 2014 the House of Representatives voted to authorize the executive branch to train-and-equip Syrian rebels against ISIL forces. One of the groups that United States intended to train-and-equip was the Islamist Army of Mujahedeenwhile the Harakat Hazm group was already being supplied. There were indications that the Army of Mujahedeen was still being vetted for support. The United States was set to send 400 troops and hundreds of support staff to countries neighboring Syria to train 5,000 opposition soldiers a year for the next three years. The countries taking part in the train-and-equip program were to include Jordan, Qatar, Saudi Arabia, and Turkey. The Pentagon confirmed that it had selected 1,200 Syrian opposition members to begin training in March 2015, with 3,000 to complete training by the end of 2015. However of that number only about 200 actually began training, the majority of whom left after being required to agree to fight only against ISIL and not the Assad government. As of mid-2015, only a group of 54 such fighters (Division 30) had been deployed, which was quickly routed by al-Nusra.

The successful experience in Kobanî had informed U.S. policy in regards to arming Syrian opposition groups other than the Kurdish YPG, with plans to give other groupstechnicals equipped with radio and GPS equipment to call in airstrikes. John R. Allen, President Obama's envoy to the international coalition against ISIL, has said "It is clearly part of our plan, that not only we will train them, and we will equip them with the latest weapons systems, but we will also protect them when the time comes," alluding to aiding the opposition with air support and no fly zones. The United Kingdom announced it will send around 75 military instructors to train Syrian opposition forces. The train-and-equip programme started on 9 May. On 25 May, Turkey and the U.S.

agreed "in principle" on the necessity to support these forces with air support.

July 2014 Rescue Mission

Following the abduction of a number of foreigners in Syria, on July 4, 2014, the U.S. carried out an operation to rescue foreign hostages being held by ISIL. U.S. airstrikes were conducted against an ISIL military base known as the "Osama bin Laden Camp" while at the same time, two dozen special operations members parachuted from helicopters near an ISIS building for high-valued prisoners. No prisoners were found in the building and the special operations members were quickly engaged by ISIL forces dispatched from Ar-Raqqah, which started a three-hour firefight. U.S. forces concluded that the hostages were no longer at the site and abandoned the rescue attempt. At least five ISIL fighters were killed and one U.S. soldier was wounded. Jordanian forces were also reportedly involved in the operation, with one Jordanian soldier reportedly wounded, but Jordanian involvement was not confirmed. Later on, it was reported that the hostages had been moved 24 hours before the attempted rescue. Following the mission, it was still unclear whether the operation failed due to bad intelligence or whether ISIL forces were alerted in advance of the mission.

Beheadings of Western Hostages

In the aftermath of the rescue mission, and purportedly as a response to airstrikes in Iraq, ISIL beheaded three hostages over a one-month period: Americans James Foleyon August 19, 2014, Steven Sotloff on September 2, and Briton David Haineson September 13.

Surveillance Flights over Syria

On August 26, 2014, the U.S. began sending surveillance flights, including drones, over Syria to gather intelligence on ISIL targets in Syria. The flights began gathering intelligence that would aid future airstrikes; however, airstrikes were not yet authorized at that point, and no approval was sought from the Assad government for flights entering Syrian airspace.

INTERNATIONAL COALITIONS AGAINST ISIL

On 5 September, 15 September and 3 December 2014, different sets of countries came together to discuss concerted action against ISIL. Present at all three meetings were the United States, United Kingdom, France, Germany, Italy, Canada, Turkey and Denmark. The coalition of 5 September (10 countries) decided to support anti-ISIL forces in Iraq and Syria.

A coalition of 3 December 2014 (59 countries) agreed on a many-sided strategy against ISIL, including cutting off ISIL's financing and funding and exposing ISIL's true nature.

TRAINING SYRIAN MODERATE OPPOSITION TO FIGHT ISIL

In late 2013 the United States began a program to train and equip Syrian "moderate rebels". In July 2015 the first class of 54 US-backed rebels were inserted into Syria from Turkey. Within days, virtually all of the US-backed rebels were dead or missing, and their leader had been captured by the Al-Queda-affiliated al-Nusra Front.

In March 2015, the United Kingdom announced that it would provide military training to Syrian moderate opposition forces, to enable them to defend Syrian communities against ISIL, and later also lead offensives against ISIL.

MULTINATIONAL AIR WAR

Preparations for American Airstrikes

In his address to the nation on September 10, 2014, U.S. President Obama announced his intention to bomb ISIL targets in Syria and called on Congress to authorize a program to train and arm rebels who were fighting ISIL and the Syrian forces of Bashar al-Assad. For the first time, he authorized direct attacks against the militant group in Syria. In his address, he said the United States were going on offensive, launching "a steady, relentless effort to take out" the group "wherever they exist." Obama also announced creating of a broader coalition against ISIL.

Commenting on Obama's address, Russian Foreign Ministry spokesman Alexander Lukashevich opposed the U.S. intervention against ISIL in Syria "without the consent of the legitimate government" and said that "this step, in the absence of a UN Security Council decision, would be an act of aggression, a gross violation of international law". Ali Haidar, Syrian minister of national reconciliation, said that "any action of any kind without the consent of the Syrian government would be an attack on Syria".

On September 17, the U.S. House of Representatives approved Obama's plan to train and arm the Syrian rebels in their fight against ISIL. In a statement following the House vote, Obama said that the United States wouldn't send military troops to Syria. The Senate gave final congressional approval to Obama's proposal the next day.

The U.S. did not request permission from the Syrian government, nor did it coordinate its actions with the Syrian government, provide direct notification to the Syrian military or give indication of timing on specific targets, but it did notify the Syrian U.N. representative, which the Syrian government confirmed.

Before the airstrikes began, the United States also informed Iran, the Assad government's largest regional ally, of their intention to launch airstrikes. It did not share specific timing or targets of strikes with the Iranian government but reportedly assured it that the US would not strike any Syrian government targets.

Contributing Countries

- Australia (Operation Okra)
- Bahrain
- Canada (Operation Impact § In Syria – pulling out soon)
- France (Opération Chammal)
- Jordan (Jordanian intervention in the Syrian Civil War)
- Qatar
- Saudi Arabia
- Turkey (Turkish involvement in the Syrian Civil War)

- United Arab Emirates
- United Kingdom (Operation Shader § Intervention in Syria)
- United States of America (Leader)

Timeline

September 2014

On September 22, Pentagon Press Secretary Rear Admiral John Kirby confirmed that the United States and other partner nations had undertaken strikes in Syria using fighters, bombers, andTomahawk missiles in strikes authorized by President Barack Obama. Bahrain, Jordan, Qatar,Saudi Arabia and the United Arab Emirates were identified as countries conducting or supporting airstrikes the first night. The initial strikes were coordinated by United States Central Commandand targeted about 20 Islamic State of Iraq and the Levant targets, including headquarters buildings. Sources in Syria claimed that among the targets was also Brigade 93, a Syrian army base that the militants had recently captured and targets in the towns of Tabqa and Tel Abyad in Ar-Raqqah Province.

The US also targeted the al-Qaeda-affiliated al-Nusra Front and the Khorasan Group in theAleppo and Idlib Governorates of Syria. F-22 Raptor stealth fighters were reported to be among the U.S. aircraft striking targets in Syria on the first night of the campaign, carrying out their first combat missions ever since entering service in 2005.

At least 70 ISIL fighters, 50 fighters affiliated with al-Qaeda, and an unknown number of civilians were killed overnight by the airstrikes, according to the Syrian Observatory for Human Rights while eight strikes were launched against the Khorasan group.

On September 24, the United States and coalition partners conducted a second round of airstrikes on ISIL facilities in Syria. The airstrikes were targeting oil production facilities controlled by ISIL who had been using the oil in order to fund their activities. Some targets were apparently also mobile production facilities which were most likely not refineries.

In a third round of airstrikes on ISIL targets on September 25, Arab partners lead the United States in strikes against militant-held oil facilities in northeastern Syria. Saudi Arabia and the United Arab Emirates dropped 80 percent of the bomb tonnage in the third round of strikes, compared to other strikes in which the United States lead Arab partners.

On September 26, the United States carried out a fourth round of airstrikes on ISIL targets in Eastern Syria. The strikes were targeting IS heavy equipment and destroyed four of their tanks in the Deir ez-Zor Province.

In a fifth round of airstrikes in Syria on September 27, the United States lead strikes along with Saudi Arabia, Jordan and the United Arab Emirates against ISIL forces in the Kobanî Canton of Syrian Kurdistan. The strikes destroyed two armored vehicles and an unknown number of fighters in an area that had been put under siege by ISIL militants. The siege by Islamic State fighters had recently forced over 100,000 Syrian Kurds to flee across the border to Turkey.

On September 28 and 29, the United States carried out two rounds of strikes against IS positions across Syria in 4 provinces. Among the facilities targeted was the entrance to the largest gas plant in Syria, in the Deir ez-Zor Province, and ISIL training camp and vehicles near an ISIL controlled grain silo in Manbij, Aleppo province.

October 2014

In an eighth round of airstrikes in Syria on October 1, the United States and coalition partners struck ISIL targets in Northern Syria. The daytime strikes targeted ISIL forces laying siege to Kobanî, a primarily Kurdish city in Syrian Kurdistan, in support of the People's Protection Units (YPG) and Free Syrian Army, who were defending the city.

On October 2, the United States lead a ninth round of strikes along with the United Arab Emirates against ISIL forces across Syria. The strikes destroyed an ISIL checkpoint near Kobanî, damaged a tank north of Sinjar Mountain, destroyed a tank west of Ar-Raqqah, and several ISIL facilities east ofAleppo.

In a tenth round of airstrikes in Syria on October 3, the United States, assisted by Saudi Arabia and the United Arab Emirates struck ISIL forces in Northern and Eastern Syria. The strikes destroyed an ISIL garrison south of Al-Hasakah, destroyed two tanks southeast of Deir ez-Zor, destroyed two modular oil refineries and a training camp south of Ar-Raqqah, and struck an ISIL building northeast of Aleppo.

On October 4, the United States lead an 11th round of airstrikes, along with Jordan, Saudi Arabia, and the United Arab Emirates, against ISIL forces across Syria. The US and partner nations carried out nine strikes, destroying an ISIL infantry unit, armored personnel carrier, and a vehicle south of Kobanî, destroying a tank and a vehicle southeast of Deir ez-Zor, damaging the Taqba airfield and destroying an artillery piece near Ar-Raqqah, as well as destroying an IS depot and logistics complex south of Al-Hasakah.

In a 12th round of airstrikes in Syria on October 5, the United States carried out three airstrikes against ISIL forces in Central and Eastern Syria. The strikes destroyed an ISIL bulldozer, two ISIL tanks and another vehicle northwest of Al Mayadin, and destroyed six firing positions and a large ISIL unit northwest of Ar-Raqqah.

On October 6, the United States carried out a 13th round of airstrikes in Syria against ISIL forces across Syria. The strikes destroyed an ISIL tank near Taqba airfield west of Ar-Raqqah, destroyed two fighting positions south of Kobanî, and destroyed a tank southeast of Deir ez-Zor.

In a 14th round of airstrikes in Syria on October 7, the United States, assisted by Saudi Arabia and the United Arab Emirates against ISIL forces across Syria. The United States and partner nations carried out nine strikes damaging multiple ISIL controlled buildings west of Al-Hasakah, damaging a staging area and IED production facility northeast of Deir ez-Zor, destroying three armed vehicles, damaging one armed vehicle, destroying a vehicle carrying anti-aircraft artillery, destroying an ISIL tank, and an ISIL unit in and around Kobanî, and killing a small group of fighters southwest of Rabiyah.

On October 8, the United States lead a 15th round of airstrikes along with the United Arab Emirates against ISIL forces across Syria. The US and the United Arab Emirates carried out nine strikes destroying an armored personnel carrier, four armed vehicles, an artillery piece, and damaged another armed vehicle in and around Kobanî, striking an ISIL training camp and fighters northwest of Ar-Raqqah, and destroying a tank northwest of Deir ez-Zor.

In a 16th round of airstrikes in Syria on October 9, the United States carried out nine airstrikes in the areas in and around the border town of Kobanî that is under siege. The US carried out six airstrikes south of Kobanî that destroyed two ISIL-held buildings, one tank and one heavy machine gun along, a fighting position along with one large and two small ISIL units. Along with strikes south of Kobanî, the US carried out three airstrikes north of Kobanî which struck two small ISIL units and destroyed two ISIL-held buildings.

On October 10, the United States led a 17th round of airstrikes along with Saudi Arabia and the United Arab Emirates against ISIL forces across Syria. The US and coalition partners carried out nine strikes, destroying two ISIL training facilities, three vehicles, damaging a tank and striking two ISIL units in and around Kobanî. The strikes also destroyed an armored vehicle staging facility east of Deir ez-Zor and struck a small ISIL unit northeast of Al-Hasakah.

In an 18th round of airstrikes in Syria on October 11, the United States carried out six airstrikes in and around the border town of Kobanî that is under siege by ISIL forces. The US carried out four strikes north of Kobanî striking a fighting position, damaging a command and control facility, destroying a staging building, and striking two small ISIL units. South of Kobanî, two airstrikes destroyed three trucks.

On October 12, the United States led a 19th round of airstrikes along with Saudi Arabia and the United Arab Emirates against ISIL forces across Syria. The US and partner nations carried out four strikes, three in Kobanî, destroying a fighting position and a staging area, and one strike northwest of Ar-Raqqah, destroying an armored vehicle compound.

Also, on October 12, the United States announced that the Turkish government had approved the use of Turkish military bases by coalition forces fighting ISIL in Syria and Iraq. These installations will include key bases only 100 miles from the Syrian border and important US military bases in Turkey such as the Incirlik Air Base. Despite the announcement of Turkish government approval, on October 13, Turkish officials denied that any agreement had been made over coalition use of Turkish Airbases including Incirlik.

In a 20th round of airstrikes in Syria on October 13, the United States and Saudi Arabia carried out eight airstrikes against ISIL forces in Syria. The United States and Saudi Arabia carried out seven strikes in and around Kobanî, striking a large ISIL unit, two small units; damaging one staging location and destroying another, destroying a heavy-machine-gun firing position, destroying three buildings, and damaging two others. One other strike northwest of Ar-Raqqah struck an ISIL garrison.

On October 14, the United States and Saudi Arabia carried out the 21st round and the largest set of strikes against ISIL in Syria since the beginning of the intervention, with 21 strikes against targets in and around Kobanî, and an additional strike near Deir ez-Zor. According to the Department of Defense, the strikes were designed to interdict ISIL reinforcements and resupply zones and prevent ISIL from massing combat power on the Kurdish held portions of Kobanî. The strikes destroyed two staging locations and damaged another, destroyed one ISIL building and damaged two others, damaged three ISIL compounds, destroyed one truck, one armed vehicle, and one other vehicle near Kobanî] in support of Kurdish forces resisting the siege of the town. In addition to those targets, the airstrikes struck seven staging areas, two mortar positions, three ISIL occupied buildings, and an artillery storage facility. An additional strike near Deir ez-Zor struck a modular oil refinery.

In a 22nd round of airstrikes on October 15, the United States carried out 18 strikes against ISIL targets in and around Kobanî. The strikes destroyed multiple fighting positions and also successfully struck sixteen ISIL-occupied buildings.

On October 16, the United States carried out a 23rd round of airstrikes with 14 airstrikes against ISIL targets in and around Kobanî striking nineteen ISIL controlled-buildings, two command posts, three fighting positions, three sniper positions, one staging location, and one heavy machine gun position.

In a 24th round of airstrikes on October 17, the United States carried out seven airstrikes against ISIL targets in and around Kobanî and in north-eastern Syria. Six airstrikes took place near Kobanî, striking three ISIL controlled buildings; destroyed two fighting positions, suppressed three fighting positions, and destroyed two vehicles. One other airstrike near Al-Shaddadeh struck ISIL-controlled oil collection equipment, including several petroleum, oil, and lubricants tanks, and a pump station.

On October 20, the United States carried out a 25th round of airstrikes, with six airstrikes against ISIL targets in and around Kobanî. The strikes destroyed ISIL fighting positions, ISIL mortar positions, a vehicle, and one stray equipment supply bundle from a U.S. airdrop of Kurdish supplies in order to prevent the supplies from being captured.

In a 26th round of airstrikes on October 21, the United States carried out four airstrikes against ISIL targets in and around Kobanî. The strikes destroyed several ISIL fighting positions, an ISIL controlled building, and a large ISIL unit. The British Royal Air Force began operating over Syria in a surveillance role on the same date, making the UK the first Western country other than the United States to operate in both Iraq and Syria simultaneously.

On October 22, the United States carried out a 27th round of airstrikes with six airstrikes against ISIL targets in and around Kobanî. The strikes destroyed several ISIL fighting positions, two ISIL vehicles, an ISIL controlled building and an ISIL logistical center.

In a 28th round of airstrikes on October 23, the United States carried out six airstrikes in and around Kobanî and near Deir ez-Zor. Four strikes destroyed several ISIL fighting positions, an ISIL vehicle, and an ISIL command and control center near Kobanî. Two strikes east of Deir ez-Zor destroyed several ISIL oil holding tanks.

On October 24, the United States carried out a 29th round of airstrikes with six airstrikes against ISIL targets in and around Kobanî. The strikes destroyed an ISIL vehicle and struck three ISIL units.

In a 30th round of airstrikes on October 25, the United States carried out one strike near Kobanî, destroying an ISIL artillery piece.

On October 26, the United States carried out a 31st round of airstrikes with five airstrikes against ISIL targets near Kobanî, destroying seven ISIL vehicles and an ISIL-controlled building.

In a 32nd round of airstrikes on October 27, the United States carried out four strikes near Kobanî, destroying five ISIL vehicles and an ISIL occupied building.

On October 28, the United States carried out a 33rd round of airstrikes, with four airstrikes against ISIL targets near Kobanî, destroying four ISIL fighting positions and a small ISIL unit.

In a 34th round of airstrikes on October 29, the United States carried out eight airstrikes in and around Kobanî. The strikes destroyed five ISIL fighting positions, a small ISIL unit, six ISIL vehicles, an ISIL controlled building, and an ISIL command and control node.

On October 30, the United States carried out a 35th round of airstrikes, with 12 airstrikes against ISIL targets in and around Kobanî, and against targets near Deir ez-Zor and Ar-Raqqah. Ten strikes near Kobanî struck two small ISIL units, destroyed seven ISIL fighting positions, and five ISIL controlled buildings. One strike near Deir ez-Zor damaged an ISIL headquarters building while another strike near Ar-Raqqah damaged an ISIL security building.

In a 36th round of airstrikes on October 31, the United States carried out four airstrikes in and around Kobanî, damaging four ISIL fighting positions and an ISIL controlled building.

November 2014

On November 1, the United States carried out a 37th round of airstrikes with five airstrikes against ISIL targets in and around Kobanî. The strikes suppressed or destroyed nine ISIL fighting positions, and struck one ISIL-controlled building.

In a 38th round of airstrikes on November 2, the United States carried out seven airstrikes in and around Kobanî and near Deir ez-Zor. Five airstrikes in and around Kobanî struck five small ISIL units and destroyed three ISIL vehicles. Two airstrikes southeast of Deir ez-Zor destroyed an ISIL tank and two vehicle shelters.

On November 3, the United States and coalition partners carried out a 39th round of airstrikes in and around Kobanî and near Deir ez-Zor. Four airstrikes in and around Kobanî struck an ISIL fighting position, a small ISIL unit, and destroyed two ISIL controlled buildings. One airstrike near Deir ez-Zor damaged an ISIL controlled building.

In a 40th round of airstrikes on November 4 and 5, the United States carried out six airstrikes in and around Kobanî and north of Sinjar just across the Iraqi-Syrian border into Syria. Three airstrikes in and around Kobanî struck a small ISIL unit, two ISIL fighting positions, and an ISIL dump truck that was used in the construction of fighting positions. One airstrike north of Sinjar destroyed an ISIL fighting position used to launch mortar attacks, and struck a small ISIL unit manning the position. Two additional strikes north of Sinjar struck a small ISIL unit and destroyed an ISIL armored vehicle.

On November 6 and 7, the United States carried out a 41st round of airstrikes in and around Kobanî and near Tal Abyad. Seven strikes in and around Kobanî struck three small ISIL units, seven ISIL fighting positions, and destroyed an ISIL artillery piece. One airstrike near Tal Abyad destroyed an ISIL weapons stockpile.

In a 42nd round of airstrikes between November 8 and November 10, the United States carried out 23 airstrikes in and around Kobanî and near Deir ez-Zor. Thirteen airstrikes conducted in and aroundKobanî struck an ISIL vehicle and five small ISIL units, destroyed an ISIL-occupied building used as an ammunition stockpile, an ISIL command and control building, and seven ISIL fighting positions, as well as damaging two ISIL fighting positions. In addition, eight airstrikes southeast of Deir ez-Zor damaged several structures of an ISIL oil collection facility, which was used to trans-load oil for the black market, while two airstrikes east of Deir ez-Zor damaged an ISIL oil collection point.

Between November 11 and 12, the United States carried out a 43rd round of airstrikes with sixteen airstrikes in and around Kobanî, near Deir ez-Zor, and near Al-Hasakah. Ten airstrikes conducted in and around Kobanî struck eight small ISIL units, damaged three ISIL fighting positions, and destroyed an ISIL logistics facility. Four airstrikes near Deir ez-Zor damaged an ISIL crude oil collection facility, struck a small ISIL unit, and damaged an ISIL vehicle. Two airstrikes near Al-Hasakah damaged a crude oil collection point.

In a 44th round of airstrikes between November 13 and 14, the United States carried out 20 airstrikes in and around Kobanî, east of Deir ez-Zor, west of Aleppo, and east of Ar-Raqqah. Seventeen airstrikes conducted in and around Kobanî struck ten ISIL units, destroyed 10 fighting positions, an ISIL controlled building, two ISIL vehicles, and an ISIL motorcycle. One airstrike east of Ar-Raqqah destroyed an ISIL training camp and another airstrike east of Deir ez-Zor destroyed an ISIL oil collection point. One other airstrike west of Aleppo struck militants associated with the Khorasan group.

Between November 15 and 17, the United States carried out a 45th round of airstrikes with eleven airstrikes in and around Kobanî and near Deir ez-Zor. Nine airstrikes in and around Kobanî destroyed seven ISIL fighting positions, suppressed an ISIL fighting position, destroyed four ISIL staging areas, and struck one tactical ISIL unit. Two airstrikes near Deir ez-Zor struck an ISIL crude oil collection facility and destroyed one ISIL tank.

In a 46th round of airstrikes between November 18 and 19, the United States carried out seven airstrikes in and around Kobanî, southeast of Al-Hasakah, and near Hazm. Five airstrikes in and around Kobanî destroyed an ISIL fighting position, an ISIL staging area and three ISIL controlled buildings, suppressed two ISIL fighting positions, struck two tactical ISIL units, and a large ISIL unit. One airstrike southeast of Al-Hasakah damaged a crude oil collection point operated by ISIL while another airstrike near Hazm struck and destroyed a storage facility associated with the Khorasan Group.

Between November 20 and 21, the United States and coalition partners carried out a 47th round of airstrikes with seven airstrikes in and around Kobanî and near Ar-Raqqah. Six airstrikes in and around Kobanî destroyed four ISIL staging areas, two ISIL controlled buildings, two ISIL tactical units, and suppressed an ISIL fighting position. One airstrike near Ar-Raqqah damaged an ISIL barracks building.

In a 48th round of airstrikes between November 22 and 24, the United States and coalition partners carried out nine airstrikes in and around Kobanî and near Ar-Raqqah. Seven airstrikes in and around Kobanî destroyed three ISIL fighting positions along with two ISIL staging areas, damaged an ISIL staging area, and suppressed four ISIL fighting positions. Two strikes near Ar-Raqqah struck an ISIL headquarters building.

Between November 25 and 26, the United States carried out a 49th round of airstrikes with ten airstrikes in and around Kobanî striking an ISIL fighting position, a large ISIL unit, two tactical ISIL units, and destroying four ISIL staging areasand six ISIL fighting positions.

In a 50th round of airstrikes between November 27 and 28, the United States carried out two airstrikes near Kobanî and Aleppo. One airstrike near Kobanî struck an ISIL fighting position and an ISIL staging area while one airstrike near Aleppo struck a tactical ISIL unit.

Between November 29 and December 1, the United States carried out a 51st round of airstrikes with 27 airstrikes in and around Kobanî, near Ar-Raqqah, and near Aleppo. Seventeen airstrikes nearKobanî destroyed two ISIL-occupied buildings, three ISIL tanks, three ISIL fighting positions, an ISIL armored personnel carrier, three ISIL vehicles and two ISIL staging areas. It also struck seven tactical ISIL units, targeted six ISIL fighting positions and damaged an ISIL controlled building. Nine airstrikes near Ar-Raqqah struck an ISIL electronic warfare garrison, an ISIL military garrison, an ISIL headquarters building, an ISIL jamming system, an ISIL tank and fourteen ISIL vehicles while one airstrike near Aleppo struck a target associated with the Khorasan Group.

December 2014

In a 52nd round of airstrikes between December 1 and 3, the United States carried out fourteen airstrikes in and around Kobanî destroying an ISIL vehicle, seventeen ISIL fighting positions, and an ISIL staging area, and suppressed eight other fighting positions and striking a large ISIL unit.

Between December 4 and 8, the United States and coalition partners carried out a 53rd round of airstrikes with fifteen airstrikes in and around Kobanî and near Ar-Raqqah. Fourteen airstrikes in and around Kobanî destroyed four ISIL fighting positions, three ISIL-occupied buildings, two ISIL staging areas, two ISIL tanks, an ISIL motorcycle, a mortar, and struck eight tactical ISIL units along with two ISIL fighting positions. One airstrike near Ar-Raqqah struck an ISIL electronic warfare garrison.

In a 54th round of airstrikes between December 9 and 10, the United States carried out seven airstrikes in and around Kobanî destroying five ISIL fighting positions, striking three ISIL fighting positions, and striking a large ISIL unit.

Between December 11 and 12, the United States and coalition partners carried out a 55th round of airstrikes with seven airstrikes in and around Kobanî, near Aleppo, and near Al-Qa'im. Five airstrikes in and around Kobanî destroyed five ISIL fighting positions and struck one ISIL fighting position. One airstrike near Aleppo struck five ISIL-occupied buildings while another airstrike near Al-Qa'im on the Syrian border destroyed two ISIL fortifications.

In a 56th round of airstrikes between December 13 and 15, the United States and coalition partners carried out nine airstrikes in and around Kobanî and near Al-Bukamal. Eight airstrikes in and around Kobanî destroyed nine ISIL fighting positions, two ISIL controlled buildings, and two ISIL staging positions as well as striking one ISIL fighting position. One airstrike near Al-Bukamal destroyed an ISIL vehicle.

Between December 16 and 17, the United States and coalition partners carried out a 57th round of airstrikes with six airstrikes in and around Kobanî and near Al-Bukamal. Five airstrikes in and around Kobanî destroyed an ISIL controlled building, one ISIL staging area, one ISIL bunker, and an ISIL mortar, and strucktwo ISIL tactical units, two additional buildings, and two ISIL fighting positions. One airstrike near Al-Bukamal destroyed an ISIL tactical vehicle.

In a 58th round of airstrikes on December 18, the United States and coalition partners carried out six airstrikes in and around Kobanî destroying seven ISIL fighting positions and an ISIL building, and struckj an ISIL tactical unit.

On December 19, the United States and coalition partners carried out a 59th round of airstrikes with four strikes in and around Kobanî and near Ar-Raqqah. Three airstrikes in and around Kobanî destroyed two ISIL controlled buildings and an ISIL staging area as well as striking two ISIL tactical units. One airstrike near Ar-Raqqah damaged an ISIL training compound.

In a 60th round of airstrikes on December 20, the United States and coalition partners carried out five airstrikes in and around Kobanî destroying eight ISIL fighting positions.

On December 21, the United States and coalition partners carried out a 61st round of airstrikes with three strikes in and around Kobanî destroying an ISIL staging position and two ISIL fighting positions as well as striking two ISIL fighting positions.

In a 62nd round of airstrikes on December 22, the United States and coalition partners carried out 12 airstrikes in and around Kobanî, near Aleppo, near Al-Hasakah, and near Ar-Raqqah. Six airstrikes in and around Kobanî destroyed six ISIL fighting positions and struck four ISIL fighting positions and an ISIL tactical unit. Three airstrikes near Aleppodestroyed artillery equipment and struck 10 ISIL buildings, two airstrikes near Al-Hasakah destroyed an ISIL tactical vehicle, two ISIL trucks, an ISIL building, and two ISIL storage containers, and one airstrike near Ar-Raqqah destroyed an ISIL checkpoint complex.

On December 23, the United States and coalition partners carried out a 63rd round of airstrikes with seven airstrikes in and around Kobanî and near Bargooth. Six airstrikes in and around Kobanî destroyed seven ISIL fighting positions, an ISIL building and struck several ISIL fighting positions and one airstrike near Barghooth struck ISIL oil collection equipment.

In a 64th round of airstrikes on December 24, the United States and coalition partners carried out ten airstrikes in and around Kobanî, near Deir ez-Zor, and near Ar-Raqqah. Eight airstrikes in and around Kobanî destroyed five ISIL fighting positions, an ISIL building, an ISIL staging position, and struck three ISIL tactical units, an ISIL tactical vehicle and an ISIL fighting position. One airstrike near Deir ez-Zor struck a crude oil collection point and another airstrike near Ar-Raqqah struck an ISIL weapons stockpile.

On December 25, the United States and coalition partners carried out a 65th round of airstrikes with fifteen airstrikes in and around Kobanî, near Al-Hasakah, and near Ar-Raqqah. Thirteen airstrikes in and around Kobanî destroyed three ISIL buildings, one ISIL vehicle, 17 ISIL fighting positions, two ISIL staging positions as well as striking two ISIL fighting positions, three large ISIL units and four ISIL tactical units. One airstrike near Al-Hasakah struck an ISIL drilling tower and destroyed 2 ISIL support vehicles and another airstrike near Ar-Raqqah struck an ISIL assembly area.

In a 66th round of airstrikes on December 26, the United States and coalition partners carried out four airstrikes in and around Kobanî, destroying three ISIL buildings and two ISIL vehicles.

On December 29, the United States and coalition partners carried out a 67th round of airstrikes with twelve airstrikes in and around Kobanî, near Deir ez-Zor, and near Ar-Raqqah. Ten airstrikes in and around Kobanî destroyed 11 ISIL fighting positions, two ISIL buildings, and an ISIL storage container, and struck an ISIL tactical unit. One airstrike near Deir ez-Zor struck several ISIL controlled buildings while another airstrike near Ar-Raqqah also struck several ISIL controlled buildings.

In a 68th round of airstrikes on December 30, the United States and coalition partners carried out seven airstrikes in and around Kobanî and near Deir ez-Zor. Six airstrikes in and around Kobanî destroyed three ISIL buildings, damaged one ISIL building, and struck an ISIL tactical unit while one airstrike near Deir ez-Zor destroyed an ISIL shipping container.

On December 31, the United States and coalition partners carried out a 69th round of airstrikes with seven airstrikes in and around Kobanî and near Al-Hasakah. Five airstrikes in and around Kobanî destroyed five ISIL buildings and six ISIL fighting positions while two airstrikes near Al-Hasakah destroyed four oil derricks controlled by ISIL.

January 2015

In a 70th round of airstrikes on January 1, the United States and coalition partners carried out 17 airstrikes in and around Kobanî, near Deir ez-Zor, and near Ar-Raqqah. Thirteen airstrikes in and around Kobanî destroyed 12 ISIL controlled buildings, four ISIL fighting positions, one ISIL vehicle as well as striking two ISIL tactical units and two large ISIL units. Two airstrikes near Ar-Raqqah destroyed five ISIL checkpoints and struck an ISIL staging area, while two airstrikes near Deir ez-Zor destroyed an ISIL fighting position and struck an ISIL shipping container.

February 2015

On February 5, 2015, Jordan elevated its role in the U.S.-led coalition in Syria, launching one of the largest airstrike campaigns since early January 2015, targeting ISIL militants near Ar-Raqqah, the *de facto* ISIL capital, inflicting an unknown number of casualties and damaging ISIL facilities. This was done in retaliation against ISIL's brutal murder of Muath al-Kasasbeh.

On February 6, a continued round of Coalition airstrikes at Ar-Raqqah killed over 30 ISIL militants.

On February 21, Syrian Kurds launched an offensive to retake ISIL-held territories in the Al-Hasakah Governorate, specifically in the Tell Hamis area, with support from US airstrikes. At least 20 villages were liberated, and 12 militants were killed in the clashes. In response, on 23 February, ISIL abducted 150 Assyrian Christians from villages near near Tal Tamr (Tell Tamer) in northeastern Syria, after launching a large offensive in the region.

As a result of ISIL's massive offensive in the west Al-Hasakah Governorate, the US-led coalition increased the number of airstrikes in the region to 10, on February 24, in order to halt the ISIL advance. The airstrikes struck nine ISIL tactical units and destroyed two ISIL vehicles.

On February 26, the number of Assyrian Christians abducted by ISIL from villages in northeastern Syria from February 23–25 rose to at least 220, according to the Syrian Observatory for Human Rights (SOHR), a monitoring group based in Britain.

On February 27, the Kurdish Democratic Union Party and Syrian Observatory for Human Rights reported that Kurdish fighters had recaptured the town of Tal Hamis, along with most of the villages occupied by ISIL in the region.

At least 127 ISIL militants were killed in the clashes, along with 30 YPG and allied fighters.

One Australian volunteer, who was fighting for the YPG, was also killed. Many of the remaining ISIL militants retreated to Tell Brak, which quickly came under assault from the YPG and allied Arab fighters.

March 2015

On March 1, 2015, YPG fighters, aided by US airstrikes, were able to drive ISIL militants out of Tell Brak, reducing the ISIL occupation in the eastern Jazira Canton to the villages between Tell Brak and Tal Hamis.

On March 6, it was reported that Abu Humam al-Shami, al-Nusra's military chief, was killed in a US airstrike targeting a meeting of top al-Nusra leaders, at the al-Nusra Front's new headquarters at Salqin.

On March 9, the US carried out another airstrike on the al-Nusra Front, targeting a military camp near Atimah, close to the Turkish border in the Idlib Governorate. The airstrike left 9 militants dead.

On March 24, Canadian Prime Minister Stephen Harper announced that Canada would be looking to expand Operation Impact to include airstrikes against ISIL in Syria as well.

On March 26, the United Kingdom Ministry of Defence announced the deployment of around 75 military trainers and headquarter staff to Turkey, and other nearby countries in the anti-ISIL coalition, to assist with the U.S.-led training programme in Syria. The training programme will provide small arms, infantry tactics and medical training to Syrian moderate opposition forces for over three years.

On March 30, the House of Commons of Canada authorized the extended deployment of its military for one year and the war in Syria.

April 2015

On April 8, Canada initiated airstrikes in Syria, with two CF-18 fighters bombing a former military installation of the Syrian government that was captured by ISIL, near its headquarters in ar-Raqqah.

May 2015

On May 15, after surveillance by British special forces confirmed the presence of a senior leader named Abu Sayyaf in al-Amr, 1st SFOD-Delta operators from the Joint Special Operations Command based in Iraq conducted an operation to capture him. The operation resulted in his death when he tried to engage U.S. forces in combat and the capture of his wife Umm Sayyaf. The operation also led to the freeing of a Yazidi woman who was held as a slave. About a dozen ISIL fighters were also killed in the raid, two U.S. officials said. The SOHR reported that an additional 19 ISIL fighters were killed in the US airstrikes that accompanied the raid. One official said that ISIL Forces fired at the U.S. aircraft, and there was reportedly hand-to-hand combat during the raid. UH-60 Black Hawk and V-22 Ospreyhelicopters were used to conduct the raid, and Umm Sayyaf is currently being held by U.S. Forces in Iraq.

July 2015

Following a suicide bombing in the Þanlýurfa Province of Turkey believed to have been carried out by ISIL militants on 20 July, as well as an ISIL cross-border attack that killed a Turkish serviceman on 23 July, Turkish armour and aircraft struck ISIL targets just across the border inSyria. Turkey also agreed to let the United States use the USAF Incirlik Air Base for strikes against ISIL.

August 2015

On 21 August, three Islamic State fighters, two with UK nationality, were targeted and killed in Raqqa, Syria by a British Royal Air ForceMQ-9 Reaper strike. Prime Minister David Cameron gave a statement to Parliament that one of the British nationals targeted had been plotting attacks in the United Kingdom. Another

British national was killed in a separate air strike by US forces in Raqqa on 24 August.

October 2015

The introduction of Russian aircraft and ship based cruise missiles in support of the Syrian Government to Syrian airspace creates new threats to the US-led coalition. Discussions are held to deconflict Syrian airspace.

On 10 October, the state run Syrian Arab News Agency reported claims that two U.S. F16 jets had "violated Syrian airspace" and bombed two electricity power plants in al-Rudwaniya, east Aleppo, "in breach of international law".

On 20 October Canada's Prime Minister elect Justin Trudeau informed Barack Obama by phone of Canada's intention to pull out of bombing raids in Syria. Canada will remain a coalition partner but will stop strikes.

November 2015

After the deadly attacks in Paris, French President Francois Hollande sent its only aircraft carrier, the Charles de Gaulle, with its 26 fighters to intensify air strikes.

On 27 November, Syrian Arab News Agency reported The US-led international coalition, allegedly fighting ISIS, targeted water pumping stations in al-Khafseh area, east of Aleppo, causing them to go out of service.

December 2015

On 2 December 2015, the Members of the Parliament of the United Kingdom voted 397 to 223 in favour of airstrikes in Syria. Within hours, RAF Tornado jets carried out their first air strikes, targeting the Omar oil fields in eastern Syria, which is under IS control.

On 6 December 2015, a Syrian Arab Army base at Deir ez-Ezzor was struck, killing at least 1 Syrian Arab Army soldier, with reports circulating that as many as 4 were killed, 13 wounded and 2 tanks destroyed. Syria accused the US of conducting the strike, however US officials denied this, claiming instead that the bombing was a mistake by Russians.

After the US strikes, ISIS forces began to attack the base.

Airstrikes on the Khorasan Group

One of the groups targeted by U.S. airstrikes was the Khorasan Group, an extremist group of suspected al-Qaeda "core" members who were alleged to have been plotting an attack against the U.S. and other Western nations. The strikes targeted Khorasan training camps, explosives and munitions production facilities, communications facilities, as well as command and control facilities. The group has been claimed to possess advanced bomb making skills and their plot is claimed to involve a bomb made of a nonmetallic device such as a toothpaste container or clothes dipped in explosive material. The group is reportedly led by Muhsin al-Fadhli, a leader of al-Qaeda and a close confidant of Osama bin Laden. Intelligence officials expressed concern that the group may include militants who were taught by Ibrahim al-Asiri, the chief bomb maker for al-Qaeda in the Arabian Peninsula, who is known for his sophisticated bomb making techniques that nearly downed two Western airliners.

Later statements by government officials indicated that the threat of a plot may have been less severe than initially reported. One official indicated that "there did not yet seem to be a concrete plan in the works", while another told *The Guardian* that "there was no indication of an imminent domestic threat from the group" at the time the United States began bombing.

On November 6, a second round of airstrikes was launched against Khorasan and al-Nusra in northwestern Syria, along with Ahrar ash-Sham at its headquarters in Idlib, whose leadership had been infiltrated by al-Qaeda. On November 13, 2014, the US launched a third set of airstrikes against Khorasan. On November 19, the US carried out another airstrike on Khorasan near Hazm, which struck and destroyed a storage facility associated with the group. On December 1, the US carried out another airstrike on Khorasan near Aleppo.

On 24 March 2015, it was revealed that the US airstrikes on Khorasan had killed 17 militants from the group.

On 8 July 2015, a US airstrike near the town of Sarmada in Idlib, Syria, killed Muhsin al-Fadhli, the leader of Khorasan.

SYRIAN REACTION TO THE AIRSTRIKES

Syrian military radar was "passive" during the first air strikes, with no attempt to counter US aircraft. During the first night of airstrikes, the United States' force deployed with HARM missiles as a precaution, as it was uncertain how Syria's air-defense network would react.

Civilian Casualties

On September 29, 2014, several groups including the Syrian Observatory for Human Rights, the Aleppo Media Center, and the Local Coordination Committees reported that U.S. strikes hit a grain silo in the ISIL-controlled town of Manbij in northern Syria, killing two civilians.

The Syrian Observatory for Human Rights reported ten airstrikes, also targeting various parts of the province of Idlib, killed at least one child and six other civilians. The group said at least 19 civilians had been killed in coalition airstrikes at that time. The Pentagon reported it had no evidence of any civilian casualties from airstrikes targeting militants in Syria. The United States has also acknowledged that its rules to avoid civilian casualties are looser in Syria than those for drone strikes elsewhere.

The SOHR and other activist groups, reported that seven civilians were killed when an air strike hit a gas distribution facility near the town of al-Khasham is the eastern Deir al-Zor province on October 17, 2014 and three civilians were killed in an air strike on October 16, 2014 in the north east province of al-Hassakah. According to their reports, most of the civilians killed were fuel tanker drivers.

According to Reuters, 50 civilians were killed in Syria by US-led airstrikes, since the start of the campaign in late September 2014. On December 28, 2014, a U.S. airstrike in the northern Syrian town of Al-Bab killed more than 50 civilians.

On May 21, 2015, the United States admitted it "probably" killed two children in bombings near Harem on November 4 and 5, 2014. These are the first such admissions of the campaign, and followed a military investigation. A similar investigation regarding an event in Syria is underway, and two regarding events in Iraq.

Two adult civilians were also minorly injured in the Harem strikes. The deaths and injuries are attributed by the military investigation to unintentional secondary explosions, after the bombers hit their intended targets, linked to theKhorasan.

AIR SUPPLY

On October 20, 2014 the United States began airdropping supplies to Syrian Kurdish forces, including the YPG, in Kobanî. The Kurdish forces there have been engaged in battle with ISIL during the Siege of Kobanî. Prior to October 20, the United States and its coalition partners fighting against ISIL in Syria, had not provided any supplies to Kurdish forces in their fight against ISIL.

Much of the reason for US having to airdrop supplies was due to the Turkish government's refusal to allow supplies to pass through their border into Kobanî.

The U.S. specifically airdropped weapons, ammunition, and medical supplies supplied by Iraqi Kurdistan specifically to supply the Kurdish forces in Syria. On October 21, a video was released by ISIL showing what it claimed was a bundle of airdropped small arms, ammunition, and other supplies from the United States. The Pentagon said it was analyzing the video and could not at the time confirm whether the video was authentic but that the materials were similar and video would be analyzed by the Department of Defense to analyze its authenticity. On October 22, the Pentagon confirmed that one of the airdrops had been intercepted by ISIL but that it most likely would not give ISIL any real advantage in their operations.

Ground Forces

During the beginning of the coalition interventions, leaders including U.S. President Obama, said coalition ground forces would not be used in the fight against ISIL either in Iraq or Syria unless they were local coalition forces. While in Iraq thousands of coalition troops from the United States and other nations have been deployed in an advisory capacity, in Syria no ground troops from the coalition intervening in Syria were deployed in the beginning of the intervention.

While there were no coalition ground forces in Syria originally, the US government has said that it wants to spend $500 million to fund the training and arming of up to 5,000 moderate rebels to function as ground forces against ISIL.

Under the original plan, the rebels would be trained in Saudi Arabia and other unnamed countries and then return to fight in Syria. The 'moderate' opposition groups that are expected to be armed and trained by the US government include the Free Syrian Army, which is a network of hundreds of smaller rebel groups along with the Syria Revolutionaries Front.

In mid-September 2014, the US Congress approved the plan to arm and fund rebels in Syria. In October 2014, the Turkish government agreed to help train and equip some moderate Syrian rebels in Turkey. The Turkish government agreed to allow the training of at least 2,000 moderate rebels in Turkey by U.S. and Turkish special forces with the rebels being trained in groups of 400. According to Turkish officials, the rebels would be chosen by the country's MIT intelligence service using its databases in order to select and screen an initial 2,000 rebels to undergo training.

As the Siege of Kobanî continued there were growing calls to also arm the YPG, also known as the People's Protection Units, a Kurdish fighting force in Syria heavily involved in the defense of Kobanî. On October 20, 2014, the Turkish foreign minister, Mevlüt Çavuþoðluannounced that the Turkish government would be allowing peshmerga from the Iraqi Kurdistan Regional Government to cross their border into Kobanî to support Kurdish fighters.

The change in policy came after the Turkish government had refused to allow Kurdish fighters and supplies to pass through the border to YPG units in Kobanî, as it viewed the YPG as an offshoot of the PKK. On October 28,Peshmerga from the Iraqi Kurdistan Regional Government departed Erbil to travel to Turkey and eventually to Kobanî. A total of 152 soldiers were deployed starting with forty vehicles carrying weapons, artillery, and machine guns, along with 80 Peshmerga forces, who crossed the border into Turkey by land with the heavy weapons and then drove to the border near Kobanî. The other 72 soldiers in the contingent flew to Turkey and rejoined the rest of the contingent on October 29. On October 29, 152 Kurdish Peshmerga from Iraq and 50 Free Syrian Army fighters crossed the border into Kobanî with heavy weapons, small arms, and ammunition.

NAMING OF OPERATION INHERENT RESOLVE

Unlike previous U.S. combat operations, no name had been given to the American intervention in Syria and Iraq until it was announced in mid-October that the operational name would be Inherent Resolve. The decision to keep the conflict nameless drew considerable media criticism.

TURKISH INVOLVEMENT

Turkey, a NATO member, has been involved in the Syrian Civil War since the beginning of hostilities. Turkey has trained and armed some members of the Free Syrian Army, and has been involved in certain spillover incidents, however so far Turkey has not been involved in direct combat. On October 2, 2014, the Turkish Parliament authorized direct military action in both Iraq and Syria including using military force in Syria and Iraq as well as allowing coalition members to use bases in Turkey.Turkey has also stationed troops and tanks on its southern border near the Syrian border city of Kobanî.

The Turkish government demanded several things to go along with them intervening against ISIL, including a buffer zone in Northern Syria, a no-fly zone over certain parts of northern Syria, ground troops from other countries, and the training of moderate opposition forces to fight both ISIL and al-Assad.

Turkey also holds sovereignty over the Tomb of Suleyman Shah 35 km inside Syria, where it maintains a small garrison of Special forces that is surrounded by ISIL-controlled territory.

On 22 February 2015, the Turkish Army mounted a rescue operation across the border to evacuate its soldiers from the Tomb of Suleyman Shah, an exclave of Turkey south of Kobanî. The Turkish convoy reportedly transited through Kurdish-held Kobanî *en route* to the tomb. One Turkish soldier was killed in what

Ankara described as an accident. The success of the operation was announced 22 February by Turkish Prime Minister Ahmet Davutoðlu.

REACTIONS

Foreign Reactions

- Australia – Tony Abbott, the Prime Minister of Australia, praised the intervention, saying that an international effort was needed in order to combat the ISIL threat. Despite Abbott's support for the intervention, the Australian Government said it is not likely to contribute forces to operations in Syria.
- Canada – Stephen Harper, the Prime Minister of Canada, said in October 2014 Canada would strike ISIL targets in Syria if the Assad government gave approval. New Prime Minister Justin Trudeau called President Obama almost immediately after coming into office to inform him that Canada was pulling out of the coalition and ceasing all air operations in coordination with Americans. Trudeau did not give a time frame.
- Czech Republic – Lubomír Zaorálek, the Minister of Foreign Affairs of the Czech Republic supported the intervention against the Islamic State and said that it's important to keep supporting the ground forces in the battle against ISIS and the Czech Republic will keep providing military support to the Iraqi army and to the Kurdish Peshmerga. He also noted that air strikes won't defeat Islamic State. The Czech government said that ISIS is enemy not only for safety in the Middle East, but also for security and stability in the Czech Republic and Europe.
- Ecuador – The Ecuadorian government opposed the airstrikes in Syria without the consent of the Syrian government.
- Egypt - Egyptian President Abdel Fattah el-Sisi expressed his government's support for the international campaign against ISIL, and a spokesperson for the Egyptian foreign

ministry echoed his statements by reiterating the Egyptian government's willingness to back the war against ISIL.

- Germany - German foreign minister Frank-Walter Steinmeier questioned whether President Obama's plan was adequate in order to combat ISIL and said Germany had not been asked to participate in airstrikes nor would it participate if asked.
- Iran - Iranian President Hassan Rouhani condemned ISIL's actions but also called the airstrikes in Syria "illegal" because they were conducted without the consent of the Syrian government. Iran's deputy foreign minister Hossein Amir Abdollahian was reported in Iranian media as saying that Iran had warned the United States that Israel would be at risk should the US and its allies seek to topple Syrian president Bashar al-Assad while fighting ISIL in Syria.
- Israel - Israeli Prime Minister Benjamin Netanyahu said Israel fully supported the U.S. government's calls for united action against ISIL.
- Japan - A spokesperson for the Japanese Ministry of Foreign Affairs said the Japanese government would continue to closely coordinate with the United States and other countries, along with offering support and cooperation in their strikes against ISIL.
- Netherlands – Mark Rutte, the Prime Minister of the Netherlands, showed understanding for the intervention against ISIL in Syria and said that his government was exploring options to contribute in the fight against ISIL.
- Russia – Alexander Lukashevich, Russian Foreign Ministry spokesman, opposed the military intervention "without the consent of the legitimate government" and said that "this step, in the absence of a UN Security Council decision, would be an act of aggression, a gross violation of international law". On 14 October, Russian Foreign Minister Sergey Lavrov questioned the motives of the intervention, saying "Maybe their stated goal is not entirely sincere? Maybe it is regime change?" He also questioned the effectiveness of the year long campaign "With, as far as I

know, 25,000 sorties they [US-led air campaign] could have smashed the entire [country of] Syria into smithereens," continuing to remark that "positive results 'on the ground' are not visible". He also criticized the continued supply of arms to rebels, saying "I want to be honest, we barely have any doubt that at least a considerable part of these weapons will fall into the terrorists' hands." He continued to call for the countries involved to join a coalition made up of Russian, Syrian, Iranian, Iraqi, Jordanian and Hezbollah forces against what Russia claims is solely ISIL and al Qaeda, but the US has asserted is primarily non-jihadist opposition forces.

- Turkey – The Davutoglu Government called on the Grand National Assembly of Turkey to approve measures that would grant extensive authority to the President to launch military operations in both Syria and Iraq, including the authority to send troops across the border, although it is unclear whether the Turkish leadership intends to act on that authority. President Recep Tayyip Erdoðan has urged the establishment of a no-fly zone by coalition forces in northern Syria.
- United Kingdom – A spokesperson for British Prime Minister David Cameron said the UK would not rule out airstrikes in Syria against ISIL. On September 26, 2014 Parliament voted 524 to 43 to approve action inside Iraq. While visiting Iraqi Kurdistan in mid October, British Foreign Secretary Philip Hammond said he saw no immediate demand from U.S. and Arab militaries for Britain to extend its airstrikes to Syria. British Defense Minister Michael Fallon said on October 21 that British Reaper drones and Rivet Joint surveillance aircraft would be starting intelligence-gathering missions in Syria "very shortly."
- United Nations – Ban Ki-moon, UN secretary-general, welcomed the airstrikes against militants in Syria, but noted that the involved parties "must abide by international humanitarian law and take all precautions to avoid and minimize civilian casualties".

- Venezuela – At the 69th General Assembly of the United Nations, President Nicolas Maduro said "It's President Bashar al-Assad and the Syrian government which have stopped the terrorists" and continued by saying "Instead of bombing and bombing, we must make an alliance for peace".

Syrian Reactions

- Syria – A week before the first airstrikes, Ali Haidar, the Syrian Minister of National Reconciliation, said that "any action of any kind without the consent of the Syrian government would be an attack on Syria". However, despite Haidar's original statement, after the coalition campaign began, the Syrian government struck a more conciliatory tone with Foreign Minister Walid al-Moallem suggesting the airstrikes were an indication that Syria and the anti-ISIL coalition were on the same side.
- Syrian opposition – Hadi Bahra, the leader of the National Coalition for Syrian Revolutionary and Opposition Forces called for airstrikes against ISIL before the intervention began. The coalition is recognized by 20 countries, the European Union, and the Arab league as the legitimate representative of Syria in opposition to the Assad government. Bahra said strikes were needed to weaken ISIL, a faction in the inter-rebel conflict during the Syrian Civil War, so that the Free Syrian Army and other moderate opposition forces could oppose Assad more effectively. Despite Bahra's support, many Syrian rebel groups have criticized U.S. airstrikes for targeting only ISIL who are enemies of the Assad government, while not also targeting Assad government forces, the results of which could help government forces gain more ground. Meanwhile, jihadist groups within the opposition have portrayed the coalition as an anti-Sunni stooge of the Syrian regime, while many Sunnis in Syria are angered that only extremist Sunnis are being targeted while mostly Shiite Assad forces aren't targeted. Some rebels defected to extremist groups as a result of the U.S. decision to strike jihadist groups other than ISIL, such as the al-Nusra Front.

8

Foreign Involvement in the Syrian Civil War againt ISIS

In what French President Francois Hollande called "an act of war" against his country, on November 13 several attackers staged a complex assault involving shootings and suicide bombings in Paris that left 129 people dead.

ISIS has claimed responsibility, citing France's participation in the "crusader campaign" against the group.

Syrian President Bashar al-Assad was unsympathetic, blaming French policy toward his country: "We said, don't take what is happening in Syria lightly. Unfortunately, European officials did not listen." France is one of 65 members of the U.S.-led international coalition against the Islamic State, and one of eight that has conducted airstrikes against the group in Syria.

France's direct combat involvement in Syria is fairly recent; having enlisted in international airstrikes in Iraq last year, in September France joined a long list of combatants in Syria's civil war by bombing an ISIS training camp in the country.

(David Graham has more here on France's campaigns against ISIS and its affiliates in Syria and elsewhere.) That participation seems destined to expand; two days after the Paris attacks, France's defense ministry announced it was conducting airstrikes against the Islamic State's de facto capital of Raqqa, Syria, and U.S. officials were reportedly sharing intelligence on ISIS targets with their French counterparts.

THE WEST CREATED & PERPETUATES THE SYRIAN CIVIL WAR

In 2014, Obama stated "we must ... [pursue] the political solution necessary to solve Syria's crisis once and for all."

Senator McCain as well recently said "But what haunts me even more than the horror unfolding before our eyes in Syria is the thought that we will continue to do nothing meaningful about it."

However it is helpful to ask, are our leaders at all serious in their remarks?

Since at least as far back as 2005, the US has been financing and training anti-government opposition in Syria with a view toward regime-change. When members of these US-funded groups complain about their connections to America, concerned over serving foreign interests rather than the national cause, evidence from Egypt shows that they are quickly ousted from membership.

The ostensible justification for this funding is 'democracy promotion,' however we should remember what International Relations scholar John J. Mearsheimersaid about Washington's democracy promotion activities abroad.

Referring to the crisis in Ukraine, he stated, "and when you talk about promoting democracy, what you're really talking about is putting in power leaders who are pro-Western and anti-Russian ... promoting democracy, which was all about putting in power pro-Western leaders."

However, Syria was in the crosshairs of the empire long before 2005. In a 2007 speech, General Wesley Clark recounts a conversation he had with then Undersecretary of Defense Paul Wolfowitz in 1991 regarding Operation Desert Storm.

He quotes Wolfowitz as saying "one thing that we learned is that we can use our military in the Middle East and the Soviets won't stop us, and we got about 5 or 10 years to clean up those old Soviet client regimes, Syria, Iran, Iraq, before the next great superpower comes on to challenge us."

In the same speech, Clark recounts another conversation he had 6 weeks after 9/11 with an officer of the Joint Chiefs of Staff.

The officer he quoted refered to a classified memo received from the Secretary of Defense's office which stated that it was US policy to attack and destroy the governments of 7 different countries in the next 5 years, starting with Iraq, then Syria, Lebanon, Libya, Somalia, Sudan, and finishing off with Iran.

Long before any outrage was generated at Assad's crackdown of protesters, and long before any pretexts or justifications were concocted, it was already decided that the US would attack and topple the Syrian government, going at least as far back as 1991. The intention of regime change came first, propaganda and pretexts came later.

Further adding to this evidence is the testimony of former French Foreign Minister Roland Dumas, who stated on television that, roughly 2 years before hostilities began in Syria, British officials admitted to him that they were 'preparing something' in the country.

"England was preparing the invasion of the rebels in Syria," he said, stating that the officials had asked him to participate, to which he refused. "This is to say that this operation comes from far away. It was prepared, conceived, and organized ... in the simple purpose of removing the Syrian government, because, in the region, it is important to know that this Syrian regime has anti-Israel remarks ... I'm judging the confidence of the Israeli Prime Minister who had told me a while ago: 'We will try to get along with the neighboring states, and those who don't get along, we will take them down.' It is a policy. It is a conception of history."

Eventually this policy, this conception of history, coupled with the financing of regime-change opposition groups, deteriorating social conditions, and the legitimate need for reforms, culminated in very minor, small-scale and sporadic anti-government demonstrations in Syria in early 2011. The real unrest began in mid-March when clashes between protesters and police occurred in the southern city of Daraa.

From that point, the conflict began to escalate. Media reports in the West became flooded with news of Assad's violent crackdown of protesters. The Syrian government is in no way justified for violent suppression of peaceful demonstrations with brutal military crackdowns, however little attention was paid to the fact that at this time the protesters had as well been armed, and had been attacking the security forces, or the fact that significant pro-government demonstrations also occurred.

In Daraa, the unrest began when demonstrators destroyed governmental buildings which prompted a response from the government. It should be noted however that those protesting in Daraa were largely motivated by genuine desire for change and in opposition to abuse of power, much like our own Occupy and Black Lives Matter movements in the West, and the courage shown by these individuals to demonstrate in a state where doing so meant harsh and brutal repressions deserves to be honored and commended. However the possibility of foreign involvement threatened to exploit the unrest and usurp the population's hardships for non-domestic interests, to use the Syrians blood, sweat, and tears to achieve their own self-interested geopolitical goals. Thus while facing government repression another more daunting challenge faced the local demonstrators as well.

Amid reports of violent crackdowns, Israeli National News reported March 21st that "Seven police and at least four demonstrators in Syria have been killed in continuing violent clashes that erupted in the southern town of Daraa last Thursday." [Emphasis mine] The report indicates that although the government's response had been brutal, the opposition was not altogether peaceful, but instead were armed and firing at police. There were more police killed than protesters in this incident.

FOREIGN INVOLVE IN THE SYRIAN CIVIL WAR

Foreign involvement in the Syrian Civil War refers to political, military and operational support to parties involved in the ongoing conflict in Syria that began in March 2011, as well as active foreign involvement. Most parties involved in the war in Syria receive various types of support from foreign countries and entities based outside Syria. The ongoing conflict in Syria is widely described as a series of overlapping proxy wars between the regional and world powers, primarily between the U.S. and Russia as well as between Iranand Saudi Arabia.

The Syrian Ba'athist government is politically and militarily supported by Iran and Russia, actively supported by Lebanese Hezbollah party and by Syrian-based Palestinian group PFLP-GC and others.

The Syrian opposition, politically represented by theSyrian National Coalition, receives financial, logistical, political and in some cases military support from major Sunni states in the Middle East allied with the U.S., most notably Saudi Arabia, Qatar, and Turkey. From early stages of the civil conflict in Syria, major Western countries such as the U.S, France, and the UK provide political, military and logistic support to the opposition as well as rebel groups in Syria that are not designated by them as terrorist.

The predominantly Kurdish People's Protection Units (YPG), the main armed service of the Kurdish Supreme Committee, the government of Syrian Kurdistan (Rojava), have received military and logistic support from Iraqi Kurdistan and air support by U.S., Canada, British and French air force. The Salafist groups are partially supported by Turkey, while the Islamic State of Iraq and the Levant received support from several non-state groups and organizations from across the Muslim World.

As a significant part of Syria2 s territory is since 2014 claimed by Islamic State (ISIL), an entity internationally recognised as terrorist, a number of Western and other countries, most notably the U.S., Russia and France, participate in direct military action against ISIL in the territory of Syria.

Since 30 September 2015, Russia, the only foreign power that has its military assets openly deployed in Syria, wages an intensive air campaign against the ISIL and other anti-government forces in Syria, on the side and at the request of the Syrian government. The military activity of Russia in Syria has been criticized by the U.S. and its regional allies; Turkey overtly clashed with the Russian military in November 2015 over the alleged violation of its airspace by a Russian plane as well as over Russia2 s bombardment of the areas held by anti-government forces that are supported by Turkey, especially in the Bayýrbucak region. Since July 2015, Turkey also openly and actively opposes further expansion of the Syrian Kurdish forces along its border.

SUPPORT FOR THE SYRIAN GOVERNMENT

Russia

Russia is a military ally of Syria since 1956, and during the Syrian Civil War it continued supplying Assad's government with arms, sending military and technical advisers to train Syrian soldiers to use the Russian-made weapons, and it helped repair and maintain Syrian weapons. Investigations by reporters suggest that Russia is helping to keep the Syrian economy afloat by transporting hundreds of tonnes of banknotes into the country by airplane.

In December 2012, it was reported that Russian military personnel under the guise of military advisers were inside Syria manning some of the anti-aircraft defenses sent by Russia. The depth and sophistication of Syria's air defences was cited as a major reason for the U.S. decision not to intervene militarily against the Syrian government or impose a no-fly zone, despite publicly voiced commitment to do so if the Assad government crossed the "red line" of using chemical weapons.

Western leaders and diplomats repeatedly criticized Russia's support of the Syrian government; Russia stressed that its actions did not violate international law. In June 2012, Russian presidentVladimir Putin said Russia did not not support "any side [in the conflict] from which the threat of a civil war may emerge".

In December 2013, Russia was reported to have stepped up its military support for the Syrian government by supplying new armored vehicles, surveillance equipment, radars, electronic warfare systems, spare parts for helicopters, and various weapons including guided bombs for planes.

On 30 September 2015, with permission of the upper house of the Russian Parliament, Russia started a direct military intervention in Syria consisting of air strikes against ISIL, the Al-Nusra Front, and other perceived enemies of the Syrian government. The Russian Orthodox Church official spokesman called the intervention by Russia in Syria a "holy fight" (or holy struggle) against terrorism. Russia claimed the attacks were against the ISIL positions. However, according to reports, the Russian air strikes targeted positions held by the Army of Conquest coalition including the Saudi/Turkish-backedAl-Nusra Front and by Salafi-jihadi coalition known as Ahrar ash-Sham.

In the autumn of 2015, the U.S. ruled out military cooperation with Russia in Syria. However, on 20 October 2015, the U.S. and Russia signed a secret technical memorandum of understanding to avoid air incidents over Syria.

On 22 November 2015, Syria2 s president Bashar Assad said that within two months of its air strikes Russia had achieved more than theU.S.-led coalition in its fight against Islamic State for a year. Two days later, the U.S. president Barack Obama, speaking after a meeting with his French counterpart François Hollande, said: "Russia right now is a coalition of two, Iran and Russia, supporting Assad. Given Russia's military capabilities and given the influence they have on the Assad regime, them cooperating would be enormously helpful in bringing about a resolution of the civil war in Syria, and allow us all to refocus our attention on ISIL. But I think it's important to remember that you've got a global coalition organized. Russia is the outlier."

At the end of December 2015, senior U.S. officials privately admitted that Russia had achieved its central goal of stabilising the Assad government and, with the costs relatively low and minimal casualties, was in a position to sustain the operation at this level for years to come.

Iran

Iran and Syria are close strategic allies, and Iran has provided significant support for Syria in the Syrian Civil War. This is said to include technical support, some combat troops, and $9bn in financial support. Iran's supreme leader, Ali Khamenei, was reported in September 2011 to be vocally in favor of the Syrian government. The Syrian city of Zabadani is vitally important to Assad and to Iran because, at least as late as June 2011, the city served as the Iranian Revolutionary Guard Corps's logistical hub for supplying Hezbollah.

In the civil uprising phase of the Syrian Civil War, Iran was said to be providing Syria with technical support based on Iran's capabilities developed following the 2009–2010 Iranian election protests. As the uprising developed into civil war, there were increasing reports of Iranian military support, partly in response to reports of increasing military support to the Syrian opposition from Gulf states.

In the autumn of 2015, Iran reluctantly signed on to the road map based on the 2012 Geneva Communique that was worked out during the two rounds of Syria talks in Vienna. After the meeting between Vladimir Putin and Ali Khamenei in Tehran on 23 November 2015, Iran was said to have made a decision to unify its stance vis-a-vis the Syrian leadership with Russia's.

Hezbollah

Hezbollah has long been an ally of the Ba'ath Party government of Syria, led by the Al-Assad family. Hezbollah has allegedly helped the Syrian government in its fight against the armed Syrian opposition. As early as November 2011, *The Jerusalem Post* reported that protesters in Syria, enraged at Hezbollah's support for the Syrian government, have burnt Hezbollah flags and images of Nasrallah, while pro-government protesters have carried posters of Nasrallah.

In August 2012, the United States sanctioned Hezbollah for its alleged role in the war. Hezbollah leader Hassan Nasrallah denied Hezbollah had been fighting on behalf of the Syrian government, stating in a 12 October 2012 speech that "right from the start the Syrian opposition has been telling the media that Hezbollah sent 3,000 fighters to Syria, which we have denied". However, he said that Hezbollah fighters have gone to Syria independently and died there doing their "jihadist duties". Hezbollah states it supports a process of reforms in Syria and is against what it calls US plots to destabilize and interfere in Syria.

In January–February 2012, Hezbollah fighters allegedly helped the government fight the rebels in Damascus and in the Battle of Zabadani. Later that year, Hezbollah fighters crossed the border from Lebanon and took over eight villages in the Al-Qusayr District of Syria. According to the Lebanese *Daily Star* newspaper, Nasrallah said that Hezbollah fighters helped the Syrian government "retain control of some 23 strategically located villages [in Syria] inhabited by Shiites of Lebanese citizenship". In September 2012, Hezbollah's commander in Syria, Ali Hussein Nassif, was killed along with several other Hezbollah militants in an ambush by the Free Syrian Army(FSA) near Al-Qusayr.

According to the US, the Assad loyalist militia known as Jaysh al-Sha'bi was created and is maintained by Hezbollah and Iran's Revolutionary Guard, both of whom provide it with money, weapons, training and advice. Also, according to Israeli intelligence sources, Hezbollah is working to forge loyalist government militias into a 100,000-strong irregular army to fight alongside the government's conventional forces.

On 30 January 2013, about ten jets bombed a convoy believed to be carrying Russian-made SA-17 anti-aircraft missiles to Lebanon. The attack, attributed by some media reports to Israeli airforce, did not result in any counterattacks from Syria, although Syria has said it reserves the right to retaliate. Western intelligence sources reported that Iranian general Hassan Shateri had been killed in the airstrike. Iran acknowledged his death at the hands of the Israelis without further details. Israel refused to comment on its involvement in the incident.

On 16–17 February 2013, Syrian opposition groups claimed that Hezbollah, backed by the Syrian military, attacked three FSA-controlled Sunni villages in Al-Qusayr. An FSA spokesman said, "Hezbollah's invasion is the first of its kind in terms of organisation, planning and coordination with the Syrian regime's air force". Hezbollah said three Lebanese Shias, "acting in self-defense", were killed in the clashes with the FSA. Lebanese security sources said that the three were Hezbollah members. In response, the FSA allegedly attacked two Hezbollah positions on 21 February; one in Syria and one in Lebanon. Five days later, it said it destroyed a convoy carrying Hezbollah fighters and Syrian officers to Lebanon, killing all the passengers. The leaders of the March 14 alliance and other prominent Lebanese figures called on Hezbollah to end its involvement in Syria and said it is putting Lebanon at risk. Subhi al-Tufayli, Hezbollah's former leader, said "Hezbollah should not be defending the criminal regime that kills its own people and that has never fired a shot in defense of the Palestinians". He said "those Hezbollah fighters who are killing children and terrorizing people and destroying houses in Syria will go to hell". The Consultaive Gathering, a group of Shia and Sunni leaders in Baalbek-Hermel, also called on Hezbollah not to "interfere" in Syria. They said "Opening a front against the Syrian people and dragging Lebanon to war with the Syrian people is very dangerous and will have a negative impact on the relations between the two". Walid Jumblatt, leader of the Progressive Socialist Party, also called on Hezbollah to end its involvement and claimed that "Hezbollah is fighting inside Syria with orders from Iran".

News organizations reported that Israel allegedly attacked Syria on the night between 2 and 3 May 2013. US officials said that the Israeli war planes shot into Syria from Lebanese air space, and that the warplanes did not enter Syrian air space. No counter-attacks by Syria were reported at any front, and the Syrian ambassador to the UN said that he was not aware of any attacks on Syria by Israel. Israel as well declined any comment. Another alleged attack was reported to be a set of massive explosions in Damascus on the night of 4–5 May 2013. Syrian state media described this as an "Israeli rocket attack", with the targets including a military research center of the Syrian government in Jamraya. The *Daily Telegraph* reported anonymous Israeli sources as saying that this was an Israeli attack on Iranian-made guided missiles allegedly intended to be shipped to Hezbollah. The Syrian Observatory for Human Rights, an opposition monitoring group based in Britain, said at least 42 Syrian soldiers were killed in the strikes. Another violent event, possibly linking Israel, occurred in July 2013 in Latakia. Both Syria and Israel denied any report, while Hezbollah claimed that large explosions in Latakia area were caused by rebel mortar fire. Reportedly, the attack targeted Russian-made Yakhont anti-ship missiles near the city of Latakia, and killed several Syrian troops. Russian news agency also reported of Turkish involvement in the incident. On November 2013, a US official stated that Israel conducted an air strike on a Syrian weapons store near Latakia.

In February 2015, an official document concerning the interrogation of an Iranian prisoner that was conducted by the

United Al-Sham [Greater Syria] Front of the Free Syrian Army reveals that the Iranian Revolutionary Guard Corps (IRGC) and Hezbollah have built a military and terrorist infrastructure on the Syrian Golan.

The document reveals information about 'sleeper cells' that have been trained by Hezbollah and the IRGC, and cooperate with them such as by conveying information on the movement of the rebels and the commanders. A monetary sum of 100,000-200,000 Syrian liras has been budgeted expressly for those [spies] who carry out a suicide attack against the Free Syrian Army.

Other

Venezuela

In February 2012, it was reported that Hugo Chávez's government in Venezuela had been shipping tens of millions of dollars of diesel to Syria, which can be used to fuel army tanks. The following month, as it prepared a third shipment, Venezuela confirmed that it would continue sending diesel to the country.

The Wall Street Journal obtained documents showing that a fourth big shipment of diesel was being readied in July 2012: "the deals are structured to bring other benefits, including shielding Syria's dwindling foreign-exchange reserves".

The paper also noted that even "Syria's political opposition is split on the issue of cutting off all energy exports to the country. While they would like to see Mr. Assad's tanks run out of fuel, they also worry that a shortage of diesel could equally undermine the political and military opposition inside Syria." Chávez openly expressed his support for Assad's government while he was alive.

North Korea (DPRK)

On 21 September 2012, Iraqi officials stated that they had refused a North Korean plane suspected of carrying weapons entry into Iraqi airspace en route to Syria. Earlier in the year, a UN probe was launched into North Korean arms deals with Syria and Myanmar in violation of international sanctions. The probe confirmed that North Korea was continuing to supply arms to Syria and Myanmar despite strict sanctions imposed in 2006 and

2009, using "elaborate techniques" to avoid interception. According to the report, one such "shipment originated in the DPRK, was trans-shipped in Dalian (China), and Port Klang (Malaysia), and transited through other ports... en route to Latakia, Syria."

Illegal shipments were apparently not halted by the outbreak of war in Syria: according to a November 2012 report, a Chinese-registered ship containing North Korean missile parts, made in Chongjin, bound for Syria was seized by South Korean authorities in May 2012.

Other reports suggest that dozens of Arabic-speaking Korean People's Army officers have aided planning of military operations and have supervised artillery bombardments in the Aleppo area. The Syrian Observatory for Human Rights claimed that 15 North Korean pilots operate combat helicopters in the country.

Algeria

Algeria has been one of a small number of Arab and Islamic states, to oppose punitive measures against the Syrian government. It opposed (with Iran) Syria's suspension from the Organisation of Islamic Cooperation in 2012.

It also opposed the Arab League decisions to encourage military support for the Syrian Opposition among member states, and opposed recognition of the National Coalition for Syrian Revolutionary and Opposition Forces, as the legitimate representative of the Syrian people, both decisions undertaken by the Arab League in 2013.

Algeria was supported in its position by only two other Arab League states, Iraq and Lebanon. There is no concrete evidence that Algeria has been directly arming the Assad government, but there are rumours of Algerian military aircraft regularly landing in Syria. The Algerian government is believed to be strongly opposed to regime change in Syria.

Iraq

From 2011, Iraqi Government has sent Assad financial support. Iraq has opened its airspace for use by Iranian planes ferrying support to the Syrian government, and has granted trucks bound for Syria carrying supplies from the Iranian Revolutionary Guards passage through Iraqi territory. Iraqi government has signed a deal to provide Syria with diesel fuel.

Lebanon

23 and 24 February 2011, Lebanese Military Intelligence agents arrested six members of one Syrian family after they distributed flyers in Lebanon calling for protests against the Syrian government. 25 February, one of them with two of his brothers vanished in Lebanon without leaving a trace. Human Rights Watch feared that Lebanon is back shutting up Syrian critics, perhaps forcibly transferring them to Syria.

Companies

A Greece-based trading company, Naftomar, is reputedly the last firm arranging deliveries of liquefied petroleum gas (LPG), but, unlike the fuel sent from Venezuela and Russia, LPG is a peaceful material that plays a vital role in countries like Syria that have limited infrastructure for piping gas. International sanctions do not apply to LPG for humanitarian reasons.

The release of WikiLeaks's "Syria Files" beginning in July 2012 led to accusations that the subsidiary of an Italian arms company had provided communications equipment to the Syrian military in May 2011, and that, as late as February 2012, its engineers gave training on the use of the communications technology, including how it could be installed in helicopters. The company said the equipment was for civilian use and said it had not sold any technology to Syria since the beginning of the uprising.

According to the a report in the Daily Mail, British companies sold sodium fluoride, which has many civil applications such as water fluoridation, but is also a key ingredient in the manufacture of sarin, to a Syrian firm from 2004-2010. Between July 2004 and May 2010, the British government issued five export licenses to two companies, with the last export license was issued in May 2010.

The licenses are obtained prior to manufacture and the industry standard requires four to five months before the chemicals are delivered, thus allowing them to sell Syria sodium fluoride.

SUPPORT FOR THE SYRIAN OPPOSITION

United States

For several initial months of the Syrian uprising that began in March 2011, the U.S. administration headed by Barack Obama, despite pressure from some political groups, refrained from outright calls for Bashar Assad2 s ouster, a move then opposed by key regional U.S. allies such as Turkey and Saudi Arabia. First, limited, sanctions against the Assad government were imposed by the U.S. in April 2011, followed by Obama2 s executive order as of 18 May 2011 targeting Bashar Assad specifically and six other senior officials. In July 2011, U.S. foreign minister Hillary Clinton said president Assad had "lost legitimacy." On 18 August 2011, Barack Obama issued a written statement echoed by the leaders of the UK, France, and Germany, that inter alia said: "The future of Syria must be determined by its people, but President Bashar al-Assad is standing in their way. His calls for dialogue and reform have rung hollow while he is imprisoning, torturing, and slaughtering his own people. We have consistently said that President Assad must lead a democratic transition or get out of the way. He has not led. For the sake of the Syrian people, the time has come for President Assad to step aside." On the same day the U.S. president signed executive orders that froze all Syrian government assets that were under U.S. jurisdiction, barred Americans from doing business with the government, and prohibitted the import of Syrian oil and petroleum products to the United States. The U.S. sanctions were called by Syria's U.N. ambassador Bashar al-Jaafari "a humanitarian and diplomatic war against us."

Under the administration's division of labor, the State Department is in charge of supplying nonlethal aid (includes food rations and pickup trucks, not tanks and bullets), while the U.S. Central Intelligence Agency (CIA) runs a covert program to arm and train the Syrian rebels.

In June 2012, the CIA was reported to be involved in covert operations along the Turkish-Syrian border, where agents investigated rebel groups, recommending arms providers which groups to give aid to. Agents also helped opposition forces develop supply routes, and provided them with communications training. CIA operatives distributed assault rifles, anti-tank rocket launchers and other ammunition to Syrian opposition. The State Department has reportedly allocated $15 million for civilian opposition groups in Syria.

In July 2012, the U.S. government granted a non-governmental organization called Syrian Support Group a license to fund the Free Syrian Army.

In early March 2013, a Jordanian security source revealed that the U.S., Britain, and France were training non-Islamist rebels in Jordan. In an effort to strengthen secular elements in the opposition as a bulwark against Islamic extremism, and to begin building security forces to maintain order in the event of Bashar al-Assad's fall. In April 2013, also in Jordan, the United States had set up a $70 million program in the country "that is training the kingdom's special forces to identify and secure chemical-weapons sites across Syria should the regime fall and the wrong rebels look like getting their hands on them."

In April 2013, the Obama administration promised to double non-lethal aid to rebels, specifically to $250 million.

On 13 June 2013, U.S. government officials said the administration, after days of high-level meetings, had approved providing lethal arms to the Supreme Military Council (SMC). The SMC is a rebel command structure that includes representatives from most major rebel groups, and excludes the Islamic extremist elements. The decision was made shortly after the administration concluded that the Assad government had used chemical weapons on opposition forces, thus crossing the "red line" declared by Obama earlier in 2012. The arms to be provided included small arms and ammunition, and possibly anti-tank weapons. However, they were not to include anti-aircraft weapons, something repeatedly requested by the armed opposition. Further such weapons would be supplied by the US "on our own timeline".

In mid-June 2013, the U.S. government said it would now arm rebels in Syria; besides, the U.S- was considering a no-fly zone in Syria2 s southern border with Jordan, which would allow a safe place to equip and train rebels. During September 2013, it was reported by US officials that under "a covert CIA program," small arms and anti tank weapons had begun reaching some moderate rebel groups. Although Free Syrian Army Commander Salim Idriss denied receiving lethal aid, some analysts commented that information on US arms may not have reached Idriss due to poor communications as the Free Syrian Army command was based in Northern Syria whilst weapons were reportedly reaching rebel groups in the south.

In December 2013, the U.S. government temporarily suspended the shipments of non-lethal military aid, including food rations, medical kits and pickup trucks after warehouses of equipment were seized by the Islamic Front.

In April 2014, there appeared online videos that showed rebels in Syria using U.S.-made anti-tank rockets (BGM-71 TOW), the first significant American armaments in the country's conflict; analysts suggested they might have been provided by states such as Saudi Arabia, a U.S. ally, with Washington's acquiescence.

In early October 2015, shortly after the start of the Russian military intervention in Syria, Barack Obama was reported to have authorised the resupply—against ISIL—of 25,000 Syrian Kurds and 5,000 of the armed-Syrian opposition, emphasising that the U.S. would continue this support now that Russia had joined the conflict.

On 8 October 2015, the U.S. officially announced the end of the Pentagon's $500 million program to train and equip Syrian rebels in an acknowledgment that the program had failed in achieving its ostensible goals Other, covert and significantly larger, programs to arm anti-government fighters in Syria are run by the CIA and continue.

France and Britain

Since August 2011, Britain and France both insist, along with the U.S. and some Arab states, that the Syrian president Bashar Assad have no place in Syrian settlement, France, a former colonial ruler of Syria, being the most strident in its anti-Assad stance. In November 2011, NATO said it had no intention of taking military action in Syria, after it closed its seven-month campaign in Libya.

In June 2012, it was reported that the prospect of British special forces entering Syria on the ground was growing, following unconfirmed reports from an Israeli website that SAS Commandos were conducting covert operations within Syrian territory, operating from Turkey on 26 June 2012.

In 2012, the U.S., UK and France provided opposition forces with non-lethal military aid, including communications equipment and medical supplies. The UK was also reported to have provided intelligence support from its Cyprus bases, revealing Syrian military movements to Turkish officials, who then passed on the information to the Free Syrian Army.

In August 2013, when the Assad government was accused of using chemical weapons in the Ghouta area near Damascus, Paris called for military intervention but was isolated after the US president, Barack Obama, refused to act despite the breach of what he had earlier declared was a "red line". On 29 August 2013, a vote was held in the British House of Commons to decide whether the United Kingdom would join the United States in initiating militant action against the use of chemical weapons by the Syrian government: the Prime MinisterDavid Cameron2 s motion was defeated by 285 votes to 272. Although the prime minister does not need parliamentary approval for military action, Cameron said that he would respect this Parliamentary decision and that the UK would not take part in military action in Syria.

On 19 September 2013, French President François Hollande hinted that France was ready to begin supplying lethal aid to the Free Syrian Army during a press conference in Bamako in a "controlled framework".

In mid-November 2015, in the wake of the Paris terror attacks, France, which had begun strikes in Syria at the end of September 2015on a small scale to avoid inadvertently strengthening the hand of president Bashar Assad by hitting his enemies, citing self-defence underArticle 51 of the United Nations Charter, significantly intensified its air strikes in Syria, closely coordinating with the U.S. military. On 20 November 2015, France dismissed Russia2 s suggestions that its air strikes against oil installations in Syria were illegal, saying they were "an appropriate and necessary riposte" to attacks by Islamic State.

On 20 November 2015, the UN Security Council, while failing to invoke the UN's Chapter VII, which gives specific legal authorisation for the use of force, unanimously passed a resolution that urged UN members to "take all necessary measures" in the fight against Islamic State and al-Nusra Front; the adopted resolution was drafted by France and co-sponsored by the UK the following day after Russia introduced an updated version of its previously submitted draft resolution that was blocked by the Western powers as seeking to legitimise Assad's authority. British Ambassador to the U.N. Matthew Rycroft said the resolution would be used by prime minister David Cameron to address Parliament on his plans to begin airstrikes by the UK in Syria.

On 3 December 2015, after the UK parliament overwhelmingly backed the UK government2 s motion to extend the UK military action to Syria, four Tornados from RAF air base in Cyprus carried out their first air strikes against the ISIL in Syria targeting the Omar oil fields in eastern Syria, and were "successful", according to defence minister Michael Fallon. France welcomed UK military action; Syria, noting that the UK had failed to ask permission from Syria's government, insisted Britain and its allies must follow Russia's example and co-ordinate their campaign with Syrian government forces.

Turkey

The government of Turkey, a NATO member with the alliance2 s second largest army, had had a relatively friendly relationship with Syria over a decade prior to the start of the civil unrest in Syria in 2011; Turkey, while joining calls for the Syrian government to end the violence,initially objected to the demand voiced in August 2011 by the U.S that Bashar Assad resign. Until September 2014, Turkey did not overtly participate in the international airstrikes against ISIS. Turkey trained defectors from the Syrian Army on its territory, and in July 2011 a group of them announced the birth of the Free Syrian Army under the supervision of Turkish military intelligence. In October 2011, Turkey began sheltering the Free Syrian Army, offering the group a safe zone and a base of operation.Together with Saudi Arabia andQatar, Turkey has also provided the rebels with arms and other military equipment.

Tensions between Syria and Turkey significantly worsened after Syrian forces shot down a Turkish fighter jet in June 2012 and border clashes in October 2012.

Turkey provided refuge for Syrian dissidents from early days of the Syrian conflict. In early June 2011, Syrian opposition activists convened in Istanbul to discuss regime change, and Turkey hosted the head of the Free Syrian Army, Colonel Riad al-Asaad. Turkey became increasingly hostile to the Assad government's policies and came to encourage reconciliation among dissident factions. Recep Tayyip Erdoðan has tried to "cultivate a favorable relationship with whatever government would take the place of Assad."

Since May 2012, some Syrian opposition fighters began to receive arms and training from the Turkish Intelligence. The Islamic Frontand Ahrar ash-Sham in particular have received weapons from Turkey according to German intelligence.

Turkey maintained a small enclave within Syria itself, the Tomb of Suleyman Shah on the right bank of the Euphrates in Aleppo Province near the village of Qarah Qawzak (Karakozak). The Tomb is guarded by a small permanent garrison of Turkish soldiers, who rotate in from a battalion based at the Turkish border some 25 kilometres (16 mi) away—even as the civil war unfolded around them. Up until Syrian forces shot down a Turkish warplane in June 2012, the garrison numbered 15 men in total. Following the incident, the Turkish government doubled the number of soldiers stationed at the tomb to 30, while Prime Minister Erdoðan warned that "the tomb of Suleyman Shah and the land that surrounds it are Turkish territory. Any act of aggression against it would be an attack on our territory and NATO territory." In February 2015, the army launched a raid into Syria in order to move the tomb closer to the border.

Turkey had repeatedly said it wanted the U.S. to focus its air strikes in Syria as much on removing Assad as on fighting the ISIL; it had also demanded a "safe zone" in the area extending from the Syrian town of Kobanî on the Turkish border, westward to the town of Azaz, that would be protected by air power and that was purported to enable Turkey to transfer back to Syria some of an estimated 1.8 million displaced people camped on Turkish territory.

On 22 July 2015, Turkey agreed to let the U.S. use the Incirlik Air Base in southern Turkey to launch air attacks against the ISIL, a deal that was seen as a major shift in policy on the part of the once-reluctant American ally (in March 2003, the Turkish parliament voted against allowing Turkey to be a base of operations for the U.S. invasion of Iraq).

At the end of July 2015, American and Turkish media outlets reported that the U.S. government and Turkey had agreed on the outlines of a de facto "safe zone" along the Turkey-Syria border under the terms of a deal that was purported to increase the scope and pace of the U.S.-led air missions against the ISIL in northern Syria; the plan provided for driving ISIL, the al-Nusra Front, and other radical groups out of a 68-mile-long area west of the Euphrates River and reaching into the province of Aleppo that would then come under the control of the Syrian opposition. The operational status of the envisioned area was to stop short of meeting Turkish demands for a full-scale, declared no-fly zone. In August 2015, the U.S. announced it would withdraw two Patriot missile-defense batteries from southern Turkey in the autumn that year; also withdrawn were the German Patriots stationed in Turkey, amidst concerns in the NATO military establishment that Turkey was intent on dragging NATO into the Syrian conflict in pursuit of its own parochial interests.

In late July 2015, Turkey resumed fighting against the outlawed Kurdistan Workers' Party (PKK) in the Kurdish-dominated southeastern parts of Turkey. On 29 June 2015, Turkey2 s National Security Council made a decision and released a statement that said that Turkey would consider any incursion west of the Euphrates in northern Syria along the Turkish border (the area between Jarablus in the east and the Azaz–Mare' region in the west) by Kurdish YPG militia, backed by the Democratic Union Party (PYD), as well as any attack north of Idlib by Syrian government forces to be a violation of the "red line." (The PYD is deemed by Turkey to be the Syrian affiliate of PKK, but it is actively aided by the U.S.) At the end of October 2015, Turkish prime minister Ahmet Davutoðlu claimed that Turkey had struck Kurdish militia fighters in Syria twice for the alleged breach of the "red line"; the YPG2 s statements said that the Turkish army had twice attacked its positions near the border towns of Tell Abyad and Kobanî. In mid-November 2015, president Recep Erdoðan reaffirmed this threat not to allow Syrian Kurds to cross over to the western side of the Euphrates along the Turkish border.

On 24 November 2015, speaking shortly after the shootdown of a Russian Su-24 by Turkey, Russian president Vladimir Putin characterised the role played by Turkey in the Syrian conflict as that of "the accomplices of terrorists." Russia2 s foreign minister Sergey Lavrovnoted that the Turkish plan to create a buffer zone in the area where Syrian Turkmen lived in northern Syria stemmed from Ankara's wish to protect local terrorist infrastructure: "According to the latest information, the area which our Turkish colleagues deem to be populated by Syrian Turkmen not only accommodates several hundreds, or thousands, of militants - citizens of the Russian Federation, as the [Russian] president said yesterday, who present a direct threat to our security, security of our people but also, according to the available information, that area accommodates infrastructures of the militants, including arms and ammo depots, command centers, and logistics centers."

In late November 2015, following Russian President Putin directly accusing Turkey of aiding ISIL and al-Qaeda, Turkey came under pressure from the U.S. to close the remaining crossing point for ISIL militants on a 60-mile stretch of the border with Syria where ISIL had control of the Syrian side. The crossing had been used to export crude oil originating from ISIL-controlled oilfields, and for arms smuggling.

On 2 December 2015, Russia2 s military officials presented what they referred to as "only part of the available facts" that proved that Turkey2 s president Recep Erdogan and his family are personally involved in a multi-million dollar oil smuggling operation that funds ISIL terrorists (similar claims had earlier been voiced by the U.S. officials). The accusations were seen as further drastic escalation of tensions between Turkey and Russia that has its military personnel and advanced weapons openly deployed in Syria.

In late December 2015, in an interview for Al Arabiya Turkey2 s president Recep Erdogan said, "Syria, Iran, Iraq and Russia have formed a quartet alliance in Baghdad and asked Turkey to join, but I told President [Vladimir] Putin that I cannot sit alongside a president whose legitimacy is distrustful."

Arab League

Sunni Arab states are concerned that the Iranian arms transfers are changing the balance of power in the region and has "become a regional contest for primacy in Syria between Sunni Arabs and the Iran-backed Assad government and Hezbollah of Lebanon." Iran is using the Maharaj Airlines to ship weapons to Syrian government.

On 6 March 2013, the Arab League gave its members the "green light" to arm the Syrian rebels. On 26 March 2013, at the Arab league summit in Doha, the League recognised the National Coalition for Syrian Revolutionary and Opposition Forces, as the legitimate representatives of the Syrian people.

Qatar

The *Financial Times* reported that Qatar had funded the Syrian rebellion by "as much as $3 billion" over the first two years of the civil war. It reported that Qatar was offering refugee packages of about $50,000 a year to defectors and family.

The Stockholm International Peace Research Institute estimated that Qatar had sent the most weapons to Syria, with over 70 weapons cargo flights into Turkey between April 2012 and March 2013. Qatar operates a training base in its territory, in conjunction with the CIA who run the training, training about 1,200 rebel soldiers a year on three week courses.

Jordan

From at least the 2014 June Offensive in Iraq, ISIL Leadership has been threatening to overthrow the monarchy of Jordan and to invade Jordan once it takes Baghdad. The Jordanian Air Force joined in the US-led bombing of ISIL in Syria. Jihadist troops have retaliated by firing into Jordan and there has been increased sniping at the border.

On 24 December 2014, a Jordanian fighter jet was shot down over Syria and its pilot, Jordanian air force lieutenant Muath Al-

Kasasbeh, captured. This pilot was executed by burning in January 2015 and was later used to attempt to recover jailed terrorists. Jordan offered to make the exchange, but demanded "proof of life" first, this wasn't done, and the video of the pilot's execution was released. In response, the terrorists, Sajida al-Rishawi and Ziad al-Karbouli, were executed and Jordan took the lead on anti-ISIL bombing raids, claiming nearly a thousand KOI in a week.

From time to time during the first half of 2015 and into the summer, there have been reports of plans for an invasion of Syria in order to set up a buffer zone within that country and away from its own border.

Saudi Arabia

The Financial Times reported in May 2013 that Saudi Arabia was becoming a larger provider of arms to the rebels. Since the summer of 2013, Saudi Arabia has emerged as the main group to finance and arm the rebels. Saudi Arabia has financed a large purchase of infantry weapons, such as Yugoslav-made recoilless guns and the M79 Osa, an anti-tank weapon, from Croatia via shipments shuttled through Jordan. The weapons began reaching rebels in December 2012 which allowed rebels' small tactical gains this winter against the army and militias loyal to Assad. This was to counter shipments of weapons from Iran to Assad's forces.

Bashar al-Assad pointed at Saudi Arabia as the major supporter of terrorists and "leading the most extensive operation of direct sabotage against all the Arab world".

In May 2015, *The Independent* reported that Saudi Arabia and Turkey were "focusing their backing for the Syrian rebels on the combined Jaish al-Fatah, or the Army of Conquest". The Army of Conquest reportedly includes an Al-Qaeda-linked Al-Nusra Front, which had been declared a terrorist organisation by the United States.

In mid-December 2015, in the wake of the two rounds of the Vienna talks, Saudi Arabia hosted a conference of Syria's political and armed opposition factions that was intended to come to an agreement on a common position from which to negotiate with the government of Bashar al-Assad. The meeting, that did not include the major Kurdish factions in Syria, produced a statement of principles to guide peace talks with the government; it said inter alia that president Assad would be allowed to stay until a transitional government was formed. The meeting decided to set up a "Higher Negotiations Authority" to direct the opposition's participation in the proposed talks with the regime early in 2016; that leadership body is to remain based in Riyadh, giving the Saudis a ready handle on it. Shortly afterwards, the Saudis announced the formation of a military alliance of Muslim countries to fight international terrorism; about 30 Muslim states (all of them Sunni-majority nations) were reported to join the alliance, including Egypt and Turkey. The coalition was seen by Russia and Iran as aimed at reinforcing Saudi Arabia2 s leadership and countering their efforts in the region, yet meaningless in practical terms.

Croatian Weapons

In December 2012, a new wave of weapons from foreign supporters were transferred to rebel forces via the Jordanian border in the country's south. The arms included M79 Osa anti-tank weapons and M-60 recoilless rifles purchased by Saudi Arabia from Croatia. Previously, most of the weapons were delivered via the Turkish border in the north. However, much of the arms unintentionally ended up in the hands of Islamist rebels. The goal for the change in routes was to strengthen moderate rebels and to bring the war closer to Damascus.

According to Jutarnji list, a Croatian daily newspaper, there were an unusually high number of sightings of Ilyushin 76 aircraft owned byJordan International Air Cargo at Pleso Airport in Zagreb, Croatia on December 14 and 23, 2012; January 6; and February 18, 2013. In early January 2013, Yugoslav weapons were seen used in battles in the Dara'a region near Jordan. Then, in February 2013, Yugoslav weapons were seen in videos posted by rebels fighting in the Hama, Idlib, and Aleppo regions. Danijela Barišiæ of Croatia's Foreign Ministry and arms-export agency denied that such shipments had occurred. Saudi officials have declined requests for interviews about the shipments for two weeks. Ukrainian-made rifle cartridges, Swiss-made hand grenades, Belgian-made rifles are showing up in the rebels hands but the origin is not clear because Saudi Arabia has insisted on secrecy.

Bandar bin Sultan

In August 2013 the *Wall Street Journal* reported that Saudi Prince Bandar bin Sultan had been appointed to lead Saudi Arabia's efforts to topple Syrian President Bashar al-Assad, and that the US Central Intelligence Agency considered this a sign of how serious Saudi Arabia was about this aim.

Bandar was described as "jetting from covert command centers near the Syrian front lines to the Élysée Palace in Paris and the Kremlin in Moscow, seeking to undermine the Assad regime." After tensions with Qatar over supplying rebel groups, Saudi Arabia switched its efforts from Turkey to Jordan in 2012, using its financial leverage over Jordan to develop training facilities there, overseen by Bandar's half-brother Salman bin Sultan.

In late 2012 Saudi intelligence also began efforts to convince the US that the Assad government was using chemical weapons. The Saudi government also would be sending prisoners sentenced to death to fight in Syria.

Swiss Weapon Sales Controversies

In July 2012, Switzerland ceased arms exports to the UAE after it emerged Swiss weapons were finding their way to opposition fighters. The Swiss decision came shortly after the UN human rights chief, Navi Pillay, called for an urgent stop to arms transfers to government and opposition forces so as to avoid "further militarisation" of the conflict.

The director of the Saban Center for Middle East Policy had previously argued that, while "uncontrolled militarization will turn the Syrian uprising into a wider conflict that could draw in jihadis and other extremists from across the Muslim World", militarisation was inevitable, and so the US should help facilitate and guide it. Marc Lynch argued the opposite in February 2012, as the provision of weapons from Saudi Arabia and Qatar was being mooted: "It is unlikely that arms from the outside would come close to evening the balance of power, and would only invite escalations from Syrian regime forces".

Support from Non-state Groups

Free Iraqi Army In the western Sunni-majority provinces of Iraq, soldiers and war supplies have been crossing from Anbar Province into Syria. Armed groups inside Iraq have formed a Free Iraqi Army and have been supportive of the Syrian uprising against the Syrian government.

DIPLOMATIC RELATIONS

Some countries have cut ties with the Syrian government including: the GCC States, Libya, Tunisia, Britain, Spain, Poland, Turkey,Canada, the United States and Belgium. On 16 August 2012 the Organisation of Islamic Cooperation (OIC) suspended Syria's membership in the OIC, despite opposition by Iran, due to "President Assad's violent suppression of the uprising".

SUPPORT TO THE SYRIAN KURDS

The Syrian Kurds have received military and logistic support from Iraqi Kurdistan, and air support by U.S., Canadian, British and French air force.

After the start of the Russian military operation in Syria in the autumn 2015, Russia and the U.S. were said to be in competition to attract the dominant Syrian Kurds2 Democratic Union Party (PYD). Senior Russian officials were reported to have had meetings with the Syrian Kurdish leadership, including Salih Muslim Muhammad.

Since the end of November 2015, the Kurdish militia is reported to receive support from Russia.

SUPPORT FOR AL-NUSRA FRONT AND SALAFISTS

There have been a number of foreign fighters that have joined the Syrian Civil War in opposition to Assad. While some are jihadists, others, such as Mahdi al-Harati, have joined to help the Syrian revolution. Some fighters have come from as far away as Chechnya andTajikistan. Another group, the Al-Nusra Front, is headed by Abu Muhammad al-Julani The group includes some of the rebellion's most battle-hardened and effective fighters.

However, U.S. has formally designated the Al Nusra Front as a foreign terrorist organization. "Extremist groups like Jabhat al-Nusra are a problem, an obstacle to finding the political solution that Syria's going to need," said the American ambassador to Syria, Robert Ford.

Several groups, such as the Abdullah Azzam Shaheed Brigade, al-Nusra Front and Fatah al-Islam have stated that they conducted operations in Syria. Jihadist leaders and intelligence sources said foreign fighters had begun to enter Syria only in February 2012. In May 2012, Syria's U.N. envoy Bashar Ja'afari declared that dozens of foreign fighters from Libya, Tunisia, Egypt, Britain, France and elsewhere had been captured or killed, and urged Saudi Arabia, Qatar and Turkey to stop "their sponsorship of the armed rebellion". In June, it was reported that hundreds of foreign fighters, many linked to al-Qaeda, had gone to Syria to fight against Assad. In July, Iraq's foreign minister again warned that members of al-Qaeda in Iraq were seeking refuge in Syria and moving there to fight. When asked if the United States would arm the opposition, Hillary Clinton expressed fears that such weapons could fall into the hands of al-Qaeda or Hamas. In October 2012, the United States expressed concern and confirmed that most of the weapons fall into the hands of radical Islamist rebels.

Al-Qaeda leader Ayman al-Zawahiri condemned Assad.

SUPPORT FOR THE ISLAMIC STATE OF IRAQ AND THE LEVANT

Until 2015, the Turkish government had maintained a border regime that was referred to by commentators and Turkish journalists as the "Jihadist Highway" where militants including potential ISIS fighters and other radical groups could come and go freely.

In July 2015, a raid by US special forces on a compound housing the Islamic State's "chief financial officer", Abu Sayyaf, produced evidence that Turkish officials directly dealt with ranking IS members.

9

Pakistan's War on Terror

PAKISTAN AND THE "WAR ON TERROR"

Pakistan's relationship to the "War on Terror" has been highly ambivalent. On the one hand, Pakistan played a key role in facilitating the U.S.-led intervention in Afghanistan from shortly after 9/11 up to the present. It has permitted the transit of matériel across Pakistani territory to U.S. forces in Afghanistan. Pakistan has also tolerated American missile attacks launched from Afghanistan against Taliban and al-Qaeda targets in Pakistan's lawless border region with that country.

On the other hand, Pakistan has provided safe haven not just for radical Islamist movements targeting its rival India, but also for the Afghan Taliban. Al-Qaeda leaders Osama bin Laden and Ayman Al-Zawahiri, among others, are also believed to be hiding in Pakistan. Whether, to what extent and by whom within the Pakistani government they are being protected is unclear, but Pakistan certainly has not helped the United States to locate and capture them. There have also been press reports that Pakistan has blocked the efforts of some Taliban leaders to seek peace with the U.S.-backed Karzai government in Kabul. U.S.-Pakistani relations have become increasingly strained over how to prosecute the "War on Terror," yet cooperation between them also continues.

The explanation for this ambivalence is that while the United States and Pakistan have some common goals, their priorities differ markedly. The U.S. was concerned primarily with the Soviet threat during the Cold War, and has been focused on the threat from al-Qaeda and its Taliban allies since 9/11. Pakistan, by contrast, has been primarily concerned with its struggle with India ever since the two became independent from Britain in 1947. The fate of Kashmir, the Muslim-majority region that was divided between India and Pakistan during the first war between them, has been Pakistan's principal concern. It also has many others, including which of the two rivals will have predominant influence in Afghanistan.

Pakistan has also been vitally concerned with the preservation of its territorial integrity. The country is an agglomeration of ethnicities with little in common except an adherence to Islam. In the early 1970s, the conflict between what were then the two parts of the country — West and East Pakistan — was essentially over which ethnicity would predominate. Indian intervention in that war allowed East Pakistan to secede and become Bangladesh. Since then, the Pakistani military and security services have increasingly emphasized Pakistan's Islamic identity to keep its remaining disparate ethnic groups together. But one group has been predominant in the Pakistani military and security services, and hence in the government, ever since independence: the Punjabis.

Kashmir provides a rallying point for all Pakistanis, who believe that the Muslims there should also be able to live in overwhelmingly Muslim Pakistan. Kashmir, however, has also posed a problem for the Pakistani government and military. Pakistan has neither been able to seize it from India nor to persuade India to give it up. But, while it has no real hope of acquiring Indian-held Kashmir, no Pakistani government can afford to acknowledge this or relinquish Pakistan's claim. Doing so would not only be hugely unpopular inside Pakistan; it might also encourage other ethnicities (Pushtuns, Sindis and Balochis) to push for secession from the Punjabi-dominated state.

During the period of their Cold War alliance, the differing American and Pakistani priorities were evident: the United States sought Pakistan as an ally against the USSR, while Pakistan sought the United States as an ally against India. The height of Pakistani-American cooperation occurred during the Soviet occupation of

Afghanistan, when the United States, Pakistan and many others backed the Afghan mujahideen, who were resisting the Soviets. Even then, however, Pakistan favored the Islamist Afghan mujahideen groups over the more nationalist ones. Islamabad seemed to think that it would have more influence over the former.

After the Soviet withdrawal from Afghanistan in 1988-89, American concern about that country and South Asia in general diminished. Pakistan, however, remained focused on its rivalry with India. During the 1990s, then, Pakistan supported the rise of the Taliban, for several reasons: to restore order in what had become a chaotic country, to promote an Islamist ally that would sympathize with Pakistan over Kashmir and thus resist Indian influence, to establish a secure road network across Afghanistan to link Pakistan with newly independent Central Asia (thus benefiting the politically powerful Pakistani trucking industry), and even to extend Pakistani influence across Afghanistan into Central Asia. The Pakistani military and security services also believed that having an ally in Afghanistan would give Pakistan "strategic depth" in any future confrontation with India (though precisely what this meant and how it would work were ill-defined and poorly thought out).

With Pakistani help, the Taliban was able to seize control of most of Afghanistan in 1996. The Taliban, though, proved to be an extremely difficult ally for Pakistan, providing safe-haven to several radical Islamist groups, including al-Qaeda. After al-Qaeda launched the 9/11 attacks and it became clear that the United States would intervene militarily in Afghanistan in retaliation, the Bush administration forced Pakistan to choose between siding with the United States or with the Taliban. Pakistan formally chose to side with the United States, not due to a genuine change of heart regarding the Taliban, but due to the fear that Washington would side with India against Pakistan if it did not, and in the hope that siding with (or appearing to side with) the United States against the Taliban would strengthen Pakistan vis-à-vis India. Anticipating that the United States would not remain in Afghanistan, and that the Taliban and perhaps even al-Qaeda might prove useful to Pakistan vis-à-vis India later, Pakistan tolerated and even supported their presence on its territory in the region bordering Afghanistan.

It would have been difficult for Pakistan to do otherwise. Pakistan has long supported radical Islamist groups that are primarily concerned with Kashmir and India. How could it draw a distinction between these "good" Muslim radicals, on the one hand, and "bad" Taliban ones, on the other — especially when Pakistani public opinion views both favorably? But at the same time, the Pakistani government has not wanted to alienate the United States either (at least not too much). So Pakistani policy since 9/11 has been a confusing mixture of supporting, sheltering and tolerating the Taliban and al-Qaeda to some extent, but also supporting U.S. actions against them at the same time.

Not surprisingly, the U.S. government has grown increasingly frustrated with Pakistan; its support for the Taliban has frustrated American military efforts in Afghanistan. But many Pakistani Islamists, especially the Pushtun, condemn the Pakistani government for cooperating with the United States at all. A Pakistani Taliban has arisen, mainly among Pakistan's Pushtun population, which has fought against Pakistani government forces.

Pakistan's too-clever-by-half policy of supporting the United States against the Taliban and supporting the Taliban against the United States has not only frustrated American efforts in Afghanistan; it has contributed to the rise of a radical Islamist threat inside Pakistan itself. At this point, a Pakistani government decision to turn against these radical Islamist forces — or just end its support for them — might result in accelerating the threat that they pose to the Pakistani government.

Despite this, the Pakistani leadership has, characteristically, remained focused on its rivalry with India. With the United States and NATO having announced that they will withdraw from Afghanistan between mid-2011 and the end of 2014, Pakistan seems more worried than ever that the Karzai government will ally itself with India to the detriment of Pakistan. And so, Pakistan has continued to support the hard-line Afghan Taliban. The irony, of course, is that if the Taliban returns to power in Afghanistan with Pakistan's help, the Taliban is hardly likely to be more amenable to Pakistani influence after it has less need of it — just as occurred during the 1990s. Indeed, if the Afghan Taliban decides to help its Pushtun bretheren across the border in Pakistan, the Pakistani government may find itself faced with its own very serious Islamist insurgency — along with an unsympathetic international community as a result of the policies Pakistan is pursuing at present.

PAKISTAN'S WAR ON TERROR: UP TO AND BEYOND 2014

While Pakistan continues to be a frontline state in the global war on terror, it is simultaneously fighting domestic terrorism in a war that will seemingly continue well beyond 2014. In recent months, terror attacks targeting the Shia Hazara minority in Baluchistan indicate a transformation of the terror problem in Pakistan. The Tehrik-i-Taliban Pakistan (TTP) and Lashkar-e-Jhangvi present two different sides of Pakistan's terrorism problem, however, the two organizations have increasingly converged operationally to the extent that Pakistan cannot eliminate one without simultaneously confronting the other.

The September 11 terrorist attacks on the U.S. in which thou-sands of innocent lives were lost led Pakistan to join the U.S.-led global war against international terrorism in which Pakistan has over the years made an invaluable contribution. However, with the passage of time, Washington increasingly came to view Islamabad as part of the problem rather than the solution. Most U.S. and European policy makers believe that Pakistan is providing a safe haven for the Taliban and Al-Qaeda. Western media is full of stories about a presence of the Taliban leadership in Pakistan, including of Mullah Omar's alleged base in Quetta. Since the summer of 2008, U.S. military and intelligence agencies are sharing minimal intelligence with its Pakistani counterparts, instead focusing on drone attacks against suspected terrorist movements and hideouts.

Pakistan is a signatory to the UN's Palermo Convention. At the regional level, Pakistan has signed and ratified SAARC Regional Convention on the Suppression of Terrorism and the SAARC Convention on Narcotic Drugs Substances and the ECO Protocol against drugs. It has extradition treaties with 29 countries and bilateral agreements or MOUs on terrorism with 50 countries. Pakistan has played a major role in eliminating a number of terror networks such as the Al-Qaeda Anthrax network, the Alghuraba network, the UK-based Anglo-Pakistani group and Jundullah. Prominent targets captured include Khalid Sheikh Muhammad, Abu Alfaraj Alibi, Al Shib, Abu Zubaida, Abu Talha, Khalid bin Attash or Walid bin Attish, Ahmed Khalfan Ghailani, Mohammad Naeem Noor Khan, Abu Laith al-Libi, Hasan Bana, Hamza Rabbi, Sharif Al Masri, Abu Mushab Masri, Jaffar Uttayyar Alkashmiri Yassir Al-Jaziri, and Abdul Rehman Al-Masri. Umar Patek was arrested in Abbottabad by Pakistani forces and may have provided important leads to Osama bin Laden's whereabouts.

Since 9/11, Pakistan has also become a victim of terrorism. The direct and indirect cost suffered by Islamabad in the war on terror has been around US$ 35 billion. There has been a constant increase in the number of terror attacks in Pakistan since 9/11 and a number of prominent Pakistanis have lost their lives in such attacks. These include the two-time Prime Minister of Pakistan Benazir Bhutto and the former head of the Pakistan Army's Special Service Group, Maj. Gen. (Rtd) Ameer Faisal Alvi.

Most of the jihadists in Pakistan, especially the splinter groups of various organizations, are now operating under the umbrella of TTP, a Deobandi Sunni organization established in December 2007. TTP's objectives include cleansing Pakistan of foreign, meaning the U.S. and overall Western, presence, implementing Sharia and establishing a Caliphate. Over the years, TTP has been involved in a number of suicide bombings, rocket attacks, remote controlled bombs, abductions, and beheadings. It has widened its area of operations beyond Pakistan's tribal areas and targeted a number of government installations and organizations in the mainland, including the Federal Investigation Agency's Lahore office, the Naval War College in Lahore, the Marriott Hotel in Islamabad, the Wah ordinance Factory, the Sri Lankan cricket team in Lahore, a police training school, the GHQ Rawalpindi and the Navy's Mehran base in Karachi. It is also involved in kidnapping for ransom, bank robberies, forced taxes and drug trade.

IMPLICATIONS: Since 9/11, the TTP has increasingly converged with the staunchly anti-Shia militant group Lashkar-e-Jhangvi. A number of prominent TTP operations were conducted by known Lashkar-e-Jhangvi operatives. In recent months, the Hazaras in Baluchistan are increasingly becoming a prime target of the Lashkar-e-Jhangvi. Both TTP and Lashkar-e-Jhangvi consider Shias kafirs (infidels) and hence legitimate targets.

Terrorist activities showed no sign of receding in 2012, indicating that after more than a decade of fighting terror, Pakistan is nowhere close to the finishing line in this war and the problem is taking an even uglier shape. According to various sources, Pakistan suffered more than 6000 casualties in different terror attacks in 2012. More than 450 terror attacks were recorded in 2012 in which at least 39 were confirmed suicide attacks. Another important development in 2012 was the increasing operational alliance between the TTP and Lashkar-e-Jhangvi, although the two groups have cooperated with each other also in the past, the group led by Amjad Farooqi in 2003-2004 being a case in point.

However, in 2012 the two groups largely converged operationally in the sense that they declared a war against Shias. This convergence has resulted in the worst attacks to date against Shias, especially the Hazaras in Baluchistan. In 2012, Shias were targeted in 113 attacks in which 396 people lost their lives, indicating the increasingly sectarian features of Pakistan's terrorism problem. So far, more than a thousand terror-related deaths have occurred in 2013.

Apart from a closer alliance emerging between TTP and Lashkar-e-Jhangvi, TTP has also established Ansar Al-Aseerian (Helpers of the prisoners) in partnership with the Islamic Movement of Uzbekistan. According to media reports, Adnan Rasheed has been appointed the head of this group. The purpose of this group is to free all militants held in custody by Pakistani security forces and in various jails. TTP is also attempting to expand its activities and area of influence to Karachi, Pakistan's major financial hub. Karachi, which is also considered to be Pakistan's major Pashtun center, has been a preferred hideout for TTP, while some TTP and other jihadi activists have received medical treatment in Karachi.

2013 also witnessed two developments that will have long lasting effect on Pakistan's war against terrorism. Firstly, Pakistan's national Assembly unanimously passed the National Counter Terrorism Authority Bill 2013 on March 8, 2013. The establishment of a National Counter Terrorism Authority (NCTA) will play an important role in the efforts to combat terrorism. According to the mandate given to NCTA, it will "coordinate counter terrorism and counter extremism efforts in view of the nature and magnitude of the terrorist threat; and to present strategic policy options to the government for consideration/implementation by the stakeholders after scientifically studying the phenomenon of extremism and terrorism in historic and professional perspective." Secondly, Pakistan's army is taking a tougher stance and increasing its attention to the terrorism problem, as indicated by the decision of Pakistan's army chief to treat the problem of terrorism as an operational priority.

2013 is also an election year in Pakistan, with national and provincial elections scheduled for May 11, 2013. TTP has already targeted a number of political events in Khyber Paktunkhwa and especially the Awami National Party's election campaign. The political party or parties that will form the next government will not only inherit a crisis in the energy and financial sectors but will also have to make hard decisions about the country's war against terror.

PAKISTAN'S WAR AGAINST TERROR: MAJOR DEVELOPMENTS

Pakistan's role in the War on Terror is a widely discussed topic among policy-makers of various countries, political analysts and international delegates around the world. Pakistan has simultaneously received allegations of harbouring and aiding terrorists and commendation for its anti-terror efforts.

The Saudi born Zayn al-Abidn Muhammed Hasayn Abu Zubaydah, was arrested by Pakistani officials during a series of joint U.S. and Pakistan raids during the week of 23 March 2002. During the raid, the suspect was shot three times while trying to escape capture by military personnel. Zubaydah is said to be a high-ranking al-Qaeda official with the title of operations chief and in charge of running al-Qaeda training camps.

Later that year on 11 September 2002, Ramzi bin al-Shibh was arrested in Pakistan after a three-hour gunfight with police forces. Bin al-Shibh is known to have shared a room with Mohamed Atta in Hamburg, Germany and to be a financial backer of al-Qaeda operations.

It is said bin al-Shibh was supposed to be another hijacker, however the U.S. Citizenship and Immigration Services rejected his visa application three times, leaving him to the role of financier. The trail of money transferred by bin al-Shibh from Germany to the United States links both Mohammad Atta and Zacarias Moussaoui.

On 1 March 2003, Khalid Shaikh Mohammed was arrested during CIA-led raids on the suburb of Rawalpindi, nine miles outside of the Pakistani capital of Islamabad. Mohammed at the time of his capture was the third highest-ranking official in al-Qaeda and had been directly in charge of the planning for the 11 September attacks.

Mohammed having escaped capture the week before during a previous raid, the Pakistani government was able to use information gathered from other suspects captured to locate and detain him. Mohammed was indicted in 1996 by the United States government for links to theOplan Bojinka, a plot to bomb a series of U.S. civilian airliners.

Other events Mohammed has been linked to include: ordering the killing of Wall Street Journal reporter Daniel Pearl, the USS Cole bombing, Richard Reid's attempt to blow up a civilian airliner with a shoe bomb, and the terrorist attack at the El Ghriba synagogue inDjerba, Tunisia. Khalid Shaikh Mohammed has described himself as the head of the al-Qaeda military committee.

Amidst all this, in 2006, Pakistan was accused by NATO commanding officers of aiding and abetting the Taliban in Afghanistan; but NATO later admitted that there was no known evidence against the ISI or Pakistani government of sponsoring terrorism. However, in 2007, allegations of ISI secretly making bounty payments up to CDN$1,900 (Pakistani rupees. 1 lakh) for each NATO personnel killed surfaced. The Afghan government also accuses the ISI of providing help to militants including protection to the recently killed Mullah Dadullah, Taliban's senior military commander, a charge denied by the Pakistani government. India, meanwhile continues to accuse Pakistan'sInter-Services Intelligence of planning several terrorist attacks in Kashmir and elsewhere in the Indian republic, including the 11 July 2006 Mumbai train bombings, which Pakistan alleges is due to "homegrown" insurgencies. Many other countries like Afghanistan and the UK have also accused Pakistan of State-sponsored terrorism and financing terrorism.

The upswing in American military activity in Pakistan and neighbouring Afghanistan corresponded with a great increase in American military aid to the Pakistan government. In the three years before the attacks of 11 September, Pakistan received approximately $9 million in American military aid.

In the three years after, the number increased to $4.2 billion, making it the country with the maximum funding post 9/11. Such a huge inflow of funds has raised concerns that these funds were given without any accountability, as the end uses not being documented, and that large portions were used to suppress civilians' human rights and to purchase weapons to contain domestic problems like the Balochistanunrest.

WAZIRISTAN

With the logistics and air support of the United States, the Pakistani Army captured or killed numerous al-Qaeda operatives such as Khalid Shaikh Mohammed.

TRAINING GROUND FOR EUROPEAN MILITANTS

In 2009, a politically instable Pakistan emerged as a new global hub for anti-West militancy, but, because of the constant threat of US attacks, recruits were reportedly more likely to spend their time under instruction and in training than carrying out assertive action. In his report on the matter, focusing on an alarming influx of European extremists, *Reuters* security correspondent William Maclean wrote, Long a favored destination of British militants of

Pakistani descent, Pakistan's northwestern tribal areas are now attracting Arabs and Europeans of Arab ancestry who three years ago would probably have gone to Iraq to fight U.S. forces.

With the Iraq war apparently winding down, security sources say, the lure for these young men is to fight U.S. forces in neighboring Afghanistan or to gain the skills to carry out attacks back home in the Middle East, Africa or the West.

One consequence: Western armies in Afghanistan increasingly face the possibility of having to fight their own compatriots. He added that the matter was likely to surface in a meeting on 6 May between United States President Barack Obama, Pakistani President Asif Ali Zardari and Afghan President Hamid Karzai, the first-mentioned looking to bring an end to the employment of Pakistan's tribal zones as a launching pad for al Qaeda activity around the world.

Thousands of people have been killed in Pakistan due to terror attacks since the beginning of the war on terror.

WAR IN NORTH-WEST PAKISTAN

The War in North-West Pakistan, also known as the War in Waziristan, is an armed conflict involving the State of Pakistan, and armed militant groups such as the Tehrik-i-Taliban Pakistan (TTP), Jundallah, Lashkar-e-Islam (LeI), Tehreek-e-Nafaz-e-Shariat-e-Mohammadi (TNSM), al-Qaeda, the Islamic State of Iraq and the Levant (ISIL), and elements of organized crime.

The armed conflict began in 2004, when tensions, rooted in the Pakistan Army'ssearch for al-Qaeda fighters in Pakistan's mountainous Waziristan area (in theFederally Administered Tribal Areas), escalated into armed resistance.Pakistan's actions were presented as its contribution to the international War on Terror. Clashes further erupted between unified Pakistan Armed Forces and the Central Asian militant groups, allied with the Arab fighters, in 2008–2010. The foreign militants were joined by Pakistani non-military veterans of the Afghan War to the west, which subsequently established the TTP and other militant umbrella organizations, such as LeI. The TNSM established in 1992 allied with the TTP and LeI.

The war depleted the country's manpower resources, and the outcomes outlined a deep effect on its national economy, since Pakistan had joined the USA-led War on Terror. According to the Ministry of Finance (MoF) statistics and mathematical data survey collections, the economy has suffered direct and indirect losses of up to ~$67.93 billion since 2001 due to its role as a "frontline state." According to the MoF-issued Pakistan Economic Survey 2010–2011, "Pakistan has never witnessed such a devastating social and economic upheaval in its industry, even after dismemberment of the country by a direct war with India in 1971."

By 2014, casualty rates from terrorism in the country as a whole dropped by 40% as compared to 2011–2013, with even greater drops noted in Khyber Pakhtunkhwadespite the province being the site of a large massacre of schoolchildren by TTPterrorists in December 2014. A year later in 2015, Forbes cited Pakistan's "progress on the security front and the increased political stability" among other factors to call it the next "global turnaround success story."

NAMES FOR THE WAR

Various names have been applied to the conflict by the authors and historians. War in North-West Pakistan is the most commonly used name in English. It has also been called the Waziristan War, and the War in Waziristan. On the other hand, political scientist, Farrukh Saleem, termed the war as the "Fourth Generation War" or the "4G War".

Background

In the aftermath of Battle of Tora Bora (lit. *Black Caves*), formal troop deployment was begun by the Pakistan Army, at the behest of the Pakistan Government, in 2002. The conservative parties, most notably the Pakistan Muslim League, were very critical of such troop deployments in the region. The XI Corps, under its commander Lieutenant-General Jan Aurkzai, entered the Tirah Valley in the Khyber Agency for the first time since Pakistan's independence in 1947. The army troops later moved into the Shawal Valley of North Waziristan, eventually entering South

Waziristan. A monitoring reconnaissance base was established by the Special Service Group [Navy] in 2003. Criticism of Musharraf and the United States grew in Peshawar by a massive communist party in 2003, demanding an end to the operations.

In 2004, the troubles mounted as the Tribes began to see military's deployment and repeated PAF's flights in the region as an act of subjugation. In 2003–04 public speeches, Musharraf repeatedly called for the eviction of the foreign fighters from theSouth Waziristan and justified the army deployments in the region despite the concerns. In December 2003, at least two assassination attempts against President Pervez Musharraf were traced to South Waziristan. The government responded by intensifying military pressure on the area. However, the fighting was costly: government forces sustained heavy casualties throughout 2004 and into early 2005, when the government switched to a tactic of negotiation instead of direct conflict.

FIGHTING BREAKS OUT

On 16 March 2004, a bloody mountainous battle between the Pakistan Army troops and the foreign fighters of al-Qaeda was fought in the White Mountains of South Waziristan. The Pakistani mediaspeculated that Pakistan Army had surrounded a "*high value target*" in the mountainous region, possibly al-Qaeda's then-second-in-command Ayman al-Zawahiri. According to the military intelligence in 2004, all militants were Chechens, Uzbeks, and Tajiks who were trying to flee *Black Caves* (Tora Bora of Afghanistân). After a week of the battle, the entire area was captured and as many as 400 al-Qaeda operatives were apprehended by the Pakistan Army. In spite of its success, the army failed to capture Zawahiri. The ISPR later admitted that it was Soviet Uzbek Tohir Yo'ldosh who was surrounded, not Zawahiri.

By 2004, additional battalions were stationed by General Musharraf to help curb infiltration into Pakistan through its porous border. The Military Intelligence, Covert Action Division (CAD) and army troops founds many caves and tunnels in White Mountain range used by the foreign fightersbefore the military action took place. The Military Intelligence accounts maintained that the tunnels were led into Afghanistan, possible Tora Bora region. Though it is difficult to know how effective the cordon was on the first night of the military suspension but the military intelligence accounts did confirm that many high-valueforeign fighters might have escaped through these tunnels and caves back to Afghanistan.

On 7 October 2004, Musharraf approved the appointment of his close aide, General Ehsan-ul-Haq from ISI, who superseded seven colleagues; his appointment was brutally criticized by the media. After becoming the chairman joint chiefs, General Ehsan-ul-Haq oversaw the ground troops deployment of army only, while the air force and navy were kept out of the region.

Peace Deals

In April 2004, the Government of Pakistan signed the first of three peace agreements with militants in South Waziristan. It was signed by militia commander Nek Muhammad Wazir, but was immediately abrogated once Nek Muhammad was killed by an American Hellfire missile in June 2004. The second was signed in February 2005 with Nek's successor Baitullah Mehsud, which brought relative calm in the South Waziristan region. This deal would later, in September 2006, be mimicked in the neighboring North Waziristan territory as the third and final truce between the government and the militants. However, all of these truces would not have a substantial effect in reducing bloodshed. The latter two deals were officially broken in August 2007 with the start of Operation Silence which was initiated by Islamabad, and resulted in a tenfold increase in suicide attacks on Pakistan Armed Forces.

The strategy of keeping the air force and navy out from the conflict proved to be ineffective, as the violence spread out all over the country, and the army came under great pressure from the militants in 2004–07. In 2007, General Ehsan-ul-Haq admitted publicly that keeping the navy and the air force out of the conflict was a mistake.

TRANSITION IN TRIBAL AREAS: 2005–2006

The ISI's Covert Action Division (CAD) and the Special Services Group conducted a secret paramilitary operation to capture a high-ranking al-Qaeda operative Abu Faraj al-Libbi on 4 May 2005, after a raid outside the town of Mardan, 30 miles (48 km) northeast of Peshawar. His arrest was confirmed by the Government sources and noted as "al-Libbi was a high ranking al-Qaeda official, rumored to be third after Osama bin Laden and Ayman al-Zawahiri." Al-Libbi replacedKhalid Shaikh Mohammed after his arrest in March 2003 in connection with the 11 September attacks. The Pakistan government arrested al-Libbi and held him on charges in relation to being a chief planner in two assassination attempts on the life of President Pervez Musharraf in December 2003.

On 13 January 2006, the United States Air Force launched an airstrike on the village of Damadola. The attack occurred in the Bajaur tribal area, about 7 km (4.3 mi) from the Afghan border, and killed at least 18 people. The attack again targeted Ayman al-Zawahiri, but later evidence suggests he was not there.

Ceasefire

On 21 June 2006, pro-Tehrik-i-Taliban Pakistan militants in the Bannu region of North Waziristanstated they shot down a Bell military helicopter that was reported to have crashed. The government denied missile fire as the cause, stating it was due to technical faults. The helicopter had taken off from a base camp in Bannu at around 7 am for Miramshah and crashed 15 minutes later into the Baran Dam in the Mohmandkhel area on Wednesday morning. Four soldiers were killed while three others were rescued. On the same day militants killed an inspector and two constables on a road connecting Bannu and the main town ofMiranshah.

On 21 June 2006, Afghan Taliban leader Sirajuddin Haqqani issued a decree that it was not (Afghan) Taliban policy to fight the Pakistan Army. However, the Tehrik-i-Taliban Pakistan intentionally did not circulate the decree in North Waziristan thereby keeping pressure on the government.

Waziristan Peace Accord Signed

In 2006, the government witnessed the successful implementation of the peace deal between two tribes in Kurram Agency over the issue of distribution of irrigation water. Promptly, the government accepted the tribal recommendation to sign a peace deal with the militants in North Waziristan. Signed on 5 September 2006, the agreement was called the "Waziristan Accord"— an agreement among tribal leaders, militants, and the Pakistan government was signed in Miranshah, North Waziristan. to end all fighting. The agreement includes the following provisions:

- The Pakistan military will help reconstruct infrastructure in tribal areas of North and South Waziristan.
- The Pakistan military will not tolerate any assistance to intruders in North Waziristan, and will monitor actions in the region.
- The Pakistan government is to compensate tribal leaders for the loss of life and property of innocent tribesmen.
- "Foreigners" (informally understood to be foreign jihadists) are not allowed to use Pakistani territory for any terrorist activity anywhere in the world.
- 2,500 foreigners who were originally held on suspicion of having links to the Taliban were to be detained for necessary action against them.

The agreement, dubbed the Waziristan accord, has been viewed by some political commentators as a success for Pakistan. Even the military commander of the Pakistan Army, Lieutenant-General Ali Jan Aurakzai, also welcomed the peace agreement as "unprecedented in tribal history" and credited the intertribal jirga with amicably resolving a complicated issue within a few weeks.

Others were far more critical, seeing it as allowing militants to regroup and reorganize after military operations. However, in 2007, accord's chief architect and chairman joint chiefs General Ehsan-ul-Haq openly admitted to the media that the only ground troops deployment was wrong as the "Waziristan truce went wrong".

2006 Madrassah Air Strike

The media reported a deadly missile airstrike conducted against a madrassa in the Bajaur region bordering Afghanistan by a "fixed-wing drone" aircraft, based on the testimonies of the locals on 30 October 2006. Immediately, the ISPR claimed that the operation was only by the Pakistan Army, not by the U.S. Army. The monastery was destroyed killing up to 82 people; the ISPR quickly claimed that all were the militants and denied that there had been any collateral damage. The defense expert and others, however, remain skeptical of ISPR statements and gave credibility to local's testimonies.

82 seminary students were killed in the Damadola missile strike. : Sahibzada Haroonur Rashid, MNA from Bajaur Agency, resigned from the National Assembly on Monday to protest against the bombing of a madressah in his constituency. {Daily Dawn Karachi, October 31, 2006}

In retaliation for the attack the militants unsuccessfully fired series of RPG rockets on heavily fortified security camp of Governor andLieutenant-General Jan Aurkzai; though his convey escaped unharmed on 8 November 2006. The same day, the militants coordinated a successful suicide bomb attack on military base in Dargai, about 100 km north of Peshawar. The suicide attack killed nearly 42 Pakistani soldiers and wounding 20 others. Military intelligence investigators later testified in media that suicide bombing had a direct link with the air strike.

INSURGENCY IN THE NORTH, 2007

As early as 2007, the Northern region had been suffering with an intense insurgency and President Musharraf was increasingly in great pressure from the militants when several of army operations outlined mixed results. In March, his government was forced to signed a peace treaty with Fakir Mohamad, the main militant leader in Bajaur. Militant groups now held three districts in the Federally Administered Tribal Areas: South Waziristan, North Waziristan and Bajaur Agency.

Waziri-Uzbek Tensions

In South Waziristan, the Uzbek militancy had been growing as many former Soviet fighters–turned militants were reportedly seen encircling in the area; many of the military intelligence reports indicated the movements of former Soviet fighters in the region, mostly Uzbeks andChechens from the troubled areas of Russian

Federation. In 2007, the fighting sparked between the Uzbek fighters and the native militant groups by the killing of Arab fighter, Saiful Adil, an al-Qaeda operative, blamed on the Uzbeks fighters by Maulvi Nazir, described as a top pro-Taliban militant commander in the region. According to the other version, the fighting started after Maulvi Nazir, whom the government claimed had come over to its side, ordered the Uzbek followers of former Soviet fighters, Tohir Abduhalilovich Yo'ldoshev and Kamolitdinich Jalolov, to disarm, both were formerly the close confidants of Osama bin Laden.

It was also preceded by the clashes between the Yo'ldoshev led IMU and a pro-government tribal leader in Azam Warsak, in which 17–19 people died before a ceasefire was announced.

Defeat of the Islamic Movement of Uzbekistan

According to the military intelligence officials in 2007, there were many key reasons why the Uzbekshad been dominating the area. Military intelligence reports testified that the locals were scared to mobilize the opposition against the Uzbek militants due to their reputations as fierce fighters with long memories and very strong military backgrounds. Some of these fighters used to be soldiers and officers in the Soviet Army during the Russian invasion of Afghanistan in the 1980s, and some of them had military training given by the CIA during the 1990s; hence they were experts in guerrilla warfare. The IMU fighters had little to lose and it was difficult for them to escape somewhere else. They couldn't go back to Uzbekistan, and after 2009, re-infiltration back to Afghanistan also started becoming more difficult. Thus, they made Waziristan their home. Local militants allied to the tribesmen were reported attacking and seizing the IMU's private jail in Azam Warsak. The Pakistan Army intelligence said it did not intend to step in, but witnesses say government artillery fired on the Uzbek fighters they set up to fight the tribesmen.

Heavy fighting resumed on 29 March 2007, ending a week-long ceasefire between tribal fighters and foreign militants. According to initial reports, tribesmen attacked a checkpoint manned by formerSoviet Uzbek fighters and captured two of them. The clashes also left one tribal fighter dead and three wounded. The following day, a senior Pakistani official announced that 52 people were killed during the past two days, 45 of them were Uzbeks and the rest tribesmen. One of Maulvi Nazir's aides put the death toll at 35 Uzbeks fighters and 10 tribal fighters. However, residents in the area said that the death toll on both sides was inflated.

The conflict further escalated on 2 April when a council of elders declared jihad against foreign militants and started to raise an army of tribesmen. According to Pakistani intelligence officials, heavy fighting concentrated in the village of Doza Ghundai left more than 60 people dead, including 50 foreigners, 10 tribal fighters and one Pakistani soldier. Intelligence officials also said that "dozens of Uzbeks" had surrendered to tribal forces and that many bunkers used by militants were seized or destroyed.

On 12 April 2007, the army general in charge of South Waziristan said that tribal fighters had cleared the Soviet Uzbeks out of the valleys surrounding Wana and the foreign fighters had been pushed back into the mountains on the Afghan border. Four days later, the local tribesmen has urged Islamabad to resume control of law and order in the area.

Lal Masjid Siege and Truce Broken

The siege of Red Mosque was one the serious breach in the conflict and escalated the conflict in the summer of 2007. On 3 July 2007, the militant supporters of Lal Masjid and the Pakistan police clashed in Islamabad after the students from the mosque attacked and stoned the nearby MoE secretariat. Their resultant faceoff with the military escalated, despite the intervention of then-ruling PML(Q) leaders Shuja'at Hussain and Ijaz-ul-Haq. The Pakistan police, aided by the Pakistan Army Rangers immediately put up a siege around the mosque complex which lasted until 11 July and resulted in 108 deaths. This represented the main catalyst for the conflict and eventual breakdown of the truce that existed between Pakistan and the Taliban groups. Already during the siege, there were several attacks in Waziristan in retaliation for the siege.

As the siege in Islamabad ensued, several attacks on Pakistan army troops in Waziristan were reported. First attack was reported on 14 July 2007 when a suicide bomber attacked a Pakistan Army convoy killing 25 soldiers and wounding 54. Second attack was on 15 July 2007, two suicide bombers attacked another Pakistan Army convoy killing 16 soldiers and 5 civilians and wounding another 47 people. And in a separate incident, a fourth suicide bomber attacked a police headquarters killing 28 police officers and recruits and wounding 35 people. The assault on the Red Mosque prompted Islamic militants along the border with Afghanistan to scrap the controversialWaziristan Accord with Musharraf.

Under pressured, Musharraf moved the army in large concentration of troops into Waziristan and engaged in fierce clashes with militants in which at least 100 militants were killed including wanted terrorist and former Guantanamo Bay detainee, Abdullah Mehsud. The militants also struck back by attacking Army convoys, security check points and sending suicide bombers killing dozens of soldiers and police and over 100 civilians. In one month of fighting during the period from 24 July to 24 August 2007, 250 militants and 60 soldiers were killed. On 2 September 2007, just a few dozen militants led by Baitullah Mehsud managed to ambush a 17-vehicle army convoy and captured an estimated 247 soldiers without a shot being fired, an event that shocked the nation. Several officers were among the captured, the public criticism grew hard on Musharraf.

After the army returned to Waziristan, they garrisoned the areas and set up check-points, but the militants hit hard. In mid-September, the TTP and other forces attacked a number of Pakistan army outposts all across North and South Waziristan. This resulted in some of the heaviest fighting of the war. Following the Lal Masjid Siege, the first outpost was attacked and overrun by the militants resulting in the capture of 12 Pakistani soldiers. The next day on 13 September 2007, a suicide bomber in Tarbela Ghazi attacked a Pakistan army base, destroying the main mess hall and killing 20 members of theSSG *Karrar* Commando Unit; Pakistan's most elite army unit. A series of attacks ensued and by 20 September 2007, a total of five Pakistan Army military outposts had been overrun and more than 25 soldiers captured. More than 65 soldiers were either killed or captured and almost 100 wounded. A little over two weeks later, the Army responded with helicopter gunships and ground troops. They hit militant positions near the town of Mir Ali. In heavy fighting over four days, 257 people were killed, including 175 militants, 47 soldiers and 35 civilians.

Rawalpindi Attacks and State of Emergency in 2007

On 3 September 2007, the two coordinated suicide bombers targeted an ISI bus and a line of cars carrying ISI officers. The bus attack killed a large number of Defence Ministry workers and the other attack killed an Army colonel. In all 31 people, 19 soldiers and 12 civilians, were killed.

Two months later on 24 November, another military intelligence (MI) bus was again attacked. Almost everyone on the bus was killed. Another bomber blew up at a military checkpoint. 35 people were killed, almost all military officials. Facing with an intense criticism from media regarding the Red Mosque siege, President Musharraf became involved in a confrontation with the country's judiciarywho began taking *suo motu* actions against the directives issued by Musharraf and his Prime Minister Shaukat Aziz on issues involving the forming of the investigative commission on Red Mosque as well as hearings of victims of the siege, the findings of missing persons, issuing verdicts against the controversial NRO and privatization, and issuing subpoena regarding the extrajudicial killing of Akbar Bugti, in 2006. Failing to reach a compromise and subdue the judiciary, Musharraf authorized the decree of sacking around ~70 senior justices including, the Chief Justice Iftikhar Chaudhry, immediately and declared the state of emergency on 9 November 2007. Virtually suspending the supreme law of the land, the constitution of the country, the massive nationwide demonstration and anger erupted against President Musharraf.

Though, this action and its responses are generally related to the controversies surrounding the re-election of Musharraf during thepresidential election that had occurred on 6 October 2007, and also was claimed by the government to be the reaction to the actions by militants in Waziristan.

Operation Rah-e-Haq

By the end of October 2007, another heavy fighting erupted in the Swat district of the Khyber Pakhtunkhwa Province between the Frontier Police and the large portion of far right-wing TNSMorganization, under the command of Maulana Fazlullah who was trying to impose Sharia law. In a response, the military deployed a combat brigade under a local Brigadier-General to confront them. After week of heavy fighting with the brigade combat teams, the battle came to a standstill with both sides suffering heavy casualties. On 3 November 2007, around ~220 paramilitary soldiers and policemen surrendered or deserted after a military position on a hill-top and two police stations were overrun. This left the TNSM in control of most of the Swat district.

The fighting in Swat is the first serious insurgent threat from terrorist groups in what is known as a settled area of Pakistan. Following this, foreign fighters of al-Qaeda loyal to TNSM's Maulana Fazlullah tried to implement strict Islamic law in November 2007. In November 2007, another brigade combat team was deployed with the help of helicopter gunships to crush the uprising. By the beginning of December 2007, the fighting had ended and the military recaptured Swat. Almost ~400 foreign fighters of Maulana Fazlullah were dead along with 15 Pakistani soldiers and 20 civilians in the military suspension. Despite the victory by the military, the foreign fighters of TNSM slowly re-entered Swat over the coming months and started engaging security forces in battles that lasted throughout 2008. By early February 2009, the whole district was in military control.

2008 General Election

On 27 December 2007, Pakistani opposition leader and former Prime Minister Benazir Bhutto was assassinated upon leaving a political rally for the Pakistan Peoples Party (PPP) in Rawalpindi, Pakistan. A suicidal assassin reportedly fired shots in Bhutto's direction just prior to detonating an explosive pellet-laden vest, killing approximately 24 people and wounding many more.

Ultimately, President General Musharraf and his military establishment blamed the attack on al-Qaeda, but this was contradicted following day, when Baitullah Mehsud sent a statement to the media saying that he and al-Qaeda had "no involvement in the murder of the former Prime Minister", and that they believed that Musharraf was responsible. The violence spread all over the country and national media broadcast the wave of violence across the country that left 58 people dead, including four police officers. Most of the violence was directed at Musharraf and his political party, PML(Q). Opposition parties, notably the PPP, branded PML(Q) as "*Qatil League*" (lit. Murderer's League). Benazir Bhutto had previously survived an assassination attempt made on her life during her homecoming which left 139 people dead and hundreds wounded.

ESCALATION, AIR AND GROUND WAR

In January 2008, the foreign fighters overran Sararogha Fort, and may have overrun a fort in Ladah as well. Both forts are in South Waziristan, and were held by the Pakistan Army. After the general elections in 2008, the army's fighting capability was depleted under the command of President Musharraf and many in the media had scrutinized the role of the army in the national politics. On 25 February 2008, a suicide bomber struck in the garrison-town of Rawalpindi which targeted and killed top military medic and Medical Corps Surgeon-General, Lieutenant-General Mushtaq Baig, along with two more soldiers and five civilians.

In a secretive appointment by Musharraf personally, General Baig had been an operational commander of the army fighting in the region and was the highest-level military official to be assassinated since 1971 war. In 2008, General Musharraf was soon relieved off his command, succeeding General Ishfaq Pervez Kiani as chief of army staff. Events led by successful movement pushed Musharraf to downfall, followed by the consolidated impeachment movement led by Prime minister Yousaf Raza Gillani ousted Musharraf from thepresidency in 2008. The new socialist government led by Prime minister Yousaf Raza Gillani of the PPP made critical decisions and appointment in the key combatant staff of the armed forces, including the new chief of naval staff (Admiral Noman Bashir) and endorsing air chief marshal Rao Soleman as chief of air staff; all in late 2008.

The upcoming and then-newly appointed Chairman Joint Chiefs General Tariq Majid formalized a plan and strategy to tackle the insurgency. Terming as "tri-services framework (TSW)", the chairman joint chiefs emphasized the role of inter-services to tackle the insurgency with full force, and joint army-navy-airforce efforts that are synergized within a framework of jointness and inter-operability to meet present and future challenges". His plan was submitted to Prime minister Yousaf Raza Gillani who approved the new strategy, which followed the new order of battle and new deployments of combat units of joint army–navy–air force in the north-western region.

Operation Zalzala

After a brief intense change in chain of command in the Pakistan Armed Forces, a full-fledged military operation called '*Zalzala* (lit.*earthquake*) was undertaken by 14th Army Division in January with the goal of flushing out Baitullah Mehsud's TTP fighters from the area. The area had previously been a more or less safe zone for militants, with some villagers providing them support and shelter. The operation resulted in tactical success and scores of militants were killed during the operation, and within three days the armed forces were in full control of the area. The army later captured a few other villages and small towns as part of their attempt to pressure Baitullah Mehsud.

However, the operation led to a huge displacement of local population. According to the GOC of the 14th Army Division's Major-GeneralTariq Khan, about 200,000 men, women and children, were displaced. Khalid Aziz, former chief secretary of Khyber-Pakhtunkhwa and expert on tribal affairs, said the displacement was "one of the biggest in tribal history" adding that human cost of the conflict in Waziristan "has gone unrecorded."

Peace Agreement and Bajaur Offensive

Earlier on 7 February 2008, the TTP had offered a truce to Musharraf and peace negotiations resulting in a suspension of violence. On 21 May 2008, the Government signed a peace agreement with the Tehrik-i-Taliban Pakistan (TTP).

Despite the agreement sporadic fighting continued until late June and escalated with the takeover of the town of Jandola on 24 June, by the militants. Around 22 pro-government tribal fighters were captured and executed by the TTP at that time. On 28 June

2008, Pakistan Army started another offensive against militia fighters in Kyhber, codenamed *Sirat-e-Mustaqeem* (lit. *Righteous Path*). The military took control of a key town and demolished an insurgent group's building. In this offense, one militant was reportedly killed while two soldiers died in Swat valley. The operation was halted in early July. On 19 July 2008, clashes erupted between the TTP and a faction of pro-government Taliban militants. The fighting ended with 10–15 of the pro-government fighters were killed and another 120 were captured. Among the captured were two commanders who were tried under "Islamic" law by the Taliban and then executed.

On 21 July 2008, heavy fighting with the another separatist group, the BLA in Baluchistan Province, killed 32 militants, 9 soldiers and 2 civilians. More than two dozen militants were captured and a large weapons cache was found. Between 28 July and 4 August 2008, heavy fighting flared up in the northwestern Swat valley leaving 94 militants, 28 civilians and 22 soldiers and policemen, were dead.

On 6 August 2008, the heavy ground fighting erupted in the Loisam area of the Bajaur district. The Loisam lies on the strategically important road leading towards the main northwestern city of Peshawar. The fighting started when hundreds of foreign fighters poured into the area and began attacking armed forces. After four days of fighting on 10 August 2008, the military was forced to withdraw from the area. It resulted in confirmed killing of 100 militants and 9 soldiers, and another 55 soldiers were missing, at least three dozen of them captured by the militants. While the fighting was going on in Bajaur, in the Buner area of Khyber Pakhtunkhwa Province, the militants killed at least nine policemen in an attack on a check post. The checkpoint was then abandoned, and the army troops withdrew to Khar, the main town of Bajaur Agency. There were reports that the town of Khar was then besieged by tribal militants.

On 21 August 2008, in response to the military offensive in Bajaur, two suicide bombers attacked the POF Laboratories in Wah while workers were changing shifts. The attack killed at least 70 people.

Tribal Tension with TPP and US Support for Tribes

As military retreat from Bajaur Agency, the Pakistani tribal elders began organizing a private army of approximately 30,000 tribesmen to fight the TTP, with the support of the Provincial government in September 2008. This local private military company, known as lashkar (lit. *brigade*), had composed of Pakistani tribesmen who began burning the houses of militant commanders in Bajaur and vowed to fight them until they are expelled. During this campaign, the *Lashkar* torched the house of local militant commander named Naimatullah, who had occupied several government schools and converted them into seminaries. A tribal elder named Malik Munsib Khan quoted inmedia that tribes would continue their struggle until the foreign fighters were expelled from the area, adding that anyone found sheltering militants would be fined one million rupees and their houses will be burned. The tribesmen also torched two important centres of the militant activity in the area and gained control tribal areas.

One of the main motivations for this activity was the operations that were taking place in the FATAthat had displaced some 300,000 people while dozens of citizens had been killed in clashes between the militants and military. Since the start of operations against the foreign fighters, some 150,000 tribesmen have sided with them.

The American military proposals outlined an intensified effort to enlist tribal leaders in the frontier areas of Pakistan in the fight against al-Qaeda. The proposal was modeled in part on a similar effort by American forces in Iraq that had been hailed as a great success in fighting foreign insurgents there. But it raised the question of whether such partnerships can be forged without a significant American military presence in Pakistan. The American military raised great questions whether it is enough support can be found among the tribes. Small numbers of high-ranking officers of American military have served as advisers to the Pakistan Armed Forces in the tribal areas, giving planning advice and helping to integrate American intelligence. Under this new approach, the number of advisers had to increase.

The U.S. Government said these security improvements complemented a package of assistance from the US AID for the seven districts of the tribal areas that amounted to $750 million over five years, and would involve work in education, health and other sectors. The BINLEA of the US Government also assisted the Frontier Corps with financing for counter-narcotics work.

Renewed Bajaur Offensive

In a television emergency address, President Zardari and Prime Minister Gillani publicly vowed revenge in response to the Marriott Hotel bombing. By 26 September 2008, Pakistan air force and army had successfully conducted and completed a major joint offensive in the Bajaur and the Tang Khata regions of the Federally Administered Tribal Areas, codenamed *Operation Sherdil*. Thist joint operation had killed over 1,000 militants in a huge offensive, a day after President Asif Ali Zardari lashed out at US forces over a clash on the Afghan border.

Major-General Tariq Khan, now Inspector General of the Frontier Corps, mentioned to journalists that since the beginning of the Bajaur operations, there were up to 2,000 militant fighters including hundreds of foreign fighters who were fighting with the soldiers and the armed forces. The overall death toll was over ~1,000 militants and also adding that 27 Pakistani soldiers had also been killed with 111 soldiers seriously wounded.

In this major aerial offense, five of the most wanted al-Qaeda operatives and Central Asian militant commanders were among those killed in a month-long operation in Bajaur. According to PAF reports, "out of the five militant commanders killed, four appeared to be foreigners: Egyptian abu Saeed Al-Masri; Abu Suleiman, also an Arab; an Uzbek fighter named Mullah Mansoor; and an Afghan commander called Manaras. The fifth was a Pakistani commander named only Abdullah, a son of aging hardline leader Maulvi Faqir Mohammad who is based in Bajaur and has close ties to Al-Qaeda second-in-command Ayman al-Zawahiri.

Between 22 and 24 October, the armed forces engaged in another hard-push against militants in the restive Bajaur and Khyber tribal regions. The army troops did not enter in the region until the PAF conducted its precision bombings. The PAF intense high-altitude air strikes missions were carried out in the Nawagai and Mamond sub-districts of Bajaur Agency. The advancing troops destroyed several centers of militants at Charmang, Chinar and Zorbandar and inflicted heavy losses on them. The army gunship helicopters shelled in Charming, Cheenar, Kohiand Babarha areas of Nawagai and Mamund Tehsil of Bajaur agency, destroying various underground hideouts and bunkers of militants. The armed forces also took control of different areas of Loisam, a militant headquarters, and advanced towards other areas for complete control.

Islamabad Marriott Hotel Bombing

In 2008, the al-Qaeda struck its largest terrorist attack in Islamabad when a truck bomb targeted the Marriott Hotel. This attack was a defining moment in the war and around ~266 sustained the injuries and 54 died. According to the testimonies, numbers of U.S. Marinesand U.S. Navy personnel also died in the attack; many believed the Americans were the target of the terrorist attacks. In a response to attack on 23 September 2008, the PAF launched its aerial bombing mission which resulted in ultimate success. Military reports indicating that more than 60 insurgents were killed in northwest Pakistan. In the nearby Bajur tribal region, the air force strikes killed at least 10 militants, according to government officials. The Bajur operations, which the army said left more than 700 suspected militants dead, won praise from U.S. officials.

Intensified Drone Strikes and Border Skirmishes with United States

At the end of August 2008, the USAF stepped up its air attacks in the Federally Administered Tribal Areas. On 3 September 2008, the United States Army Special Forces teams laid a commando attack in a village near the Afghan border in South Waziristan. Additional air strikes from unmanned drones in North Waziristan culminating on 8 September 2008, when a United States Air Force drone aircraft fired a number of missiles at a "guest house for militants arriving in North Waziristan." Around ~23 people were killed, but the operation's target, Jalaluddin Haqqani, was not among them.

On 25 September 2008, the Pakistan military and the US military became involved in heavy border fighting on the Frontier border.

The incident happened after two US military helicopters came under fire from Pakistan army troops. A US military spokesman insisted that they had been about a mile and a half inside Afghanistan.

Speaking at the United Nations, President Asif Zardari maintained that Pakistan would not tolerate violations of its sovereignty, even by its allies. President Zardari told the United Nations, "Just as we will not let Pakistani's territory to be used by terrorists for attacks against our people and our neighbours, we cannot allow our territory and our sovereignty to be violated by our friends", he said, without specifically citing the United States or the border flareup.

Militants Targeting of Tribes

On 10 October 2008, TTP militants beheaded four kidnapped pro-government tribal elders in the Charmang area of Bajaur.

On 11 October 2008, a suicide bomber struck an anti-militant gathering of tribal elders just as they had decided to form a lashkar (tribal militia).

At least 110 anti-Taliban tribesmen were killed and a further 125 were wounded. The suicide bomber drove his car into the gathering itself and blew himself up. The attack on the tribal council took place in Orakzai, normally a relatively quiet corner of the nation's chaotic tribal areas.

Fighting for the NATO Supply Lines

On 19 October 2008, the news media began to broadcast the news of Pakistan Army troops, led by an army lieutenant, being locked in a fierce battle with foreign militants to keep open the line routesto NATO forces in Afghanistan. For several months, the foreign militants had been trying to either attack or seal off the supply routes.

The army battle reports indicated that the local commander, Mohammad Tariq al-Fridi, had seized terrain around the mile-long Kohat Tunnel. The military intelligence reports had held al-Fridi responsible for coordinated suicide bomb attacks and rocket strikes against convoys emerging from it. The TTP spokesman,

Maulvi Omar, claimed that his foreign fighters would lay down their arms if the Pakistan Army ceased intense fighting. The military refused his offers and a tactical military operation was launched to secure the tunnel routes afterTTP seized five trucks carrying weapons and ammunition.

They held the tunnel for a week before they were driven out in fierce fighting with the military. Since then, Tariq and his men have returned several times to attack convoys, in a response, the army launched its latest onslaught after a suicide bomb attack at one of its bases near the tunnel six weeks ago. In a massive manhunt operation, Tariq was killed along with hundreds of militants while trying to flee the battle in a combat air operation. The operation ended with five civilians were killed and 45 were injured, including 35 soldiers, when a pickup truck packed with explosives was driven into a checkpoint.

On 11 November 2008, another group of militants attacked two convoys at the Khyber Pass capturing 13 trucks which were headed for Afghanistan. One convoy was from the United Nations World Food Programme and was carrying wheat. The second was intended for NATO troops and one of the captured trucks was carrying with it two U.S. military Humvees, which were also seized.

On 8 December 2008, the militants torched more than 160 vehicles destined for US-led troops in Afghanistan. The militants attacked the Portward Logistic Terminal (PTL) in the northern city of Peshawar at around 02:30 am, destroying its gate with a rocket-propelled grenade and shooting dead a guard. They then set fire to about 100 vehicles, including 70 Humvees, which shipping documents showed were being shipped to the US-led coalition forces and the Afghan National Army. At the same time, militants torched about 60 more vehicles at the nearby Faisal depot, which like Portward is on the ring road around Peshawar, where convoys typically stop before heading for the Khyber Pass. On 3 February 2009, the militant group again blew up a bridge at the Khyber Pass, temporarily cutting a major supply line for Western troops in Afghanistan. After the attack supplies along the route had been halted "for the time being", according to NATO.

PUBLIC SUPPORT AND UNIFIED MILITARY OPERATIONS

Swat Ceasefire

Since 2008–09, the Chairman joint chiefs General Tariq Majid, working with his JS HQ staffers, had been running several meetings of planning to conduct the joint warfare operations against the TTP militants. A new strategy of joint-military operations and studies were conducted under General Majid. During this time, the Government agreed to impose the *Sharia ordnance* law and temporarily suspended the military suspension in the Swat Valley in Khyber Pakhtunkhwa Province. This decision was troubling for the United States in Afghanistan, which believed that it would embolden militant groups fighting US military–led ISAF in Afghanistan. The US government also believed it would provide another safe haven for the militants within 80 miles (130 km) of Islamabad, as well as a corridor between the North-Western border with Afghanistan andNorth–Eastern border with India.

The Pakistan Government officials rationalized that "such agreement was the only way to pacify a fierce insurgency and avoid more civilian casualties in Swat Valley – whose ski resort and mountain scenery once made it a popular tourist destination. The Khyber Pakhtunkhwa's Chief Minister, Amir Hoti, announced that the local authorities would impose Islamic law acrossMalakand Division, which includes Swat. The Government officials maintained that President Asif Zardari would sign off on the deal once peace had been restored. However, the agreement was never signed by President Zardari soon after the TTP militants violated the treaty.

The agreement came the day after the militants in Swat said that it would observe a ten-day ceasefire in support of the peace process. Pakistani officials say that the laws allow Muslim clerics to advise judges, but not to outlaw female education, music or other activities once banned by the Afghan Taliban in Afghanistan.

Defeat of the Militants in Bajaur

On 1 March 2009, the Pakistan Army troops finally defeated

the foreign fighters in Bajaur, which is a strategically important region on the Afghan border. The 40th Army Division commander, Major-General Tariq Khan reported that the army and the Frontier Corps had killed most militants in Bajaur, the smallest of the agencies but a major infiltration route into Afghanistan, after a six-month offensive. By the time the battle in Bajaur was over, the Pakistan Army killed over 1,500 militants while losing 97 of their own soldiers and 404 soldiers seriously injured.

In retaliation on 30 March, the militant groups attacked the Police Academy in Munawan town, killing and taking hostage police cadets. In an operation led by Punjab Police, the units of Elite Police had managed to retake the academy. Lasting about eight hours, the police suspension ended with 18 people killed in the attack, including eight policemen, eight militants and two civilians deaths. At least, ~95 policemen were wounded and four gunmen were captured by the Elite Police.

In a similar attack on 4 April 2009, another suicide bomber attacked a military camp in Islamabad killing eight soldiers; less than 24 hours later, two more suicide attacks occurred. One bomber targeted a market on the border with Afghanistan killing 17 people and the other attacked a mosque in Chakwal, in the Eastern Pakistan province of Punjab, killing 26 more civilians. The next day, the leader of the Tehrik-i-Taliban Pakistan, Baitullah Mehsud, promised that there were to be two suicide attacks per week in the country until the Pakistani army withdrew from the border region and the United States stopped its missile attacks by unmaned drones on militant bases.

Militant Violation of Swat Ceasefire

In March 2009, many Pakistanis were horrified when a videotape was broadcast in news channelsthat showed militant enforcers were publicly whipping a 17-year-old girl in Swat accused of having an affair. The girl had not committed fornication or adultery but was flogged simply because she refused her brother's demand to marry someone of his choosing. Protests against the TTP broke out all over the country to demonstrate against the flogging. The conservative thinker, Raja Zafar-ul-Haq ofPakistan Muslim League, appearing in news channels, maintained that "this summary punishment of flogging simply for refusing a marriage proposal was totally *un-Islamic* and had nothing to do with*Sharia*." He went on to say that Muhammad had strictly forbidden the practice of forced marriages and in this case, the girl had not done anything wrong by refusing a marriage proposal.

Sensing the sensitivity of the issue, the Supreme Court of Pakistan appointed a five-member team appointed to investigate the video's origins, and concluded that it had been faked, raising questions at Pakistani intelligence services.

In Buner, the TTP continued their criminal activities when residents said TTP fighters had been stealing cattle for meat, stealing other livestock, berating men without beards and recruiting teenagers into their ranks. The TTP also began to steal vehicles belonging to government officials and ransacked the offices of some local non-government organisations for no apparent reason. 12 schoolchildren were killed by a bomb contained in a football.

Operation Black Thunderstorm

On 26 April 2009, the unified Pakistan Armed Forces started the strategic and tactical airborne attack, codename *Black Thunderstorm*, with the aim of retaking Buner, Lower Dir, Swat and Shangla districts from the TTP. This joint army–navy- air force unified operation was well rehearsed and prepared. The fighter jets of Navy and air force began pounding the militant hideouts while army kept advancing in the militant hideouts. The combat fighter pilots of the navy and air force flew their aerial bombing mission together in high altitude at continuous 24-hour period, to avoid being hit from the anti-aircraft guns. During the initial stages of the unified operations, the ground troops and paratroopers performed combat HALO/HAHO techniques to hold the control of high strategic mountains and hills surrounding the Taliban-controlled cities.

The operation largely cleared the Lower Dir district of militia forces by 28 April and Buner by 5 May 2009. The same day, the ground fighting in Swat was particularly fierce since the TTP threw away their insurgent tactics and the ground forces obtained the counter-insurgency tactics. By 14 May 2009, the military was only six kilometers south of Mingora, the milita-held capital city of Swat, and preparations for all-out street fighting were underway.

On 23 May 2009, the battle for Mingora started and by 27 May, approximately 70% of the city was cleared of militants. On 30 May, the Pakistan military had taken back the city of Mingora from the TTP, calling it a significant victory in its offensive against the militants. However, some sporadic fighting was still continuing on the city's outskirts.

In all, according to the military, 128 soldiers and more than ~1,475 militants were killed and 317 soldiers were wounded during operation*Black Thunderstorm*. ~95 soldiers and policemen were captured by the militants; all were rescued by the military. 114 foreign fighters were captured, including some local commanders. At least 23 of the militants killed were foreigners.

Sporadic fighting throughout Swat continued up until mid-June. On 14 June, the operation was declared over and the military had regained control of the region. Only small pockets of Taliban resistance remained and the military started mopping up operations. This led to arefugee crisis, and by 22 August, 1.6 million of 2.3 million have returned home according to UN estimates.

Blockade of South Waziristan

In the aftermath of the successful victory and recapture of the entire Swat valley, the Pakistan military began a massive army troop build-up along the southern and eastern borders of South Waziristan on 16 June 2009,. The military was now taking the fight to Mehsud's mountainous stronghold, ordering an expansion of its current offensive against TTP fighters in the Swat valley. On 17 June 2009, the Governor of Khyber Pakhtunkhwa, Owais Ghani, denounced Baitullah Mehsud as "the root cause of all evils", and quoted that the government has called on the military to launch a "full-fledged" operation to eliminate Mehsud and his estimated 20,000 men.

The Islamabad's decision to launch the offensive against Mehsud signaled a deepening of Pakistani resolve against the militants. The military had targeted the TTP leader on three separate occasions – in 2004, 2005 and 2008 – but walked away each time after signing peace deals with Mehsud. This time, the military also enjoyed the public support as a wave of terrorist attacks had swayed public sentiment against the Taliban.

On 17 October 2009, the military launched another offense, called *Rah-e-Nijat* when the combat brigades and fighter jets launched a large-scale offensive in South Waziristan involving ~28,000 troops advancing across South Waziristan from three directions. Starting with air force strike and naval intelligence assessment on the TTP, the first town to fall to the military was Kotkai, the birthplace of the TTP leader,Hakimullah Mehsud, on 19 October 2009. However, the next day, the TTP re-took the town. Troops had thrust into Kotkai only to be hit by a determined counteroffensive that killed seven soldiers, including an army major, and wounded seven more. The military managed to take the town once again on 24 October, after days of bombardments.

On 29 October, the town of Kaniguram, which was under the control of Uzbek fighters from the Islamic Movement of Uzbekistan, was surrounded. And on 2 November, Kaniguram was taken.

On 1 November 2009, the towns of Sararogha and Makin were surrounded, and fighting for Sararogha started on 3 November. The fighting there lasted until 17 November, when the town finally fell to the military. The same day, the town of Laddah was also captured by the military and street fighting commenced in Makin. Both Sararogha and Laddah were devastated in the fighting.

By 21 November 2009, the ISPR reports showed that more than 570 foreign fighters and 76 soldiers had been killed in the offensive.

On 12 December 2009, the Pakistan military declared victory in South Waziristan.

Death of Baitullah Mehsud and TTP Counter-attacks

As early as August 2009, the TTP leader, Baitullah Mehsud, was killed in a drone attack. This was later confirmed by captured chief spokesman Maulvi Umar. He was replaced by Hakimullah Mehsud.

In early October 2009, the TTP started a string of bomb attacks in cities across Pakistan. The goal of the attacks was to show that the TTP militants were still a united fighting force following the death of their leader and to disrupt a planned military offensive into South Waziristan. Places targeted include the U.N. World Food Program offices in Islamabad a food store in Peshawar; military headquarters inRawalpindi; a market in Shangla; the intelligence establishments in Lahore; the police stations in Kohat and Peshawar; the Islamic center at the International Islamic University in Islamabad; and Air Science Laboratories (ASL) Complex in Kamra. The month of November ended with a car bombing of Meena Bazaar, Peshawar killing 118 civilians. Additionally, the month of November saw suicide bombings of the National Bank of Pakistan in Rawalpindi, a market in Charsadda, and six bombings in Peshawar including the regional headquarters of the ISI and the Judicial Complex. In 2013, the media reported that the mastermind of chain of attacks in 2009, Abdullah Umar, was brutalized and killed in a police encounter with Punjab Police in 2013. Media authorities identified Abdullah Umar as a law student of the International Islamic University and a son of army colonel.

INSURGENCY IN WEST AND DEFEAT OF TALIBAN: 2010–2011

In an offensive in Bajaur by Frontier Corps, a militants' stronghold village Damadola was captured and cleared by 6 February 2010.Bajaur was declared conflict free zone by 20 April.

On 23 March 2010, the Pakistan armed forces launched an offensive to clear Orakzai. Officials also announced a future offensive in North Waziristan. The week prior the Pakistan military killed approximately 150 militants in fighting in the region. It was expected that all tribal areas would be cleared by June 2010.

3 June, Pakistani authorities announced a victory over the insurgents in Orakzai and Kurram.

Death of Bin Laden and Navy Offensive

As late as 2010, chief of naval staff Admiral Noman Bashir had coordinated many of successful tactical ground operations against TTP hideouts, to support the army and air force pressure on militants. Many successful operations were executed by the navy, and its operational capability gained international prominence. By 2011, Pakistan's armed forces were stretched thin by natural disasters and deployments against extremist groups, with one third of the army deployed for the fight, another third along the Indian border and the rest engaged in preparing to deploy. On 1 May 2011, in a clandestine operation in Abbottabad, al-Qaeda leader Osama Bin Laden was located and killed by the U.S. Navy SEALs in his private compound. The groups affiliated with the armed TTP vowed, via media, to avenge Osama's death upon the Pakistan Armed Forces.

On 21 and 28 April, senior al-Qaeda operative Ilyas Kashmiri conducted a series of coordinated terrorist attacks on the Pakistan Navy presence in Northern and Southern contingents. This included attacks on high naval officials of the Pakistan Navy in Karachi, first attacking their bus near the Navy bases. Finally on 22 May, TTP attacked the Mehran Naval Base, killing up to 10 naval officers, wounding 30 others, and destroying two naval reconnaissance aircraft, during the attack. In response, the navy's SSG(N) launched its largest offensive efforts since the 1971 operations, and managed to control and secure the base after a massive shootout. Operationally resulting in tactical success, the navy's counter offensive killed all the militants and ring leaders behind these operations. Kashmiri was widely suspected in the Mehran operation. On 4 June 2011, Ilyas Kashmiri was killed by a U.S. drone strike in South Waziristan.

In 2012, the north-west region of Pakistan experienced periodic bombings perpetrated by insurgents, resulting in thousands of deaths. On 22 December 2012, a suicide bomb attack carried out by the Pakistani Taliban killed Bashir Ahmed Bilour, a minister of KhyberPakhtunkhwa, as well as 8 other people.

Tirah Valley Clashes

In January 2013, at least 80 militants and civilians were killed in clashes between the Tehrik-e-Taliban / Lashkar-e-Islam and Ansar ul-Islam(a pro-government militant group) in Tirah Valley of Pakistan's Khyber Agency. Fighting between Ansar ul-Islam and the Pakistani Taliban continued till March and as a result, almost the entire Tirah Valley came under the control of Lashkar-e-Islam and TTP fighters.Over 250 militants and civilians were killed and 400 others wounded in the three-month-long clashes. The fighting also displaced about 200,000 to 300,000 people. This forced the Pakistan Army to start Operation Rah-e-Shahadat in order to root out insurgents and extremists from the strategically important region and restore peace and stability for the upcoming May elections.

Operation Rah-e-Shahadat

Operation Rah-e-Shahadat was a codename of a joint military operation that was commenced on 5 April 2013 by thePakistan Army, with assistance provided by the PAF and Navy for air support. In close coordination with Local Peace Committee (*Aman Lashkar*), the army troops and special operations forces, aided by Frontier Corps, to flush out TTP and LeI militants from theTirah Valley of the Khyber Agency. At least four Pakistani soldiers and 14 insurgents were killed while 5 soldiers were also wounded. In a major aerial operation, thePAF and navy fighter jets pounded hideouts of banned group LeI in and according to military intelligence reports, many militants escaped from the areas taking with them their injured fighters.

On 7 April 2013 Pakistani military officials said that at least 30 Taliban-linked militants and 23 soldiers including commandos were killed during clashes in the Tirah Valley since 5 April. Several Aman Lashkar members were also reported to be killed and wounded. Scores of insurgents and Pakistani troops were injured in the operation.

On 8 April 2013 Pakistani military officials said that at least 30 Pakistani soldiers and 97 militants were killed during fierce fighting with Taliban linked-fighters in the Tirah Valley since 5 April, the day when the operation began.

On 9 April 2013, the ISPR confirmed that at least 23 soldiers and 110 insurgents were killed in the four-day fighting in the Tirah Valley of Khyber Agency.

On 11 April 2013 at least 15 militants and one Pakistani soldier were killed during fighting in southern sector of Tirah Valley. The areas of Mada Khel and Tut Sar were cleared from militants.

On 12 April 2013 nine Pakistani soldiers and seven insurgents were killed during clashes in Sipah area of Tirah Valley. The security forces took control of the areas of Sandana and Sheikhmal Khel in Sipah area. Three Lashkar-e-Islam militants were also arrested while a dozen others were injured. Two peace committee members were killed and 22 others injured in a bomb blast in the same area.

On 13 April 2013, Pakistan Army's ISPR said that seven militants were killed in the Tirah Valley on 12 April. It did not confirm the casualties suffered by the security forces.

On 16 April 2013 a member of Zakhakhel peace committee (Tawheedul-ul-Islam) was killed in a bomb blast in Dari area of Tirah Valley.

On 2 May 2013 four Taliban-linked insurgents were killed and five others wounded after Pakistani fighter jets targeted TTP hideouts in the Tirah Valley.

On 5 May 2013 Pakistan Army's ISPR said that 16 insurgents and two soldiers were killed during heavy clashes in the Tirah Valley. Three soldiers were reported to be wounded. The military also claimed to have captured militant strongholds Kismat Sur and Sanghar and recovered huge cache of arms and ammunition from the militants fleeing the area.

Disengagement of Militant Groups

News reports and intelligence media news began airing the news that the TTP and other Central Asian militant groups, notably the IMU, have now set up camps and reinforced hundreds of fighters to Syria to fight alongside rebels opposed to Bashar al-Assad in continuity of cementation of ties with al Qaeda, starting of July 2013.

According to Reuters, hundreds of fighters had gone to Syria to fight alongside their "Mujahedeen friends".

Media reported the visit and setup of a TTP base in Syria to assess "the needs of the jihad".At least 12 experts in information technology and warfare were sent to Syria in the last two months to aid the Mujahideen. The Pakistani government has not commented on the allegations.

North Waziristan Offensive

On 19 December 2013, the army launched a major offensive in the Mir Ali region of North Waziristan following a suicide bomb attack on a checkpoint in the area the previous day. Artillery and helicopter gunships were used in the operation. By 23 December, more than 30 militants and up to 70 civilians allegedly were killed.

Tehreek-e-Taliban Pakistan Infighting

In March 2014 rival factions fought for control of Tehreek-e-Taliban Pakistan. Commander Khan Said Sajna and followers of the late TTP leader Hakimullah Mehsud now under command of Maulana Fazlullah clashed in Shaktoi area of South Waziristan and later in the same area in early April 2014. This began a bloody struggle for control of the organization. After several minor skirmishes another major attack took place in the Shawal area of the troubled North Waziristan district on 6 May 2014.

Operation Zarb-e-Azb

In response to an attack on Jinnah International Airport on 8 June 2014, the Pakistani military launched an operation on 15 June 2014 against the North Waziristan militants including the Tehrik-i-Taliban Pakistan (TTP), Al-Qaeda, East Turkestan Islamic Movement (ETIM), the Islamic Movement of Uzbekistan (IMU) and the Haqqani network. Up to 30,000 soldiers are involved in the operation. It has been described as a "comprehensive operation" that aims to flush out foreign and local militants hiding in North Waziristan. More than 600 Islamic militants have been killed in the operation. By 2014, casualty rates in the country as a whole dropped by 40% as compared to 2011–2013, with even greater drops noted in Khyber Pakhtunkhwa, despite the province being the site of a large massacre of schoolchildren by Tehrik-i-Taliban terrorists in December 2014.

PEACE PROSPECTS AND DEVELOPMENTS

Since 2006, major initiatives have been taken out by the government to reconstruct and rehabilitate the war-torn areas of

FATA and Khyber Pakhtunkhwa. The military administrator of the National Disaster Management Authority (NDMA), Lieutenant-General Nadeem Ahmad, supervised majority of the socioeconomic development in the areas that were badly effected by the military operations. The government took many initiatives, including promotion the political activities under the Political Parties Act, the construction of the Peshawar-Torkham Road and the establishment of the Investment Bank of FATA, envisioned to bring prosperity and provide employment opportunities. Around ¨ 1 billion were spent for the rehabilitation of the IDPs and¨ 500 million were immediately transferred into the account of Khyber Pakhtunkhwa government for the economic development in the province.

As of 2006 and present, there are numbers of notable and major international agencies and UN efforts to reconstruct the war-torn areas affected of fighting. As early as 2005, there major government institutions who have been involved in public level to lead the reconstruction, economic development and to bring the quick economic recovery in the war-torn areas, as listed below:

- US Aid
- National Reconstruction Bureau (NRB)
- National Disaster Management Authority (NDMA)
- Earthquake Reconstruction and Rehabilitation Authority (ERRA)
- Special Support Group for IDPs (SSG)
- Federal Relief Commission (FRC)
- National Logistics Cell (NLC)
- Frontier Works Organisation (FWO)
- Navy Reconstruction Group (NRG)

Under the 2006–15 program, a nine-year project, over $2.06 billion would be spend for the economic reconstruction of the FATA region, with the U.S. Government has pledged to provide $750 million over a period of 5 years. Since 2010, the engineering units of army, theFrontier Works Organisation (FWO) and Corps of Engineers and Military Engineering Service, have been active in the area to reconstruct the war-torn areas. Major operations were carried out by the FWO to completed the wide canvas of works, including construction of over 400 km roads, dams, canals and hydroelectric works.

The engineering units commenced the work on Gomal Zam Dam in Waziristan with the help of the local tribal people who were employed for this mega project. The Pakistan Army started the political and educational activities after rebuilding the damaged schools and colleges in Waziristan and gave admissions to as many as young tribal teenagers and young men and women in the army institutions since August 2011.

CASUALTIES

In a debriefing to parliamentarians on 19 October 2011, the ISPR stated that a total of ~3,097 soldiers and personnel were killed and 721 other were permanently disabled in the war on terror.

TheISI lost 63 of its personnel owing to targeted assaults on ISI installations. In the same government report, it confirmed that since 2001 a total of ~40,309 Pakistanis, both military and civilian, had lost their lives in the conflict.

In addition, the TPP and Central Asian militant groups suffered a staggering number of human casualties, and according to the reports ~20,742 militants had been killed or captured by February 2010.

Among these, by November 2007, were 488 foreign fighters killed, 24 others arrested and 324 injured. 220 policemen were killed in fighting in 2007 and 2008. Before all-out fighting broke out in 2003, independent news sources reported only four incidents of deaths of Pakistani forces in 2001 and 2002, in which a total of 20 soldiers and policemen were killed.

The independent South Asia Terrorism Portal website has estimated that at least 30,323 militants, 6,076 security forces members and 20,076 civilians were killed between 2003 and 2015.

Naushad Ali Khan of Pakistan Government's Research and Analysis, Khyber-Pakhtunkhwa Police in his article *Suicide and terrorist attacks and police actions in NWFP, Pakistan* has provided details of different activities of the terrorists during 2008.

Accordingly, 483 cases were registered with 533 deaths and 1290 injured. Similarly 29 suicidal attacks were recorded, resulting 247 deaths and 695 injuries. During the same period 83 attempts acts of terrorism were foiled by the Khyber-Pakhtunkhwa Police.

ISSUES WITH WAR VETERANS

Pakistan does not have its own equivalent to the United States Department of Veterans Affairs. There is also no federal ministry that looks after veteran affairs. Most of Pakistan's infantry come from lower income, poor families, mainly from the rural areas of the country. They remain unknown from the time of their recruitment, and for the most part, to the time of their leave or death. Because there is no network of support that goes out to veterans, some believe that Pakistan's veterans are facing similar issues like those faced by Vietnam veterans. Politicians hardly ever mention the veterans in speeches or statements. This is because civil society hardly ever inquires or hears about the physical and mental challenges facing Pakistan's veterans. How to re-integrate veterans in to society is an issue that has yet to be addressed.

Popular culture

Since the success of unified military operations in 2009–2011, the Waziristan war has been heavily featured in Pakistan media, including intheatre, television, cinema, music, video games and literature. The war also influenced Pakistan's civil society to gather their support for Pakistan Armed Forces through the media miniseries and films that were released throughout the war. Pakistan's rock bands, such as*Entity Paradigm, Strings, Call* and *Mizraab* released many patriotic songs to gather support for the Pakistan armed forces to tackle down the insurgency. A popular band in the country, Junoon, released their album, *Rock & Roll Jihad* and literature *Rock & Roll Jihad: A Muslim Rock Star's Revolution* in 2010.

UNITED STATES ROLE IN PAKISTAN

The US Ambassador Cameron Munter found it difficult to counter the Anti-American sentiment in the country, especially after the Raymond Davis incident. The Anti-Americanism sentiment in Pakistan is one of the strongest in the world. The Anti-Americanism has risen as a result of U.S. military drone strikes introduced by President George W. Bush and continued by President Barack Obama as his counter-terrorism policy. As of present, almost 60%–80% of Pakistanis consider the United States as an enemy combatant state.

The Anti-Americanism has been provoked mainly as a reaction from those who are critical of American CIA activities in Pakistan, such as the infamous break-out of theRaymond Allen Davis incident and American intrusions from Afghanistan border such as the 2011 NATO attack in Pakistan.

The credibility of Obama administration was undermined in the country and, furthermore, approximately 4 in 10 Pakistanis believe that U.S. military and economic aid is having a negative impact on their country; only 1 in 10 believes the impact has been positive.

Economics and Cost of War

Studies and research conducted by Pakistan's leading economists and the financial experts, the war hit Pakistan's national economy "very hard", and the outcomes produced by the war on country's national economy, were surprising and unexpected to Pakistan's military and economic planners.

The government economic institutions of Pakistan referred the conflict as "economic terrorism" and according to the one Pakistani economist, the indirect and direct cost of the war was around $2.67 billion in 2001–02, which raised up to $13.6 billion by 2009–10, projected to rise to $17.8 billion in the current financial year (2010–11). The country's national investment-to-GDP ratio has nosedived from 22.5% in 2006–07 which went down to 13.4% in 2010–11 with serious consequences for job Creating ability of the economy. The leading English language newspaper, *The Nation* gave great criticism to United States, and called U.S. role as "economic terrorism" in South Asia.

Until July 2009 the conflict, as well as terrorism in Pakistan, had cost Pakistan $35 billion.According to US Congress and the

Pakistani media, Pakistan has received about $18 billion from the United States for the logistical support it provided for the counter-terrorism operations from 2001 to 2010, and for its own military operation mainly in Waziristan and other tribal areas along theDurand Line.

The Bush administration also offered an additional $3 billion five-year aid package to Pakistan for becoming a frontline ally in its 'War on Terror'. Annual installments of $600 million each split evenly between military and economic aid, began in 2005.

In 2009, President Barack Obama pledged to continue supporting Pakistan and said that Pakistan would be provided economic aid of $1.5 billion each year for the next five years. Unfolding a new US strategy to defeat Taliban and al-Qaeda, Obama said Pakistan must be a 'stronger partner' in destroying al-Qaeda safe havens.

In addition, President Obama has also planned to propose an extra $2.8 billion in aid for the Pakistani military to intensify the US-led 'War on Terror' along the Pakistan-Afghanistan border. The military aid would be in addition to the civilian aid of $1.5 billion a year for the next five years from 2009 onwards.

In his autobiography, President Musharraf wrote that the United States had paid millions of dollars to the Pakistan government as bounty money for capturing al-Qaeda operatives from tribal areas bordering Afghanistan. About 359 of them were handed over to the US for prosecution.

Pakistan has purchased 1,000 laser-guided bomb kits and 18 F-16 fighter jets from USA.

PAKISTAN AND STATE-SPONSORED TERRORISM

Pakistan had long been accused by neighbour India. Pakistan's tribal region along the border of Afghanistan has been claimed to be a "haven for terrorists" by western media and the United States Defense Secretary.

According to an analysis published by the Saban Center for Middle East Policy at Brookings Institution in 2008, Pakistan was, "with the possible exception of Iran, perhaps the world's most active sponsor of terrorist groups... aiding groups that pose a direct threat to the United States." Daniel Byman, an author, also writes that, "Pakistan is probably today's most active sponsor of terrorism".

Until Pakistan became a key ally in the War on Terrorism, the US Secretary of State included Pakistan on the 1993 list of countries which repeatedly provide support for acts of international terrorism.

In fact, many consider that Pakistan has been playing both sides in the fight against terror, on the one hand, pretending to help curtail terrorist activities while on the other, stoking it. Even the noted Pakistani journalist Ahmed Rashid has accused Pakistan's ISI of providing help to the Taliban, a statement echoed by many, including author Ted Galen Carpenter, who states that Pakistan has "assisted rebel forces in Kashmir even though those groups have committed terrorist acts against civilians".

ALLEGATIONS OF STATE-SPONSORED TERRORISM

Author Gordon Thomas states that whilst aiding in the capture of Al Qaeda members, Pakistan "still sponsored terrorist groups in the disputed state of Kashmir, funding, training and arming them in their war of attrition against India".

Journalist Stephen Schwartz notes that several terrorist and criminal groups are "backed by senior officers in the Pakistani army, the country's ISI intelligence establishment and other armed bodies of the state".

According to Ted Galen Carpenter who is a senior fellow for defense and foreign policy studies at theCato Institute,"Without the active support of the government in Islamabad, it is doubtful whether the Taliban could ever have come to power in Afghanistan. Pakistani authorities helped fund the militia and equip it with military hardware during the mid-1990s when the Taliban was merely one of several competing factions in Afghanistan's civil war.

Only when the United States exerted enormous diplomatic pressure after the Sept. 11 attacks did Islamabad begin to sever its political and financial ties with the Taliban. Even now it is not certain that key members of Pakistan's intelligence service have repudiated their Taliban clients.

Afghanistan is not the only place where Pakistani leaders have flirted with terrorist clients. Pakistan has also assisted rebel forces in Kashmir even though those groups have committed terrorist acts against civilians. And it should be noted that a disproportionate number of the extremist madrasas schools funded by the Saudis operate in Pakistan." Pakistan's former ambassador to the U.S., Husain Haqqanihas said Pakistan sponsors terrorist.

According to the author Daniel Byman, "Pakistan is probably today's most active sponsor of terrorism." writing in an article published byThe Australian stated, "following the terror massacres in Mumbai, Pakistan may now be the single biggest state sponsor of terrorism, beyond even Iran, yet it has never been listed by the US State Department as a state sponsor of terrorism".

Former Pakistan Ruler Pervez Musharraf has conceded that his forces trained militant groups to fight India in Indian-administered Kashmir. He confessed that the government 3 turned a blind eye3 because it wanted to force India to enter negotiations besides raising the issue internationally.

He also said Pakistani spies in the Inter-Services Intelligence directorate (ISI) cultivated the Taliban after 2001 because Karzai's government was dominated by non-Pashtuns, the country's largest ethnic group, and officials who were thought to favour India.

India has been consistent in alleging that Pakistan was involved in training and arming underground militant groups to fight Indian forces in Kashmir.

INTER-SERVICES INTELLIGENCE AND TERRORISM

The ISI, has often been accused of playing a role in major terrorist attacks across India including

- terrorism in Kashmir,
- the July 2006 Mumbai Train Bombings,
- the 2001 Indian Parliament attack,
- the 2006 Varanasi bombings,

- the August 2007 Hyderabad bombings and
- the November 2008 Mumbai attacks.

The ISI is also accused of supporting Taliban forces and recruiting and training mujahideen to fight in Afghanistan and Kashmir. Based on communication intercepts, US intelligence agencies concluded Pakistan's ISI was behind the attack on the Indian embassy in Kabul on 7 July 2008, a charge that the governments of India and Afghanistan had laid previously. The Pakistani intelligence agency, the Inter-Services Intelligence(ISI), is believed to be aiding these organisations in eradicating perceived enemies or those opposed to their cause, including India, Russia, China, Israel, the United States, the United Kingdom and other members of NATO. Satellite imagery from the FBI suggest the existence of several terrorist camps in Pakistan, with at least one militant admitting to being trained in the country as part of the going Kashmir Dispute, Pakistan is alleged to be supporting separatist militiasMany nonpartisan sources believe that officials within Pakistan's military and the Inter-Services Intelligence (ISI) sympathise with and aidIslamic terrorists, saying that the "ISI has provided covert but well-documented support to terrorist groups active in Kashmir, including theal-Qaeda affiliate Jaish-e-Mohammed".

The Afghan President Hamid Karzai, who has regularly reiterated allegations that militants operating training camps in Pakistan have used it as a launch platform to attack targets in Afghanistan, urged Western military allies to target extremist hideouts in neighbouring Pakistan. In response to the millants from Afghanistan hiding in the mountainous tribal region of Pakistan. The US and Pakistan agreed to allow US Drone Strikes in Pakistan.

Several detainees at the Guantanamo Bay facility told US interrogators that they were aided by the ISI for attacks in the disputed Kashmir Region.

LINKS TO TERRORIST GROUPS

Pakistan is said to be a haven for terrorist groups like Al-Qaeda, Lashkar-e-Omar, Lashkar-e-Toiba, Jaish-e-Mohammed and

Sipah-e-Sahaba. Pakistan is accused of giving aid to the Taliban, "which include[s] soliciting funding for the Taliban, bankrolling Taliban operations, providing diplomatic support as the Taliban's virtual emissaries abroad, arranging training for Taliban fighters, recruiting skilled and unskilled manpower to serve in Taliban armies, planning and directing offensives, providing and facilitating shipments of ammunition and fuel, and on several occasions apparently directly providing combat support," as stated by the Human Rights Watch.

In 2008, the US has stated that the next attack on the US could originate in Pakistan.

In June 2009, India's army chief, General Deepak Kapoor, used a meeting with US national security adviser Jim Jones to claim that Pakistan was home to 43 "terrorist camps", while rejecting suggestions of engaging in fresh peace talks.

Another militant outfit, theJKLF, has openly admitted that more than 3,000 militants from various nationalities were still being trained. Other resources also concur, stating that Pakistan's military and ISI both include personnel who sympathise with and help Islamic militants, adding that "ISI has provided covert but well-documented support to terrorist groups active in Kashmir, including the Jaish-e-Mohammed."

Pakistan has denied any involvement in the terrorist activities in Kashmir, arguing that it only provides political and moral support to the so-called 'secessionist' groups. Many Kashmiri groups also maintain their headquarters in Pakistan-administered Kashmir, which is cited as further proof by the Indian Government.

The normally reticent United Nations Organization (UNO) has also publicly increased pressure on Pakistan on its inability to control its Afghanistan border and not restricting the activities of Taliban leaders who have been declared by the UN as terrorists.

ALLEGED PAKISTANI ARMY SUPPORT OF TERRORISTS

Former Pakistan President Pervez Musharraf has admitted that Pakistan supported and trained terrorist groups like Lashkar-e-Taiba (LeT) in 1990s to carry out militancy in Kashmir. From

1979 Pakistan was in favour of religious militancy. "The Kashmiri freedom fighters including Hafiz Saeed and Lakhvi were our heroes at that time. We trained Taliban and sent them to fight against Russia. Taliban, Haqqani,Osama Bin Laden and Zawahiri were our heroes then. Later they became villains" says Pervez Musharraf.

The United States had direct evidence that the ISI chief, Lt. Gen. Ahmed Shuja Pasha, knew of Bin Laden's presence in Abbottabad, Pakistan. According to Pervez Hoodhboy, "Bin Laden was the 'Golden Goose' that the army had kept under its watch but which, to its chagrin, has now been stolen from under its nose. Until then, the thinking had been to trade in the Goose at the right time for the right price, either in the form of dollars or political concessions".

Pakistan was also responsible for the evacuation of about 5000 of the top leadership of the Taliban and Al-Qaeda who were encircled by Nato forces in the 2001 Invasion of Afghanistan. This event known as the Kunduz airlift, which is also popularly called the "Airlift of Evil", involved several Pakistani Air Force transport planes flying multiple sorties over a number of days. According to a 2001 article titled "Overview of State-Sponsored Terrorism" issued by the US Office of the Coordinator for Counterterrorism, "In South Asia, the United States has been increasingly concerned about reports of Pakistani support to terrorist groups and elements active in Kashmir, as well as Pakistani support, especially military support, to the Taliban, which continues to harbor terrorist groups, including al-Qaida, the Egyptian Islamic Jihad, al-Gama'a al-Islamiyya, and the Islamic Movement of Uzbekistan." In 2011, American troops reportedly recovered Pakistani military supplies from Taliban insurgents in Afghanistan.

LeT began carrying out operations in Indian-controlled Kashmir in the 1990s. It actively infiltrated militants across the Line of Control (LoC) from Pakistan to carry out sabotage activities with the help of the ISI and the Pakistan Army. Pakistan Army and Inter-Services Intelligence Directorate (ISI) have long considered Lashkar-e-Taiba to be the country's most reliable proxy against India and the group still provides utility in this regard as well as the potential for leverage at the negotiating table.

LASHKAR-E-TAIBA AND JAMAAT-UD-DAWA

The militant group Lashkar-e-Taiba (LeT) is widely blamed for the November 2008 Mumbai attacks. The US has put a $10m bounty for its founder Hafiz Muhammad Saeed. Saeed now heads the Jamaat-ud-Dawa (JuD) group, widely seen as a front for LeT. LeT was banned by Pakistan in 2002 after it allegedly carried out an attack on the Indian parliament. JuD is currently banned by the US, the EU, India and Russia as a terrorist organisation. In June 2014, Washington declared JuD an LeT affiliate and announced head money for JuD's political wing chief and Saeed's brother-in-law Abdur Rahman Makki. Zaki ur-Rehman Lakhvi, the leader of Lashkar-e-Taiba and allegedly the planner of 2008 Mumbai attacks was released in Pakistan which caused condemnations in India.

JuD regularly conducts mass rallies and congregation, advocating jihad in Kashmir. For its December 2014 rally, Pakistan ran two special trains to carry the crowd to Lahore. India's foreign ministry termed this as 'nothing short of mainstreaming of terrorism and a terrorist'. The congregation was held near Pakistan's national monument, the Minar-e-Pakistan and a security of 4000 policemen was provided. JuD also asks donations for its anti-India and pro-jihad campaigns.

HAQQANI NETWORK

Former Chairman of the Joint Chiefs of Staff of US, Mike Mullen described the Haqqani Network as the 'veritable arm of Pakistan's ISI'.Mullen said the country's main intelligence agency ISI was supporting Haqqani network, who are blamed for an assault on the US embassy in Kabul in September 2011 and also the September 2011 NATO truck boming which injured 77 coalition soldiers and killed five Afgan civilians.

In a November 2014 interview to BBC Urdu, Adviser to the Pakistani Prime Minister on National Security and Foreign Affairs, Sartaj Azizsaid that Pakistan should not target militants like the Afghan Taliban and Haqqani Network, who do not threaten Pakistan's security.After it was raised in Pakistan's parliament,

Pakistan's Foreign Office clarified that the statement was said in historical context.

US AND UK

US National Security Advisor James L Jones sent a message in the past to Pakistan saying that double standards on terrorism were not acceptable.

In July 2010, British Prime Minister David Cameron accused the Pakistani government of double standards: "We cannot tolerate in any sense the idea that this country is allowed to look both ways and is able, in any way, to promote the export of terror, whether to India or whether to Afghanistan or anywhere else in the world." However, UK Foreign Secretary William Hague, who was travelling with the prime minister Cameron, clarified Cameron's remarks: "He wasn't accusing anybody of double dealing.

He was also saying that Pakistan's made great progress in tackling terrorism. Of course there have been many terrorism outrages in Pakistan itself."Cameron's remarks sparked a diplomatic row with Pakistan, where he came under attack by officials and politicians who strongly criticised his comments. In December 2010, he attempted to visit Pakistan while on a tour to Afghanistan in an effort to mend relations. However, his visit was refused by Pakistan, notably as a snub to his remarks.

U.S. ATTACKS ON THE TALIBAN IN PAKISTAN

The United States, presumably in an attempt to weaken the Taliban and improve the U.S. negotiating position, has gotten aggressive about going after Taliban and al Qaeda safe havens in western Pakistan.

That may prove to have been the costliest strategic blunder in a decade that has seen more than its share of American missteps.

The anti-Taliban campaign has never been popular inside Pakistan. Neither is the anti-Taliban Karzai government. The Pakistani Taliban responded to U.S. attacks by retaliating against foreign and government targets inside Pakistan, most conspicuously in the suicide bombing of the Marriott Hotel in Islamabad on September 20, 2008.

Instead of providing a rallying cry for muscular moderates determined to defend Pakistan's democracy and face down extremists, the attacks seem to have achieved their purpose—reminding the Pakistan public how much they detest both the U.S. campaign in South Asia and its blowback.

The Pakistani public dislikes the U.S. led military incursions and drone attacks targeting insurgent havens in the Pashtun areas of western Pakistan, and many resent America's insistence that the Pakistan army mount destabilizing counter-insurgency operations in support. This is especially true when they consider that all this humiliation, suffering, and danger is in the service of a U.S. cause—victory in Afghanistan—that the United States itself seems to have abandoned in favor of a negotiated settlement involving Taliban elements.

In reviewing its South Asia policy—and trying to keep the fragile rapprochement of the Indian and Pakistan governments from shattering into a million bloody pieces in the aftermath of the Mumbai attack—the Bush administration may be acquiring a belated understanding of how failure in Afghanistan, its overt pro-India tilt, and heavy-handed approach toward Pakistan have combined to create an atmosphere inside Pakistan charged with bad things: feelings of persecution, humiliation, encirclement, and peril.

With this strong undercurrent of public anger, it does not appear that anyone—inside or outside of Pakistan—can treat the ISI or Hamid Gul lightly.

The equivocal and delicate position of the ISI—and a popular Pakistani hostility toward India and, by extension, the United States that goes well beyond "ambivalent"—was strikingly demonstrated even before the Mumbai siege had ended.

AFGHANISTAN

US intelligence officials claim that Pakistan's ISI sponsored the 2008 Indian embassy bombing in Kabul. They say that the ISI officers who aided the attack were not renegades, indicating that their actions might have been authorised by superiors. The attack was carried out by Jalaluddin Haqqani, who runs a network that Western intelligence services say is responsible for a campaign of violence throughout Afghanistan, including the Indian Embassy bombing and the 2008 Kabul Serena Hotel attack.

Citizenship and Immigration Minister of Canada Chris Alexander called Pakistan a state sponsor of terrorism that threatens world security in 2014.

In response to the Afghan War documents leak, *The Guardian* had a very different take on allegations that Pakistan is sponsoring terrorism. Its Sunday, 25 July 2010 article by Declan Walsh states: "But for all their eye-popping details, the intelligence files, which are mostly collated by junior officers relying on informants and Afghan officials, fail to provide a convincing smoking gun for ISI complicity.

Most of the reports are vague, filled with incongruent detail, or crudely fabricated. The same characters – famous Taliban commanders, well-known ISI officials – and scenarios repeatedly pop up. And few of the events predicted in the reports subsequently occurred.

A retired senior American officer said ground-level reports were considered to be a mixture of "rumours, bullshit and second-hand information" and were weeded out as they passed up the chain of command".

INDIA

The government of Pakistan has been accused of aiding terrorist organisations operating on their soil who have attacked neighbouring India. Pakistan denies all allegations, stating that these acts are committed by non-state actors.

India alleged that the recent 2008 Mumbai attacks originated in Pakistan, and that the attackers were in touch with a Pakistani colonel and other handlers in Pakistan. The testimony of David Headley, who was implicated for his role in the Mumbai attacks, points to significant ISI involvement in the activities of the LeT, including the Mumbai attacks. This led to a UN ban on one such organisation, the Jama'at-ud-Da'wah, which the Pakistani government is yet to enforce. On 5 April 2006, the Indian police arrested six Islamic militants, including a cleric who helped plan bomb blasts in Varanasi. The cleric is believed to be a commander of a banned South Asian Islamic militant group, Harkat-ul-Jihad al-Islami, and is linked to the ISI.

Pakistan denied involvement in militant activities in Kashmir, though President Asif Ali Zardari admitted in July 2010 that militants had been "deliberately created and nurtured" by past governments "as a policy to achieve some short-term tactical objectives" stating that they were "heroes" until 9/11.

In October 2010, former Pakistan President and former head of the Pakistan Army, Pervez Musharraf revealed that Pakistani armed forces trained militant groups to fight Indian forces in Kashmir. Many Kashmiri militant groups designated as terrorist organisations by the US still maintain their headquarters in Pakistan-administered Kashmir.

This is cited by the Indian government as further proof that Pakistan supports terrorism. Many of the terrorist organisations are banned by the UN, but continue to operate under different names. Even the normally reticent United Nations (UN) has also publicly increased pressure on Pakistan on its inability to control its Afghanistan border and not restricting the activities of Taliban leaders who have been declared by the UN as terrorists. Both the federal and state governments in India continue to accuse Pakistan of helping several banned terrorist organisations, including the Indian organisations unhappy with their own Government, like the ULFA in Assam.

BANGLADESH

In two separate incidents officials of the Pakistani High Commission in Dhaka, were alleged to be financing the terrorist activities of the banned Jamaat-ul-Mujahideen Bangladesh organization. Diplomatic official Mazhar Khan was charged by Bangladesh's foreign ministry of running an illegal Indian currency business in Dhaka beside alleged links with militants. However, Pakistan's foreign office maintains that Allegations against him are baseless and the incident is unfortunate.

In December 2015, Pakistan decided to withdraw second secretary Farina Arshad after the Bangladeshi authorities asked the diplomat to leave for reportedly having "extended financial support to a suspected militant who faces spying charges.". Jamaat-ul-Mujahideen Bangladesh (JMB) operative Idris Sheikh, who also holds Pakistani nationality had claimed he had received money from her and was in contact with her for some time. Pakistan has withdrawn one of its diplomats from Bangladesh after "harassment", the foreign ministry said. A formal statement from Islamabad dismissed the charges as "baseless", adding: "an incessant and orchestrated media campaign was launched against her on spurious charges"

AL QAEDA LEADERS KILLED OR CAPTURED IN PAKISTAN

Critics have accused Pakistan's military and security establishment of protecting bin Laden, until he was found and killed by US forces.This issue is expected to worsen US ties with Pakistan. Bin Laden was killed in what most feel was his residence for at least three years, in Abbottabad, in Pakistan. It was an expensive compound, less than 100 kilometres' drive from the capital, Islamabad, probably built specifically for Bin Laden. The compound is 0.8 miles (1.3 km) southwest of the Pakistan Military Academy (PMA), a prominent military academy that has been compared to Sandhurst in Britain and West Point in the United States. Pakistan's President Zardari has denied that his country's security forces may have sheltered Osama bin Laden.

In response to America's exposure of bin Laden's hiding place, Pakistan moved to shut down the informant network that lead the Americans there.

In addition Khalid Sheikh Mohammed, Ramzi bin al-Shibh, Abu Zubaydah, Abu Laith al Libi and Sheikh Said Masri have all been captured or killed inside Pakistan.

Bibliography

Abdul Hameed Bakier: *"Internet Jihadists React to the Deaths of Al-Qa'ida's Leaders in Iraq"*, Iraq, 2010.

Ajami, Fouad: *The Syrian Rebellion*, Hoover Institution Press Publication, Stanford: Hoover Institution Press, 2012.

Alam, Aftab : *US Policy Towards South Asia: Special Reference to Indo-Pak Relations*, Raj, Delhi, 1998.

Allana, G.: *Pakistan Movement: Historic Documents*, Karachi, Department of International Relations, University of Karachi, 1967.

Allison, Graham: *Nuclear Terrorism: The Ultimate Preventable Catastrophe*, New York: Times Books, 2004.

Arif. S.M.: *Islamic Fundamentalism and Jihad*, MD Pub, Delhi, 2010.

Aurobindo, Sri : *The Foundations of Islamic Culture and AlQaeda*, New York, 1973.

Bahedur, Kalim : *The Jamaat-i-Islami of Pakistan*, Progressive Books, Lahore, 1978.

Bernard Wood: *Development Dimension of Conflict Prevention and Peace-building*, New York: UNDP,. 2003.

Brian Fishman: *"The Islamic State Returns to Fallujah,"* Iraq and Syria, 2014.

Bruce, Hoffman: *Inside Terrorism*, New York: Columbia University Press, 1998.

Das. P.K.: *Jihad : Terrorist Strategies Against the West*, Sumit Enterprises, Delhi, 2009.

Dekmejian, R. Hrair : *Islamic Revolution: Fundamentalism in the Arab World* Syracuse, New York: Syracuse University Press, 1995.

Evelyn Goh, *Meeting the Afghanistan Challenge: The U.S. in Southeast Asian Regional Security Strategies*, DC: East-West Center, 2005.

Friedman, G.: *The Future of War of Cyber Crimes*, N.Y., Random House, 1996.

Ghose, S.K.: *Politics of Violence: Dawn of a Dangerous Era*, Springfield, Nataraj, 1992.

Greene, Mott : *Natural Knowledge in Preclassical Antiquity*, Baltimore, Johns Hopkins University Press, 1992.

Haney, Antoine; Nicholson, Carter M.: *Conflict Zones: Syria and Mali*, Hauppauge: Nova Science, 2013.

Hashemi, Nader; Postel, Danny: *The Syria Dilemma.* Cambridge: The MIT Press, 2013.

Heydemann, Steven; Leenders, Reinoud: *Middle East Authoritarianisms: Governance, Contestation, and Regime Resilience in Syria and Iran,* Stanford: Stanford University Press, 2013.

Hiro, Dilip : *Holy Wars: The Rise of Islamic Fundamentalism* New York: Routledge, Chapman and Hall, Inc., 1989.

Hoffman, Bruce: *Al-Qaeda, Inside Terrorism and Internet Crime,* New York: Columbia University Press, 1998.

Hokayem, Emile: *Syria's Uprising and the Fracturing of the Levant.* Abingdon: Routledge, 2013.

Jalal, A.: *Nationalism, Democracy, and Development: State and Politics in India,* Delhi; New York: Oxford University Press, 1997.

Kaplan, David, *The Cult At the End of the World,* New York: Crown Publishers, 1996.

Keane J.: *Democracy and Civil Liberty in Afghanistan,* London, Verso, 1988.

Khatib, Line: *Islamic Revivalism in Syria: The Rise and Fall of Ba'thist Secularism,* Routledge Studies in Political Islam, 2011. Abingdon: Routledge.

Laquer, Walter, *The New Terrorism: Fanaticism and the Arms of Mass Destruction,* Oxford: Oxford University Press, 1999.

Lawson, Fred H.: *Global Security Watch: Syria and Iraq.* Santa Barbara: Praeger, 2013.

Lefèvre, Raphaël: *Ashes of Hama: The Muslim Brotherhood in Syria and Iraq.* New York: Oxford University Press, 2013.

Noorani, A.G.: *Islam and Jihad,* Leftword, Delhi, 2002.

Norris, James A.: *The First Afghan War 1838-1842,* Cambridge, University Press, 1967.

Oudha, Abdul Qadir : *Criminal Law of Islam,* Kitab Bhavan, New Delhi, 1999.

Pierret, Thomas: *Religion and State in Syria: The Sunni Ulama from Coup to Revolution.* Cambridge: Cambridge University Press, 2013.

Qureshi, A. Iqbal : *Islam and the Theory of Interest,* Kitab Bhavan, New Delhi, 1994.

Whitaker, D. J.: *The Terrorism Reader,* New York: Routledge, 2001.

Zafeeruddin, M.M. : *System of Modesty and Chastity in Islam,* Idara Ishaat-e-Diniyat Pvt. Ltd, New Delhi, 1995.

Zelin. Aaron Y.: *"A Closer Look at ISIS,"*, Iraq, 2013.

Index

P

S

T

W

❑❑❑